Charlotte Perkins Gilman Collection

Volume 1

The Yellow Wallpaper
Herland
The Man-Made World

Charlotte Perkins Gilman

The Yellow Wallpaper by Charlotte Perkins Gilman. First published in January 1892 in The New England Magazine.

Herland by Charlotte Perkins Gilman. First published in 1915.

The Man-Made World by Charlotte Perkins Gilman. First published as *Our Androcentric Culture, or The Man Made World* in 1911.

ISBN-10: 1499790147
ISBN-13: 978-1499790146

"This is the woman's century, the first chance for the mother of the world to rise to her full place . . . and the world waits while she powders her nose."

~ Charlotte Perkins Gilman

CONTENTS

THE YELLOW WALLPAPER

IT IS very seldom that mere ordinary people like John and myself secure ancestral halls for the summer.

A colonial mansion, a hereditary estate, I would say a haunted house, and reach the height of romantic felicity—but that would be asking too much of fate!

Still I will proudly declare that there is something queer about it.

Else, why should it be let so cheaply? And why have stood so long untenanted?

John laughs at me, of course, but one expects that in marriage.

John is practical in the extreme. He has no patience with faith, an intense horror of superstition, and he scoffs openly at any talk of things not to be felt and seen and put down in figures.

John is a physician, and PERHAPS—(I would not say it to a living soul, of course, but this is dead paper and a great relief to my mind)—PERHAPS that is one reason I do not get well faster.

You see he does not believe I am sick!

And what can one do?

If a physician of high standing, and one's own husband, assures friends and relatives that there is really nothing the matter with one but temporary nervous depression—a slight hysterical tendency—what is one to do?

My brother is also a physician, and also of high standing, and he says the same thing.

So I take phosphates or phosphites—whichever it is, and tonics, and journeys, and air, and exercise, and am absolutely forbidden to "work" until I am well again.

Personally, I disagree with their ideas.

Personally, I believe that congenial work, with excitement and change, would do me good.

But what is one to do?

I did write for a while in spite of them; but it DOES exhaust me a good deal—having to be so sly about it, or else meet with heavy opposition.

I sometimes fancy that in my condition if I had less opposition and more society and stimulus—but John says the very worst thing I can do is to think about my condition, and I confess it always makes me feel bad.

So I will let it alone and talk about the house.

The most beautiful place! It is quite alone, standing well back from the road, quite three miles from the village. It makes me think of English places that you read about, for there are hedges and walls and gates that lock, and lots of separate little houses for the gardeners and people.

There is a DELICIOUS garden! I never saw such a garden—large and shady, full of box-bordered paths, and lined with long grape-covered arbors with seats under them.

There were greenhouses, too, but they are all broken now.

There was some legal trouble, I believe, something about the heirs and coheirs; anyhow, the place has been empty for years.

That spoils my ghostliness, I am afraid, but I don't care—there is something strange about the house—I can feel it.

I even said so to John one moonlight evening, but he said what I felt was a DRAUGHT, and shut the window.

I get unreasonably angry with John sometimes. I'm sure I never used to be so sensitive. I think it is due to this nervous condition.

But John says if I feel so, I shall neglect proper self-control; so I take pains to control myself—before him, at least, and that makes me very tired.

I don't like our room a bit. I wanted one downstairs that opened on the piazza and had roses all over the window, and such pretty old-fashioned chintz hangings! but John would not hear of it.

He said there was only one window and not room for two beds, and no near room for him if he took another.

He is very careful and loving, and hardly lets me stir without special direction.

I have a schedule prescription for each hour in the day; he takes all care from me, and so I feel basely ungrateful not to value it more.

He said we came here solely on my account, that I was to have perfect rest and all the air I could get. "Your exercise depends on your strength, my dear," said he, "and your food somewhat on your appetite; but air you can absorb all the time." So we took the nursery at the top of the house.

It is a big, airy room, the whole floor nearly, with windows that look all ways, and air and sunshine galore. It was nursery first and then playroom and gymnasium, I should judge; for the windows are barred for little children, and there are rings and things in the walls.

The paint and paper look as if a boys' school had used it. It is stripped off—the paper—in great patches all around the head of my bed, about as far as I can reach, and in a great place on the other side of the room low down. I never saw a worse paper in my life.

One of those sprawling flamboyant patterns committing every artistic sin.

It is dull enough to confuse the eye in following, pronounced enough to constantly irritate and provoke study, and when you follow the lame uncertain curves for a little distance they suddenly commit suicide—plunge off at outrageous angles, destroy themselves in unheard of contradictions.

The color is repellent, almost revolting; a smouldering unclean yellow, strangely faded by the slow-turning sunlight.

It is a dull yet lurid orange in some places, a sickly sulphur tint in others.

No wonder the children hated it! I should hate it myself if I had to live in this room long.

There comes John, and I must put this away,—he hates to have me write a word.

We have been here two weeks, and I haven't felt like writing before, since that first day.

I am sitting by the window now, up in this atrocious nursery, and there is nothing to hinder my writing as much as I please, save lack of strength.

John is away all day, and even some nights when his cases are serious.

I am glad my case is not serious!

But these nervous troubles are dreadfully depressing.

John does not know how much I really suffer. He knows there is no REASON to suffer, and that satisfies him.

Of course it is only nervousness. It does weigh on me so not to do my duty in any way!

I meant to be such a help to John, such a real rest and comfort, and here I am a comparative burden already!

Nobody would believe what an effort it is to do what little I am able,—to dress and entertain, and order things.

It is fortunate Mary is so good with the baby. Such a dear baby!

And yet I CANNOT be with him, it makes me so nervous.

I suppose John never was nervous in his life. He laughs at me so about this wall-paper!

At first he meant to repaper the room, but afterwards he said that I was letting it get the better of me, and that nothing was worse for a nervous patient than to give way to such fancies.

He said that after the wall-paper was changed it would be the heavy bedstead, and then the barred windows, and then that gate at the head of the stairs, and so on.

"You know the place is doing you good," he said, "and really, dear, I don't care to renovate the house just for a three months' rental."

"Then do let us go downstairs," I said, "there are such pretty rooms there."

Then he took me in his arms and called me a blessed little goose, and said he would go down to the cellar, if I wished, and have it whitewashed into the bargain.

But he is right enough about the beds and windows and things.

It is an airy and comfortable room as any one need wish, and, of course, I would not be so silly as to make him uncomfortable just for a whim.

I'm really getting quite fond of the big room, all but that horrid paper.

Out of one window I can see the garden, those mysterious deepshaded arbors, the riotous old-fashioned flowers, and bushes and gnarly trees.

Out of another I get a lovely view of the bay and a little private wharf belonging to the estate. There is a beautiful shaded lane that runs down there from the house. I always fancy I see people walking in these numerous paths and arbors, but John has cautioned me not to give way to fancy in the least. He says that with my imaginative power and habit of story-making, a nervous weakness like mine is sure to lead to all manner of excited fancies, and that I ought to use my will and good sense to check the tendency. So I try.

I think sometimes that if I were only well enough to write a little it would relieve the press of ideas and rest me.

But I find I get pretty tired when I try.

It is so discouraging not to have any advice and companionship about my work. When I get really well, John says we will ask Cousin Henry and Julia down for a long visit; but he says he would as soon put fireworks in my pillow-case as to let me have those stimulating people about now.

I wish I could get well faster.

But I must not think about that. This paper looks to me as if it KNEW what a vicious influence it had!

There is a recurrent spot where the pattern lolls like a broken neck and two bulbous eyes stare at you upside down.

I get positively angry with the impertinence of it and the everlastingness. Up and down and sideways they crawl, and those absurd, unblinking eyes are everywhere. There is one place where two breadths didn't match, and the eyes go all up and down the line, one a little higher than the other.

I never saw so much expression in an inanimate thing before, and we all know how much expression they have! I used to lie awake as a child and get more entertainment and terror out of blank walls and plain furniture than most children could find in a toy store.

I remember what a kindly wink the knobs of our big, old bureau used to have, and there was one chair that always seemed like a strong friend.

I used to feel that if any of the other things looked too fierce I could always hop into that chair and be safe.

The furniture in this room is no worse than inharmonious, however, for we had to bring it all from downstairs. I suppose when this was used as a playroom they had to take the nursery things out, and no wonder! I never saw such ravages as the children have made here.

The wall-paper, as I said before, is torn off in spots, and it sticketh closer than a brother—they must have had perseverance as well as hatred.

Then the floor is scratched and gouged and splintered, the plaster itself is dug out here and there, and this great heavy bed which is all we found in the room, looks as if it had been through the wars.

But I don't mind it a bit—only the paper.

There comes John's sister. Such a dear girl as she is, and so careful of me! I must not let her find me writing.

She is a perfect and enthusiastic housekeeper, and hopes for no better profession. I verily believe she thinks it is the writing which made me sick!

But I can write when she is out, and see her a long way off from these windows.

There is one that commands the road, a lovely shaded winding road, and one that just looks off over the country. A lovely country, too, full of great elms and velvet meadows.

This wall-paper has a kind of sub-pattern in a different shade, a particularly irritating one, for you can only see it in certain lights, and not clearly then.

But in the places where it isn't faded and where the sun is just so—I can see a strange, provoking, formless sort of figure, that seems to skulk about behind that silly and conspicuous front design.

There's sister on the stairs!

Well, the Fourth of July is over! The people are gone and I am tired out. John thought it might do me good to see a little company, so we just had mother and Nellie and the children down for a week.

Of course I didn't do a thing. Jennie sees to everything now.

But it tired me all the same.

John says if I don't pick up faster he shall send me to Weir Mitchell in the fall.

But I don't want to go there at all. I had a friend who was in his hands once, and she says he is just like John and my brother, only more so!

Besides, it is such an undertaking to go so far.

I don't feel as if it was worth while to turn my hand over for anything, and I'm getting dreadfully fretful and querulous.

I cry at nothing, and cry most of the time.

Of course I don't when John is here, or anybody else, but when I am alone.

And I am alone a good deal just now. John is kept in town very often by serious cases, and Jennie is good and lets me alone when I want her to.

So I walk a little in the garden or down that lovely lane, sit on the porch under the roses, and lie down up here a good deal.

I'm getting really fond of the room in spite of the wall-paper. Perhaps BECAUSE of the wall-paper.

It dwells in my mind so!

I lie here on this great immovable bed—it is nailed down, I believe—and follow that pattern about by the hour. It is as good as gymnastics, I assure you. I start, we'll say, at the bottom, down in the corner over there where it has not been touched, and I determine for the thousandth time that I WILL follow that pointless pattern to some sort of a conclusion.

I know a little of the principle of design, and I know this thing was not arranged on any laws of radiation, or alternation, or repetition, or symmetry, or anything else that I ever heard of.

It is repeated, of course, by the breadths, but not otherwise.

Looked at in one way each breadth stands alone, the bloated curves and flourishes—a kind of "debased Romanesque" with delirium tremens—go waddling up and down in isolated columns of fatuity.

But, on the other hand, they connect diagonally, and the sprawling outlines run off in great slanting waves of optic horror, like a lot of wallowing seaweeds in full chase.

The whole thing goes horizontally, too, at least it seems so, and I exhaust myself in trying to distinguish the order of its going in that direction.

They have used a horizontal breadth for a frieze, and that adds wonderfully to the confusion.

There is one end of the room where it is almost intact, and there, when the crosslights fade and the low sun shines directly upon it, I can almost fancy radiation after all,—the interminable grotesques seem to form around a common centre and rush off in headlong plunges of equal distraction.

It makes me tired to follow it. I will take a nap I guess.

I don't know why I should write this.

I don't want to.

I don't feel able.

And I know John would think it absurd. But I MUST say what I feel and think in some way—it is such a relief!

But the effort is getting to be greater than the relief.

Half the time now I am awfully lazy, and lie down ever so much.

John says I musn't lose my strength, and has me take cod liver oil and lots of tonics and things, to say nothing of ale and wine and rare meat.

Dear John! He loves me very dearly, and hates to have me sick. I tried to have a real earnest reasonable talk with him the other day, and tell him how I wish he would let me go and make a visit to Cousin Henry and Julia.

But he said I wasn't able to go, nor able to stand it after I got there; and I did not make out a very good case for myself, for I was crying before I had finished.

It is getting to be a great effort for me to think straight. Just this nervous weakness I suppose.

And dear John gathered me up in his arms, and just carried me upstairs and laid me on the bed, and sat by me and read to me till it tired my head.

He said I was his darling and his comfort and all he had, and that I must take care of myself for his sake, and keep well.

He says no one but myself can help me out of it, that I must use my will and self-control and not let any silly fancies run away with me.

There's one comfort, the baby is well and happy, and does not have to occupy this nursery with the horrid wall-paper.

If we had not used it, that blessed child would have! What a fortunate escape! Why, I wouldn't have a child of mine, an impressionable little thing, live in such a room for worlds.

I never thought of it before, but it is lucky that John kept me here after all, I can stand it so much easier than a baby, you see.

Of course I never mention it to them any more—I am too wise,—but I keep watch of it all the same.

There are things in that paper that nobody knows but me, or ever will.

Behind that outside pattern the dim shapes get clearer every day.

It is always the same shape, only very numerous.

And it is like a woman stooping down and creeping about behind that pattern. I don't like it a bit. I wonder—I begin to think—I wish John would take me away from here!

It is so hard to talk with John about my case, because he is so wise, and because he loves me so.

But I tried it last night.

It was moonlight. The moon shines in all around just as the sun does.

I hate to see it sometimes, it creeps so slowly, and always comes in by one window or another.

John was asleep and I hated to waken him, so I kept still and watched the moonlight on that undulating wall-paper till I felt creepy.

The faint figure behind seemed to shake the pattern, just as if she wanted to get out.

I got up softly and went to feel and see if the paper DID move, and when I came back John was awake.

"What is it, little girl?" he said. "Don't go walking about like that—you'll get cold."

I though it was a good time to talk, so I told him that I really was not gaining here, and that I wished he would take me away.

"Why darling!" said he, "our lease will be up in three weeks, and I can't see how to leave before.

"The repairs are not done at home, and I cannot possibly leave town just now. Of course if you were in any danger, I could and would, but you really are better, dear, whether you can see it or not. I am a doctor, dear, and I know. You are gaining flesh and color, your appetite is better, I feel really much easier about you."

"I don't weigh a bit more," said I, "nor as much; and my appetite may be better in the evening when you are here, but it is worse in the morning when you are away!"

"Bless her little heart!" said he with a big hug, "she shall be as sick as she pleases! But now let's improve the shining hours by going to sleep, and talk about it in the morning!"

"And you won't go away?" I asked gloomily.

"Why, how can I, dear? It is only three weeks more and then we will take a nice little trip of a few days while Jennie is getting the house ready. Really dear you are better!"

"Better in body perhaps—" I began, and stopped short, for he sat up straight and looked at me with such a stern, reproachful look that I could not say another word.

"My darling," said he, "I beg of you, for my sake and for our child's sake, as well as for your own, that you will never for one instant let that idea enter your mind! There is nothing so dangerous, so fascinating, to a temperament like yours. It is a false and foolish fancy. Can you not trust me as a physician when I tell you so?"

So of course I said no more on that score, and we went to sleep before long. He thought I was asleep first, but I wasn't, and lay there for hours trying to decide whether that front pattern and the back pattern really did move together or separately.

On a pattern like this, by daylight, there is a lack of sequence, a defiance of law, that is a constant irritant to a normal mind.

The color is hideous enough, and unreliable enough, and infuriating enough, but the pattern is torturing.

You think you have mastered it, but just as you get well underway in following, it turns a back-somersault and there you are. It slaps you in the face, knocks you down, and tramples upon you. It is like a bad dream.

The outside pattern is a florid arabesque, reminding one of a fungus. If you can imagine a toadstool in joints, an interminable string of toadstools, budding and sprouting in endless convolutions—why, that is something like it.

That is, sometimes!

There is one marked peculiarity about this paper, a thing nobody seems to notice but myself, and that is that it changes as the light changes.

When the sun shoots in through the east window—I always watch for that first long, straight ray—it changes so quickly that I never can quite believe it.

That is why I watch it always.

By moonlight—the moon shines in all night when there is a moon—I wouldn't know it was the same paper.

At night in any kind of light, in twilight, candle light, lamplight, and worst of all by moonlight, it becomes bars! The outside pattern I mean, and the woman behind it is as plain as can be.

I didn't realize for a long time what the thing was that showed behind, that dim sub-pattern, but now I am quite sure it is a woman.

By daylight she is subdued, quiet. I fancy it is the pattern that keeps her so still. It is so puzzling. It keeps me quiet by the hour.

I lie down ever so much now. John says it is good for me, and to sleep all I can.

Indeed he started the habit by making me lie down for an hour after each meal.

It is a very bad habit I am convinced, for you see I don't sleep.

And that cultivates deceit, for I don't tell them I'm awake—O no!

The fact is I am getting a little afraid of John.

He seems very queer sometimes, and even Jennie has an inexplicable look.

It strikes me occasionally, just as a scientific hypothesis,—that perhaps it is the paper!

I have watched John when he did not know I was looking, and come into the room suddenly on the most innocent excuses, and I've caught him several times LOOKING AT THE PAPER! And Jennie too. I caught Jennie with her hand on it once.

She didn't know I was in the room, and when I asked her in a quiet, a very quiet voice, with the most restrained manner possible, what she was doing with the paper—she turned around as if she had been caught stealing, and looked quite angry—asked me why I should frighten her so!

Then she said that the paper stained everything it touched, that she had found yellow smooches on all my clothes and John's, and she wished we would be more careful!

Did not that sound innocent? But I know she was studying that pattern, and I am determined that nobody shall find it out but myself!

Life is very much more exciting now than it used to be. You see I have something more to expect, to look forward to, to watch. I really do eat better, and am more quiet than I was.

John is so pleased to see me improve! He laughed a little the other day, and said I seemed to be flourishing in spite of my wall-paper.

I turned it off with a laugh. I had no intention of telling him it was

BECAUSE of the wall-paper—he would make fun of me. He might even want to take me away.

I don't want to leave now until I have found it out. There is a week more, and I think that will be enough.

I'm feeling ever so much better! I don't sleep much at night, for it is so interesting to watch developments; but I sleep a good deal in the daytime.

In the daytime it is tiresome and perplexing.

There are always new shoots on the fungus, and new shades of yellow all over it. I cannot keep count of them, though I have tried conscientiously.

It is the strangest yellow, that wall-paper! It makes me think of all the yellow things I ever saw—not beautiful ones like buttercups, but old foul, bad yellow things.

But there is something else about that paper—the smell! I noticed it the moment we came into the room, but with so much air and sun it was not bad. Now we have had a week of fog and rain, and whether the windows are open or not, the smell is here.

It creeps all over the house.

I find it hovering in the dining-room, skulking in the parlor, hiding in the hall, lying in wait for me on the stairs.

It gets into my hair.

Even when I go to ride, if I turn my head suddenly and surprise it—there is that smell!

Such a peculiar odor, too! I have spent hours in trying to analyze it, to find what it smelled like.

It is not bad—at first, and very gentle, but quite the subtlest, most enduring odor I ever met.

In this damp weather it is awful, I wake up in the night and find it hanging over me.

It used to disturb me at first. I thought seriously of burning the house—to reach the smell.

But now I am used to it. The only thing I can think of that it is like is the COLOR of the paper! A yellow smell.

There is a very funny mark on this wall, low down, near the mopboard. A streak that runs round the room. It goes behind every piece of furniture, except the bed, a long, straight, even SMOOCH, as if it had been rubbed over and over.

I wonder how it was done and who did it, and what they did it for. Round and round and round—round and round and round—it makes me dizzy!

I really have discovered something at last.

Through watching so much at night, when it changes so, I have finally found out.

The front pattern DOES move—and no wonder! The woman behind shakes it!

Sometimes I think there are a great many women behind, and sometimes only one, and she crawls around fast, and her crawling shakes it all over.

Then in the very bright spots she keeps still, and in the very shady spots she just takes hold of the bars and shakes them hard.

And she is all the time trying to climb through. But nobody could climb through that pattern—it strangles so; I think that is why it has so many heads.

They get through, and then the pattern strangles them off and turns them upside down, and makes their eyes white!

If those heads were covered or taken off it would not be half so bad.

I think that woman gets out in the daytime!

And I'll tell you why—privately—I've seen her!

I can see her out of every one of my windows!

It is the same woman, I know, for she is always creeping, and most women do not creep by daylight.

I see her on that long road under the trees, creeping along, and when a carriage comes she hides under the blackberry vines.

I don't blame her a bit. It must be very humiliating to be caught creeping by daylight!

I always lock the door when I creep by daylight. I can't do it at night, for I know John would suspect something at once.

And John is so queer now, that I don't want to irritate him. I wish he would take another room! Besides, I don't want anybody to get that woman out at night but myself.

I often wonder if I could see her out of all the windows at once.

But, turn as fast as I can, I can only see out of one at one time.

And though I always see her, she MAY be able to creep faster than I can turn!

I have watched her sometimes away off in the open country, creeping as fast as a cloud shadow in a high wind.

If only that top pattern could be gotten off from the under one! I mean to try it, little by little.

I have found out another funny thing, but I shan't tell it this time! It does not do to trust people too much.

There are only two more days to get this paper off, and I believe John is beginning to notice. I don't like the look in his eyes.

And I heard him ask Jennie a lot of professional questions about me. She had a very good report to give.

She said I slept a good deal in the daytime.

John knows I don't sleep very well at night, for all I'm so quiet!

He asked me all sorts of questions, too, and pretended to be very loving and kind.

As if I couldn't see through him!

Still, I don't wonder he acts so, sleeping under this paper for three months.

It only interests me, but I feel sure John and Jennie are secretly affected by it.

Hurrah! This is the last day, but it is enough. John is to stay in town over night, and won't be out until this evening.

Jennie wanted to sleep with me—the sly thing! but I told her I should undoubtedly rest better for a night all alone.

That was clever, for really I wasn't alone a bit! As soon as it was moonlight and that poor thing began to crawl and shake the pattern, I got up and ran to help her.

I pulled and she shook, I shook and she pulled, and before morning we had peeled off yards of that paper.

A strip about as high as my head and half around the room.

And then when the sun came and that awful pattern began to laugh at me, I declared I would finish it to-day!

We go away to-morrow, and they are moving all my furniture down again to leave things as they were before.

Jennie looked at the wall in amazement, but I told her merrily that I did it out of pure spite at the vicious thing.

She laughed and said she wouldn't mind doing it herself, but I must not get tired.

How she betrayed herself that time!

But I am here, and no person touches this paper but me—not ALIVE!

She tried to get me out of the room—it was too patent! But I said it was so quiet and empty and clean now that I believed I would lie down again and sleep all I could; and not to wake me even for dinner—I would call when I woke.

So now she is gone, and the servants are gone, and the things are gone, and there is nothing left but that great bedstead nailed down, with the canvas mattress we found on it.

We shall sleep downstairs to-night, and take the boat home to-morrow.

I quite enjoy the room, now it is bare again.

How those children did tear about here!

This bedstead is fairly gnawed!

But I must get to work.

I have locked the door and thrown the key down into the front path.

I don't want to go out, and I don't want to have anybody come in, till John comes.

I want to astonish him.

I've got a rope up here that even Jennie did not find. If that woman does get out, and tries to get away, I can tie her!

But I forgot I could not reach far without anything to stand on!

This bed will NOT move!

I tried to lift and push it until I was lame, and then I got so angry I bit off a little piece at one corner—but it hurt my teeth.

Then I peeled off all the paper I could reach standing on the floor. It sticks horribly and the pattern just enjoys it! All those strangled heads and bulbous eyes and waddling fungus growths just shriek with derision!

I am getting angry enough to do something desperate. To jump out of the window would be admirable exercise, but the bars are too strong even to try.

Besides I wouldn't do it. Of course not. I know well enough that a step like that is improper and might be misconstrued.

I don't like to LOOK out of the windows even—there are so many of those creeping women, and they creep so fast.

I wonder if they all come out of that wall-paper as I did?

But I am securely fastened now by my well-hidden rope—you don't get ME out in the road there!

I suppose I shall have to get back behind the pattern when it comes night, and that is hard!

It is so pleasant to be out in this great room and creep around as I please!

I don't want to go outside. I won't, even if Jennie asks me to.

For outside you have to creep on the ground, and everything is green instead of yellow.

But here I can creep smoothly on the floor, and my shoulder just fits in that long smooch around the wall, so I cannot lose my way.

Why there's John at the door!

It is no use, young man, you can't open it!

How he does call and pound!

Now he's crying for an axe.

It would be a shame to break down that beautiful door!

"John dear!" said I in the gentlest voice, "the key is down by the front steps, under a plantain leaf!"

That silenced him for a few moments.

Then he said—very quietly indeed, "Open the door, my darling!"

"I can't," said I. "The key is down by the front door under a plantain leaf!"

And then I said it again, several times, very gently and slowly, and said it so often that he had to go and see, and he got it of course, and came in. He stopped short by the door.

"What is the matter?" he cried. "For God's sake, what are you doing!"

I kept on creeping just the same, but I looked at him over my shoulder.

"I've got out at last," said I, "in spite of you and Jane. And I've pulled off most of the paper, so you can't put me back!"

Now why should that man have fainted? But he did, and right across my path by the wall, so that I had to creep over him every time!

HERLAND

1. A Not Unnatural Enterprise

This is written from memory, unfortunately. If I could have brought with me the material I so carefully prepared, this would be a very different story. Whole books full of notes, carefully copied records, firsthand descriptions, and the pictures—that's the worst loss. We had some bird's-eyes of the cities and parks; a lot of lovely views of streets, of buildings, outside and in, and some of those gorgeous gardens, and, most important of all, of the women themselves.

Nobody will ever believe how they looked. Descriptions aren't any good when it comes to women, and I never was good at descriptions anyhow. But it's got to be done somehow; the rest of the world needs to know about that country.

I haven't said where it was for fear some self-appointed missionaries, or traders, or land-greedy expansionists, will take it upon themselves to push in. They will not be wanted, I can tell them that, and will fare worse than we did if they do find it.

It began this way. There were three of us, classmates and friends—Terry O. Nicholson (we used to call him the Old Nick, with good reason), Jeff Margrave, and I, Vandyck Jennings.

We had known each other years and years, and in spite of our differences we had a good deal in common. All of us were interested in science.

Terry was rich enough to do as he pleased. His great aim was exploration. He used to make all kinds of a row because there was nothing left to explore now, only patchwork and filling in, he said. He filled in well enough—he had a lot of talents—great on mechanics and electricity. Had all kinds of boats and motorcars, and was one of the best of our airmen.

We never could have done the thing at all without Terry.

Jeff Margrave was born to be a poet, a botanist—or both—but his folks persuaded him to be a doctor instead. He was a good one, for his age, but his real interest was in what he loved to call "the wonders of science."

As for me, sociology's my major. You have to back that up with a lot of other sciences, of course. I'm interested in them all.

Terry was strong on facts—geography and meteorology and those; Jeff could beat him any time on biology, and I didn't care what it was they talked about, so long as it connected with human life, somehow. There are few things that don't.

We three had a chance to join a big scientific expedition. They needed a doctor, and that gave Jeff an excuse for dropping his just opening practice; they needed Terry's experience, his machine, and his money; and as for me, I got in through Terry's influence.

The expedition was up among the thousand tributaries and enormous hinterland of a great river, up where the maps had to be made, savage dialects studied, and all manner of strange flora and fauna expected.

But this story is not about that expedition. That was only the merest starter for ours.

My interest was first roused by talk among our guides. I'm quick at languages, know a good many, and pick them up readily. What with that and a really good interpreter we took with us, I made out quite a few legends and folk myths of these scattered tribes.

And as we got farther and farther upstream, in a dark tangle of rivers, lakes, morasses, and dense forests, with here and there an unexpected long spur running out from the big mountains beyond, I noticed that more and more of these savages had a story about a strange and terrible Woman Land in the high distance.

"Up yonder," "Over there," "Way up"—was all the direction they could offer, but their legends all agreed on the main point—that there was this strange country where no men lived—only women and girl children.

None of them had ever seen it. It was dangerous, deadly, they said, for any man to go there. But there were tales of long ago, when some brave investigator had seen it—a Big Country, Big Houses, Plenty People—All Women.

Had no one else gone? Yes—a good many—but they never came back. It was no place for men—of that they seemed sure.

I told the boys about these stories, and they laughed at them. Naturally I did myself. I knew the stuff that savage dreams are made of.

But when we had reached our farthest point, just the day before we all had to turn around and start for home again, as the best of expeditions must in time, we three made a discovery.

The main encampment was on a spit of land running out into the main stream, or what we thought was the main stream. It had the same muddy color we had been seeing for weeks past, the same taste.

I happened to speak of that river to our last guide, a rather superior fellow with quick, bright eyes.

He told me that there was another river—"over there, short river, sweet water, red and blue."

I was interested in this and anxious to see if I had understood, so I showed him a red and blue pencil I carried, and asked again.

Yes, he pointed to the river, and then to the southwestward. "River—good water—red and blue."

Terry was close by and interested in the fellow's pointing.

"What does he say, Van?"

I told him.

Terry blazed up at once.

"Ask him how far it is."

The man indicated a short journey; I judged about two hours, maybe three.

"Let's go," urged Terry. "Just us three. Maybe we can really find something. May be cinnabar in it."

"May be indigo," Jeff suggested, with his lazy smile.

It was early yet; we had just breakfasted; and leaving word that we'd be back before night, we got away quietly, not wishing to be thought too gullible if we failed, and secretly hoping to have some nice little discovery all to ourselves.

It was a long two hours, nearer three. I fancy the savage could have done it alone much quicker. There was a desperate tangle of wood and water and a swampy patch we never should have found our way across alone. But there was one, and I could see Terry, with compass and notebook, marking directions and trying to place landmarks.

We came after a while to a sort of marshy lake, very big, so that the circling forest looked quite low and dim across it. Our guide told us that boats could go from there to our camp—but "long way—all day."

This water was somewhat clearer than that we had left, but we could not judge well from the margin. We skirted it for another half hour or so, the ground growing firmer as we advanced, and presently we turned the corner of a wooded promontory and saw a quite different country—a sudden view of mountains, steep and bare.

"One of those long easterly spurs," Terry said appraisingly. "May be hundreds of miles from the range. They crop out like that."

Suddenly we left the lake and struck directly toward the cliffs. We heard running water before we reached it, and the guide pointed proudly to his river.

It was short. We could see where it poured down a narrow vertical cataract from an opening in the face of the cliff. It was sweet water. The guide drank eagerly and so did we.

"That's snow water," Terry announced. "Must come from way back in the hills."

But as to being red and blue—it was greenish in tint. The guide seemed not at all surprised. He hunted about a little and showed us a quiet marginal pool where there were smears of red along the border; yes, and of blue.

Terry got out his magnifying glass and squatted down to investigate.

"Chemicals of some sort—I can't tell on the spot. Look to me like dyestuffs. Let's get nearer," he urged, "up there by the fall."

We scrambled along the steep banks and got close to the pool that foamed and boiled beneath the falling water. Here we searched the border and found traces of color beyond dispute. More—Jeff suddenly held up an unlooked-for trophy.

It was only a rag, a long, raveled fragment of cloth. But it was a well-woven fabric, with a pattern, and of a clear scarlet that the water had not faded. No savage tribe that we had heard of made such fabrics.

The guide stood serenely on the bank, well pleased with our excitement.

"One day blue—one day red—one day green," he told us, and pulled from his pouch another strip of bright-hued cloth.

"Come down," he said, pointing to the cataract. "Woman Country—up there."

Then we were interested. We had our rest and lunch right there and pumped the man for further information. He could tell us only what the others had—a land of women—no men—babies, but all girls. No place for men—dangerous. Some had gone to see—none had come back.

I could see Terry's jaw set at that. No place for men? Dangerous? He looked as if he might shin up the waterfall on the spot. But the guide would not hear of going up, even if there had been any possible method of scaling that sheer cliff, and we had to get back to our party before night.

"They might stay if we told them," I suggested.

But Terry stopped in his tracks. "Look here, fellows," he said. "This is our find. Let's not tell those cocky old professors. Let's go on home with 'em, and then come back—just us—have a little expedition of our own."

We looked at him, much impressed. There was something attractive to a bunch of unattached young men in finding an undiscovered country of a strictly Amazonian nature.

Of course we didn't believe the story—but yet!

"There is no such cloth made by any of these local tribes," I announced, examining those rags with great care. "Somewhere up yonder they spin and weave and dye—as well as we do."

"That would mean a considerable civilization, Van. There couldn't be such a place—and not known about."

"Oh, well, I don't know. What's that old republic up in the Pyrenees somewhere—Andorra? Precious few people know anything about that, and it's been minding its own business for a thousand years. Then there's Montenegro—splendid little state—you could lose a dozen Montenegroes up and down these great ranges."

We discussed it hotly all the way back to camp. We discussed it with care and privacy on the voyage home. We discussed it after that, still only among ourselves, while Terry was making his arrangements.

He was hot about it. Lucky he had so much money—we might have had to beg and advertise for years to start the thing, and then it would have been a matter of public amusement—just sport for the papers.

But T. O. Nicholson could fix up his big steam yacht, load his specially-made big motorboat aboard, and tuck in a "dissembled" biplane without any more notice than a snip in the society column.

We had provisions and preventives and all manner of supplies. His previous experience stood him in good stead there. It was a very complete little outfit.

We were to leave the yacht at the nearest safe port and go up that endless river in our motorboat, just the three of us and a pilot; then drop the pilot when we got to that last stopping place of the previous party, and hunt up that clear water stream ourselves.

The motorboat we were going to leave at anchor in that wide shallow lake. It had a special covering of fitted armor, thin but strong, shut up like a clamshell.

"Those natives can't get into it, or hurt it, or move it," Terry explained proudly. "We'll start our flier from the lake and leave the boat as a base to come back to."

"If we come back," I suggested cheerfully.

"'Fraid the ladies will eat you?" he scoffed.

"We're not so sure about those ladies, you know," drawled Jeff. "There may be a contingent of gentlemen with poisoned arrows or something."

"You don't need to go if you don't want to," Terry remarked drily.

"Go? You'll have to get an injunction to stop me!" Both Jeff and I were sure about that.

But we did have differences of opinion, all the long way.

An ocean voyage is an excellent time for discussion. Now we had no eavesdroppers, we could loll and loaf in our deck chairs and talk and talk—there was nothing else to do. Our absolute lack of facts only made the field of discussion wider.

"We'll leave papers with our consul where the yacht stays," Terry planned. "If we don't come back in—say a month—they can send a relief party after us."

"A punitive expedition," I urged. "If the ladies do eat us we must make reprisals."

"They can locate that last stopping place easy enough, and I've made a sort of chart of that lake and cliff and waterfall."

"Yes, but how will they get up?" asked Jeff.

"Same way we do, of course. If three valuable American citizens are lost up there, they will follow somehow—to say nothing of the glittering attractions of that fair land—let's call it 'Feminisia,'" he broke off.

"You're right, Terry. Once the story gets out, the river will crawl with expeditions and the airships rise like a swarm of mosquitoes." I laughed as I thought of it. "We've made a great mistake not to let Mr. Yellow Press in on this. Save us! What headlines!"

"Not much!" said Terry grimly. "This is our party. We're going to find that place alone."

"What are you going to do with it when you do find it—if you do?" Jeff asked mildly.

Jeff was a tender soul. I think he thought that country—if there was one—was just blossoming with roses and babies and canaries and tidies, and all that sort of thing.

And Terry, in his secret heart, had visions of a sort of sublimated summer resort—just Girls and Girls and Girls—and that he was going to be—well, Terry was popular among women even when there were other men around, and it's not to be wondered at that he had pleasant dreams of what might happen. I could see it in his eyes as he lay there, looking at the long blue rollers slipping by, and fingering that impressive mustache of his.

But I thought—then—that I could form a far clearer idea of what was before us than either of them.

"You're all off, boys," I insisted. "If there is such a place—and there does seem some foundation for believing it—you'll find it's built on a sort of matriarchal principle, that's all. The men have a separate cult of their own, less socially developed than the women, and make them an annual visit—a sort of wedding call. This is a condition known to have existed—here's just a survival. They've got some peculiarly isolated valley or tableland up there, and their primeval customs have survived. That's all there is to it."

"How about the boys?" Jeff asked.

"Oh, the men take them away as soon as they are five or six, you see."

"And how about this danger theory all our guides were so sure of?"

"Danger enough, Terry, and we'll have to be mighty careful. Women of that stage of culture are quite able to defend themselves and have no welcome for unseasonable visitors."

We talked and talked.

And with all my airs of sociological superiority I was no nearer than any of them.

It was funny though, in the light of what we did find, those extremely clear ideas of ours as to what a country of women would be like. It was no use to tell ourselves and one another that all this was idle speculation. We were idle and we did speculate, on the ocean voyage and the river voyage, too.

"Admitting the improbability," we'd begin solemnly, and then launch out again.

"They would fight among themselves," Terry insisted. "Women always do. We mustn't look to find any sort of order and organization."

"You're dead wrong," Jeff told him. "It will be like a nunnery under an abbess—a peaceful, harmonious sisterhood."

I snorted derision at this idea.

"Nuns, indeed! Your peaceful sisterhoods were all celibate, Jeff, and under vows of obedience. These are just women, and mothers, and where there's motherhood you don't find sisterhood—not much."

"No, sir—they'll scrap," agreed Terry. "Also we mustn't look for inventions and progress; it'll be awfully primitive."

"How about that cloth mill?" Jeff suggested.

"Oh, cloth! Women have always been spinsters. But there they stop—you'll see."

We joked Terry about his modest impression that he would be warmly received, but he held his ground.

"You'll see," he insisted. "I'll get solid with them all—and play one bunch against another. I'll get myself elected king in no time—whew! Solomon will have to take a back seat!"

"Where do we come in on that deal?" I demanded. "Aren't we Viziers or anything?"

"Couldn't risk it," he asserted solemnly. "You might start a revolution—probably would. No, you'll have to be beheaded, or bowstrung—or whatever the popular method of execution is."

"You'd have to do it yourself, remember," grinned Jeff. "No husky black slaves and mamelukes! And there'd be two of us and only one of you—eh, Van?"

Jeff's ideas and Terry's were so far apart that sometimes it was all I could do to keep the peace between them. Jeff idealized women in the best Southern style. He was full of chivalry and sentiment, and all that. And he was a good boy; he lived up to his ideals.

You might say Terry did, too, if you can call his views about women anything so polite as ideals. I always liked Terry. He was a man's man, very much so, generous and brave and clever; but I don't think any of us in college days was quite pleased to have him with our sisters. We weren't very stringent, heavens no! But Terry was "the limit." Later on—why, of course a man's life is his own, we held, and asked no questions.

But barring a possible exception in favor of a not impossible wife, or of his mother, or, of course, the fair relatives of his friends, Terry's idea seemed to be that pretty women were just so much game and homely ones not worth considering.

It was really unpleasant sometimes to see the notions he had.

But I got out of patience with Jeff, too. He had such rose-colored halos on his womenfolks. I held a middle ground, highly scientific, of course, and used to argue learnedly about the physiological limitations of the sex.

We were not in the least "advanced" on the woman question, any of us, then.

So we joked and disputed and speculated, and after an interminable journey, we got to our old camping place at last.

It was not hard to find the river, just poking along that side till we came to it, and it was navigable as far as the lake.

When we reached that and slid out on its broad glistening bosom, with that high gray promontory running out toward us, and the straight white fall clearly visible, it began to be really exciting.

There was some talk, even then, of skirting the rock wall and seeking a possible footway up, but the marshy jungle made that method look not only difficult but dangerous.

Terry dismissed the plan sharply.

"Nonsense, fellows! We've decided that. It might take months—we haven't got the provisions. No, sir—we've got to take our chances. If we get back safe—all right. If we don't, why, we're not the first explorers to get lost in the shuffle. There are plenty to come after us."

So we got the big biplane together and loaded it with our scientifically compressed baggage: the camera, of course; the glasses; a supply of concentrated food. Our pockets were magazines of small necessities, and we had our guns, of course—there was no knowing what might happen.

Up and up and up we sailed, way up at first, to get "the lay of the land" and make note of it.

Out of that dark green sea of crowding forest this high-standing spur rose steeply. It ran back on either side, apparently, to the far-off white-crowned peaks in the distance, themselves probably inaccessible.

"Let's make the first trip geographical," I suggested. "Spy out the land, and drop back here for more gasoline. With your tremendous speed we can reach that range and back all right. Then we can leave a sort of map on board—for that relief expedition."

"There's sense in that," Terry agreed. "I'll put off being king of Ladyland for one more day."

So we made a long skirting voyage, turned the point of the cape which was close by, ran up one side of the triangle at our best speed, crossed over the base where it left the higher mountains, and so back to our lake by moonlight.

"That's not a bad little kingdom," we agreed when it was roughly drawn and measured. We could tell the size fairly by our speed. And from what we could see of the sides—and that icy ridge at the back end—"It's a pretty enterprising savage who would manage to get into it," Jeff said.

Of course we had looked at the land itself—eagerly, but we were too high and going too fast to see much. It appeared to be well forested about the edges, but in the interior there were wide plains, and everywhere parklike meadows and open places.

There were cities, too; that I insisted. It looked—well, it looked like any other country—a civilized one, I mean.

We had to sleep after that long sweep through the air, but we turned out early enough next day, and again we rose softly up the height till we could top the crowning trees and see the broad fair land at our pleasure.

"Semitropical. Looks like a first-rate climate. It's wonderful what a little height will do for temperature." Terry was studying the forest growth.

"Little height! Is that what you call little?" I asked. Our instruments measured it clearly. We had not realized the long gentle rise from the coast perhaps.

"Mighty lucky piece of land, I call it," Terry pursued. "Now for the folks—I've had enough scenery."

So we sailed low, crossing back and forth, quartering the country as we went, and studying it. We saw—I can't remember now how much of this we noted then and how much was supplemented by our later knowledge, but we could not help seeing this much, even on that excited day—a land in a state of perfect cultivation, where even the forests looked as if they were cared for; a land that looked like an enormous park, only it was even more evidently an enormous garden.

"I don't see any cattle," I suggested, but Terry was silent. We were approaching a village.

I confess that we paid small attention to the clean, well-built roads, to the attractive architecture, to the ordered beauty of the little town. We had our glasses out; even Terry, setting his machine for a spiral glide, clapped the binoculars to his eyes.

They heard our whirring screw. They ran out of the houses—they gathered in from the fields, swift-running light figures, crowds of them. We stared and stared until it was almost too late to catch the levers, sweep off and rise again; and then we held our peace for a long run upward.

"Gosh!" said Terry, after a while.

"Only women there—and children," Jeff urged excitedly.

"But they look—why, this is a CIVILIZED country!" I protested. "There must be men."

"Of course there are men," said Terry. "Come on, let's find 'em."

He refused to listen to Jeff's suggestion that we examine the country further before we risked leaving our machine.

"There's a fine landing place right there where we came over," he insisted, and it was an excellent one—a wide, flat-topped rock, overlooking the lake, and quite out of sight from the interior.

"They won't find this in a hurry," he asserted, as we scrambled with the utmost difficulty down to safer footing. "Come on, boys—there were some good lookers in that bunch."

Of course it was unwise of us.

It was quite easy to see afterward that our best plan was to have studied the country more fully before we left our swooping airship and trusted ourselves to mere foot service. But we were three young men. We had been talking about this country for over a year, hardly believing that there was such a place, and now—we were in it.

It looked safe and civilized enough, and among those upturned, crowding faces, though some were terrified enough, there was great beauty—on that we all agreed.

"Come on!" cried Terry, pushing forward. "Oh, come on! Here goes for Herland!"

2. Rash Advances

Not more than ten or fifteen miles we judged it from our landing rock to that last village. For all our eagerness we thought it wise to keep to the woods and go carefully.

Even Terry's ardor was held in check by his firm conviction that there were men to be met, and we saw to it that each of us had a good stock of cartridges.

"They may be scarce, and they may be hidden away somewhere—some kind of a matriarchate, as Jeff tells us; for that matter, they may live up in the mountains yonder and keep the women in this part of the country—sort of a national harem! But there are men somewhere—didn't you see the babies?"

We had all seen babies, children big and little, everywhere that we had come near enough to distinguish the people. And though by dress we could not be sure of all the grown persons, still there had not been one man that we were certain of.

"I always liked that Arab saying, 'First tie your camel and then trust in the Lord,'" Jeff murmured; so we all had our weapons in hand, and stole cautiously through the forest. Terry studied it as we progressed.

"Talk of civilization," he cried softly in restrained enthusiasm. "I never saw a forest so petted, even in Germany. Look, there's not a dead bough—the vines are trained—actually! And see here"—he stopped and looked about him, calling Jeff's attention to the kinds of trees.

They left me for a landmark and made a limited excursion on either side.

"Food-bearing, practically all of them," they announced returning. "The rest, splendid hardwood. Call this a forest? It's a truck farm!"

"Good thing to have a botanist on hand," I agreed. "Sure there are no medicinal ones? Or any for pure ornament?"

As a matter of fact they were quite right. These towering trees were under as careful cultivation as so many cabbages. In other conditions we should have found those woods full of fair foresters and fruit gatherers; but an airship is a conspicuous object, and by no means quiet—and women are cautious.

All we found moving in those woods, as we started through them, were birds, some gorgeous, some musical, all so tame that it seemed almost to contradict our theory of cultivation—at least until we came upon occasional little glades, where carved stone seats and tables stood in the shade beside clear fountains, with shallow bird baths always added.

"They don't kill birds, and apparently they do kill cats," Terry declared. "MUST be men here. Hark!"

We had heard something: something not in the least like a birdsong, and very much like a suppressed whisper of laughter—a little happy sound, instantly smothered. We stood like so many pointers, and then used our glasses, swiftly, carefully.

"It couldn't have been far off," said Terry excitedly. "How about this big tree?"

There was a very large and beautiful tree in the glade we had just entered, with thick wide-spreading branches that sloped out in lapping fans like a beech or pine. It was trimmed underneath some twenty feet up, and stood there like a huge umbrella, with circling seats beneath.

"Look," he pursued. "There are short stumps of branches left to climb on. There's someone up that tree, I believe."

We stole near, cautiously.

"Look out for a poisoned arrow in your eye," I suggested, but Terry pressed forward, sprang up on the seat-back, and grasped the trunk. "In my heart, more likely," he answered. "Gee! Look, boys!"

We rushed close in and looked up. There among the boughs overhead was something—more than one something—that clung motionless, close to the great trunk at first, and then, as one and all we started up the tree, separated into three swift-moving figures and fled upward. As we climbed we could catch glimpses of them scattering above us. By the time we had reached about as far as three men together dared push, they had left the main trunk and moved outward, each one balanced on a long branch that dipped and swayed beneath the weight.

We paused uncertain. If we pursued further, the boughs would break under the double burden. We might shake them off, perhaps, but none of us was so inclined. In the soft dappled light of these high regions, breathless with our rapid climb, we rested awhile, eagerly studying our objects of pursuit; while they in turn, with no more terror than a set of frolicsome children in a game of tag, sat as lightly as so many big bright birds on their precarious perches and frankly, curiously, stared at us.

"Girls!" whispered Jeff, under his breath, as if they might fly if he spoke aloud.

"Peaches!" added Terry, scarcely louder. "Peacherinos—apricot-nectarines! Whew!"

They were girls, of course, no boys could ever have shown that sparkling beauty, and yet none of us was certain at first.

We saw short hair, hatless, loose, and shining; a suit of some light firm stuff, the closest of tunics and kneebreeches, met by trim gaiters. As bright and smooth as parrots and as unaware of danger, they swung there before us, wholly at ease, staring as we stared, till first one, and then all of them burst into peals of delighted laughter.

Then there was a torrent of soft talk tossed back and forth; no savage sing-song, but clear musical fluent speech.

We met their laughter cordially, and doffed our hats to them, at which they laughed again, delightedly.

Then Terry, wholly in his element, made a polite speech, with explanatory gestures, and proceeded to introduce us, with pointing finger. "Mr. Jeff Margrave," he said clearly; Jeff bowed as gracefully as a man could in the fork of a great limb. "Mr. Vandyck Jennings"—I also tried to make an effective salute and nearly lost my balance.

Then Terry laid his hand upon his chest—a fine chest he had, too, and introduced himself; he was braced carefully for the occasion and achieved an excellent obeisance.

Again they laughed delightedly, and the one nearest me followed his tactics.

"Celis," she said distinctly, pointing to the one in blue; "Alima"—the one in rose; then, with a vivid imitation of Terry's impressive manner, she laid a firm delicate hand on her gold-green jerkin—"Ellador." This was pleasant, but we got no nearer.

"We can't sit here and learn the language," Terry protested. He beckoned to them to come nearer, most winningly—but they gaily shook their heads. He suggested, by signs, that we all go down together; but again they shook their heads, still merrily. Then Ellador clearly indicated that we should go down, pointing to each and all of us, with unmistakable firmness; and further seeming to imply by the sweep of a lithe arm that we not only go downward, but go away altogether—at which we shook our heads in turn.

"Have to use bait," grinned Terry. "I don't know about you fellows, but

I came prepared." He produced from an inner pocket a little box of purple velvet, that opened with a snap—and out of it he drew a long sparkling thing, a necklace of big varicolored stones that would have been worth a million if real ones. He held it up, swung it, glittering in the sun, offered it first to one, then to another, holding it out as far as he could reach toward the girl nearest him. He stood braced in the fork, held firmly by one hand—the other, swinging his bright temptation, reached far out along the bough, but not quite to his full stretch.

She was visibly moved, I noted, hesitated, spoke to her companions. They chattered softly together, one evidently warning her, the other encouraging. Then, softly and slowly, she drew nearer. This was Alima, a tall long-limbed lass, well-knit and evidently both strong and agile. Her eyes were splendid, wide, fearless, as free from suspicion as a child's who has never been rebuked. Her interest was more that of an intent boy playing a fascinating game than of a girl lured by an ornament.

The others moved a bit farther out, holding firmly, watching. Terry's smile was irreproachable, but I did not like the look in his eyes—it was like a creature about to spring. I could already see it happen—the dropped necklace, the sudden clutching hand, the girl's sharp cry as he seized her and drew her in. But it didn't happen. She made a timid reach with her right hand for the gay swinging thing—he held it a little nearer—then, swift as light, she seized it from him with her left, and dropped on the instant to the bough below.

He made his snatch, quite vainly, almost losing his position as his hand clutched only air; and then, with inconceivable rapidity, the three bright creatures were gone. They dropped from the ends of the big boughs to those below, fairly pouring themselves off the tree, while we climbed downward as swiftly as we could. We heard their vanishing gay laughter, we saw them fleeting away in the wide open reaches of the forest, and gave chase, but we might as well have chased wild antelopes; so we stopped at length somewhat breathless.

"No use," gasped Terry. "They got away with it. My word! The men of this country must be good sprinters!"

"Inhabitants evidently arboreal," I grimly suggested. "Civilized and still arboreal—peculiar people."

"You shouldn't have tried that way," Jeff protested. "They were perfectly friendly; now we've scared them."

But it was no use grumbling, and Terry refused to admit any mistake. "Nonsense," he said. "They expected it. Women like to be run after. Come on, let's get to that town; maybe we'll find them there. Let's see, it was in this direction and not far from the woods, as I remember."

When we reached the edge of the open country we reconnoitered with our field glasses. There it was, about four miles off, the same town, we concluded, unless, as Jeff ventured, they all had pink houses. The broad green fields and closely cultivated gardens sloped away at our feet, a long easy slant, with good roads winding pleasantly here and there, and narrower paths besides.

"Look at that!" cried Jeff suddenly. "There they go!"

Sure enough, close to the town, across a wide meadow, three bright-hued figures were running swiftly.

"How could they have got that far in this time? It can't be the same ones," I urged. But through the glasses we could identify our pretty tree-climbers quite plainly, at least by costume.

Terry watched them, we all did for that matter, till they disappeared among the houses. Then he put down his glass and turned to us, drawing a long breath. "Mother of Mike, boys—what Gorgeous Girls! To climb like that! to run like that! and afraid of nothing. This country suits me all right. Let's get ahead."

"Nothing venture, nothing have," I suggested, but Terry preferred "Faint heart ne'er won fair lady."

We set forth in the open, walking briskly. "If there are any men, we'd better keep an eye out," I suggested, but Jeff seemed lost in heavenly dreams, and Terry in highly practical plans.

"What a perfect road! What a heavenly country! See the flowers, will you?"

This was Jeff, always an enthusiast; but we could agree with him fully.

The road was some sort of hard manufactured stuff, sloped slightly to shed rain, with every curve and grade and gutter as perfect as if it were Europe's best. "No men, eh?" sneered Terry. On either side a double row of trees shaded the footpaths; between the trees bushes or vines, all fruit-bearing, now and then seats and little wayside fountains; everywhere flowers.

"We'd better import some of these ladies and set 'em to parking the United States," I suggested. "Mighty nice place they've got here." We rested a few moments by one of the fountains, tested the fruit that looked ripe, and went on, impressed, for all our gay bravado by the sense of quiet potency which lay about us.

Here was evidently a people highly skilled, efficient, caring for their country as a florist cares for his costliest orchids. Under the soft brilliant blue of that clear sky, in the pleasant shade of those endless rows of trees, we walked unharmed, the placid silence broken only by the birds.

Presently there lay before us at the foot of a long hill the town or village we were aiming for. We stopped and studied it.

Jeff drew a long breath. "I wouldn't have believed a collection of houses could look so lovely," he said.

"They've got architects and landscape gardeners in plenty, that's sure," agreed Terry.

I was astonished myself. You see, I come from California, and there's no country lovelier, but when it comes to towns—! I have often groaned at home to see the offensive mess man made in the face of nature, even though I'm no art sharp, like Jeff. But this place! It was built mostly of a sort of dull rose-colored stone, with here and there some clear white houses; and it lay abroad among the green groves and gardens like a broken rosary of pink coral.

"Those big white ones are public buildings evidently," Terry declared. "This is no savage country, my friend. But no men? Boys, it behooves us to go forward most politely."

The place had an odd look, more impressive as we approached. "It's like an exposition." "It's too pretty to be true." "Plenty of palaces, but where are the homes?" "Oh there are little ones enough—but—." It certainly was different from any towns we had ever seen.

"There's no dirt," said Jeff suddenly. "There's no smoke," he added after a little.

"There's no noise," I offered; but Terry snubbed me—"That's because they are laying low for us; we'd better be careful how we go in there."

Nothing could induce him to stay out, however, so we walked on.

Everything was beauty, order, perfect cleanness, and the pleasantest sense of home over it all. As we neared the center of the town the houses stood thicker, ran together as it were, grew into rambling palaces grouped among parks and open squares, something as college buildings stand in their quiet greens.

And then, turning a corner, we came into a broad paved space and saw before us a band of women standing close together in even order, evidently waiting for us.

We stopped a moment and looked back. The street behind was closed by another band, marching steadily, shoulder to shoulder. We went on—there seemed no other way to go—and presently found ourselves quite surrounded by this close-massed multitude, women, all of them, but—

They were not young. They were not old. They were not, in the girl sense, beautiful. They were not in the least ferocious. And yet, as I looked from face to face, calm, grave, wise, wholly unafraid, evidently assured and determined, I had the funniest feeling—a very early feeling—a feeling that I traced back and back in memory until I caught up with it at last. It was that sense of being hopelessly in the wrong that I had so often felt in early youth when my short legs' utmost effort failed to overcome the fact that I was late to school.

Jeff felt it too; I could see he did. We felt like small boys, very small boys, caught doing mischief in some gracious lady's house. But Terry showed no such consciousness. I saw his quick eyes darting here and there, estimating numbers, measuring distances, judging chances of escape. He examined the close ranks about us, reaching back far on every side, and murmured softly to me, "Every one of 'em over forty as I'm a sinner."

Yet they were not old women. Each was in the full bloom of rosy health, erect, serene, standing sure-footed and light as any pugilist. They had no weapons, and we had, but we had no wish to shoot.

"I'd as soon shoot my aunts," muttered Terry again. "What do they want with us anyhow? They seem to mean business." But in spite of that businesslike aspect, he determined to try his favorite tactics. Terry had come armed with a theory.

He stepped forward, with his brilliant ingratiating smile, and made low obeisance to the women before him. Then he produced another tribute, a broad soft scarf of filmy texture, rich in color and pattern, a lovely thing, even to my eye, and offered it with a deep bow to the tall unsmiling woman who seemed to head the ranks before him. She took it with a gracious nod of acknowledgment, and passed it on to those behind her.

He tried again, this time bringing out a circlet of rhinestones, a glittering crown that should have pleased any woman on earth. He made a brief address, including Jeff and me as partners in his enterprise, and with another bow presented this. Again his gift was accepted and, as before, passed out of sight.

"If they were only younger," he muttered between his teeth. "What on earth is a fellow to say to a regiment of old Colonels like this?"

In all our discussions and speculations we had always unconsciously assumed that the women, whatever else they might be, would be young. Most men do think that way, I fancy.

"Woman" in the abstract is young, and, we assume, charming. As they get older they pass off the stage, somehow, into private ownership mostly, or out of it altogether. But these good ladies were very much on the stage, and yet any one of them might have been a grandmother.

We looked for nervousness—there was none.

For terror, perhaps—there was none.

For uneasiness, for curiosity, for excitement—and all we saw was what might have been a vigilance committee of women doctors, as cool as cucumbers, and evidently meaning to take us to task for being there.

Six of them stepped forward now, one on either side of each of us, and indicated that we were to go with them. We thought it best to accede, at first anyway, and marched along, one of these close at each elbow, and the others in close masses before, behind, on both sides.

A large building opened before us, a very heavy thick-walled impressive place, big, and old-looking; of gray stone, not like the rest of the town.

"This won't do!" said Terry to us, quickly. "We mustn't let them get us in this, boys. All together, now—"

We stopped in our tracks. We began to explain, to make signs pointing away toward the big forest—indicating that we would go back to it—at once.

It makes me laugh, knowing all I do now, to think of us three boys—nothing else; three audacious impertinent boys—butting into an unknown country without any sort of a guard or defense. We seemed to think that if there were men we could fight them, and if there were only women—why, they would be no obstacles at all.

Jeff, with his gentle romantic old-fashioned notions of women as clinging vines. Terry, with his clear decided practical theories that there were two kinds of women—those he wanted and those he didn't; Desirable and Undesirable was his demarcation. The latter as a large class, but negligible—he had never thought about them at all.

And now here they were, in great numbers, evidently indifferent to what he might think, evidently determined on some purpose of their own regarding him, and apparently well able to enforce their purpose.

We all thought hard just then. It had not seemed wise to object to going with them, even if we could have; our one chance was friendliness—a civilized attitude on both sides.

But once inside that building, there was no knowing what these determined ladies might do to us. Even a peaceful detention was not to our minds, and when we named it imprisonment it looked even worse.

So we made a stand, trying to make clear that we preferred the open country. One of them came forward with a sketch of our flier, asking by signs if we were the aerial visitors they had seen.

This we admitted.

They pointed to it again, and to the outlying country, in different directions—but we pretended we did not know where it was, and in truth we were not quite sure and gave a rather wild indication of its whereabouts.

Again they motioned us to advance, standing so packed about the door that there remained but the one straight path open. All around us and behind they were massed solidly—there was simply nothing to do but go forward—or fight.

We held a consultation.

"I never fought with women in my life," said Terry, greatly perturbed, "but I'm not going in there. I'm not going to be—herded in—as if we were in a cattle chute."

"We can't fight them, of course," Jeff urged. "They're all women, in spite of their nondescript clothes; nice women, too; good strong sensible faces. I guess we'll have to go in."

"We may never get out, if we do," I told them. "Strong and sensible, yes; but I'm not so sure about the good. Look at those faces!"

They had stood at ease, waiting while we conferred together, but never relaxing their close attention.

Their attitude was not the rigid discipline of soldiers; there was no sense of compulsion about them. Terry's term of a "vigilance committee" was highly descriptive. They had just the aspect of sturdy burghers, gathered hastily to meet some common need or peril, all moved by precisely the same feelings, to the same end.

Never, anywhere before, had I seen women of precisely this quality. Fishwives and market women might show similar strength, but it was coarse and heavy. These were merely athletic—light and powerful. College professors, teachers, writers—many women showed similar intelligence but often wore a strained nervous look, while these were as calm as cows, for all their evident intellect.

We observed pretty closely just then, for all of us felt that it was a crucial moment.

The leader gave some word of command and beckoned us on, and the surrounding mass moved a step nearer.

"We've got to decide quick," said Terry.

"I vote to go in," Jeff urged. But we were two to one against him and he loyally stood by us. We made one more effort to be let go, urgent, but not imploring. In vain.

"Now for a rush, boys!" Terry said. "And if we can't break 'em, I'll shoot in the air."

Then we found ourselves much in the position of the suffragette trying to get to the Parliament buildings through a triple cordon of London police.

The solidity of those women was something amazing. Terry soon found that it was useless, tore himself loose for a moment, pulled his revolver, and fired upward. As they caught at it, he fired again—we heard a cry—.

Instantly each of us was seized by five women, each holding arm or leg or head; we were lifted like children, straddling helpless children, and borne onward, wriggling indeed, but most ineffectually.

We were borne inside, struggling manfully, but held secure most womanfully, in spite of our best endeavors.

So carried and so held, we came into a high inner hall, gray and bare, and were brought before a majestic gray-haired woman who seemed to hold a judicial position.

There was some talk, not much, among them, and then suddenly there fell upon each of us at once a firm hand holding a wetted cloth before mouth and nose—an order of swimming sweetness—anesthesia.

3. A Peculiar Imprisonment

From a slumber as deep as death, as refreshing as that of a healthy child, I slowly awakened.

It was like rising up, up, up through a deep warm ocean, nearer and nearer to full light and stirring air. Or like the return to consciousness after concussion of the brain. I was once thrown from a horse while on a visit to a wild mountainous country quite new to me, and I can clearly remember the mental experience of coming back to life, through lifting veils of dream. When I first dimly heard the voices of those about me, and saw the shining snowpeaks of that mighty range, I assumed that this too would pass, and I should presently find myself in my own home.

That was precisely the experience of this awakening: receding waves of half-caught swirling vision, memories of home, the steamer, the boat, the airship, the forest—at last all sinking away one after another, till my eyes were wide open, my brain clear, and I realized what had happened.

The most prominent sensation was of absolute physical comfort. I was lying in a perfect bed: long, broad, smooth; firmly soft and level; with the finest linen, some warm light quilt of blanket, and a counterpane that was a joy to the eye. The sheet turned down some fifteen inches, yet I could stretch my feet at the foot of the bed free but warmly covered.

I felt as light and clean as a white feather. It took me some time to conscientiously locate my arms and legs, to feel the vivid sense of life radiate from the wakening center to the extremities.

A big room, high and wide, with many lofty windows whose closed blinds let through soft green-lit air; a beautiful room, in proportion, in color, in smooth simplicity; a scent of blossoming gardens outside.

I lay perfectly still, quite happy, quite conscious, and yet not actively realizing what had happened till I heard Terry.

"Gosh!" was what he said.

I turned my head. There were three beds in this chamber, and plenty of room for them.

Terry was sitting up, looking about him, alert as ever. His remark, though not loud, roused Jeff also. We all sat up.

Terry swung his legs out of bed, stood up, stretched himself mightily. He was in a long nightrobe, a sort of seamless garment, undoubtedly comfortable—we all found ourselves so covered. Shoes were beside each bed, also quite comfortable and goodlooking though by no means like our own.

We looked for our clothes—they were not there, nor anything of all the varied contents of our pockets.

A door stood somewhat ajar; it opened into a most attractive bathroom, copiously provided with towels, soap, mirrors, and all such convenient comforts, with indeed our toothbrushes and combs, our notebooks, and thank goodness, our watches—but no clothes.

Then we made a search of the big room again and found a large airy closet, holding plenty of clothing, but not ours.

"A council of war!" demanded Terry. "Come on back to bed—the bed's all right anyhow. Now then, my scientific friend, let us consider our case dispassionately."

He meant me, but Jeff seemed most impressed.

"They haven't hurt us in the least!" he said. "They could have killed us—or—or anything—and I never felt better in my life."

"That argues that they are all women," I suggested, "and highly civilized. You know you hit one in the last scrimmage—I heard her sing out—and we kicked awfully."

Terry was grinning at us. "So you realize what these ladies have done to us?" he pleasantly inquired. "They have taken away all our possessions, all our clothes—every stitch. We have been stripped and washed and put to bed like so many yearling babies—by these highly civilized women."

Jeff actually blushed. He had a poetic imagination. Terry had imagination enough, of a different kind. So had I, also different. I always flattered myself I had the scientific imagination, which, incidentally, I considered the highest sort. One has a right to a certain amount of egotism if founded on fact—and kept to one's self—I think.

"No use kicking, boys," I said. "They've got us, and apparently they're perfectly harmless. It remains for us to cook up some plan of escape like any other bottled heroes. Meanwhile we've got to put on these clothes—Hobson's choice."

The garments were simple in the extreme, and absolutely comfortable, physically, though of course we all felt like supes in the theater. There was a one-piece cotton undergarment, thin and soft, that reached over the knees and shoulders, something like the one-piece pajamas some fellows wear, and a kind of half-hose, that came up to just under the knee and stayed there—had elastic tops of their own, and covered the edges of the first.

Then there was a thicker variety of union suit, a lot of them in the closet, of varying weights and somewhat sturdier material—evidently they would do at a pinch with nothing further. Then there were tunics, knee-length, and some long robes. Needless to say, we took tunics.

We bathed and dressed quite cheerfully.

"Not half bad," said Terry, surveying himself in a long mirror. His hair was somewhat longer than when we left the last barber, and the hats provided were much like those seen on the prince in the fairy tale, lacking the plume.

The costume was similar to that which we had seen on all the women, though some of them, those working in the fields, glimpsed by our glasses when we first flew over, wore only the first two.

I settled my shoulders and stretched my arms, remarking: "They have worked out a mighty sensible dress, I'll say that for them." With which we all agreed.

"Now then," Terry proclaimed, "we've had a fine long sleep—we've had a good bath—we're clothed and in our right minds, though feeling like a lot of neuters. Do you think these highly civilized ladies are going to give us any breakfast?"

"Of course they will," Jeff asserted confidently. "If they had meant to kill us, they would have done it before. I believe we are going to be treated as guests."

"Hailed as deliverers, I think," said Terry.

"Studied as curiosities," I told them. "But anyhow, we want food. So now for a sortie!"

A sortie was not so easy.

The bathroom only opened into our chamber, and that had but one outlet, a big heavy door, which was fastened.

We listened.

"There's someone outside," Jeff suggested. "Let's knock."

So we knocked, whereupon the door opened.

Outside was another large room, furnished with a great table at one end, long benches or couches against the wall, some smaller tables and chairs. All these were solid, strong, simple in structure, and comfortable in use—also, incidentally, beautiful.

This room was occupied by a number of women, eighteen to be exact, some of whom we distinctly recalled.

Terry heaved a disappointed sigh. "The Colonels!" I heard him whisper to Jeff.

Jeff, however, advanced and bowed in his best manner; so did we all, and we were saluted civilly by the tall-standing women.

We had no need to make pathetic pantomime of hunger; the smaller tables were already laid with food, and we were gravely invited to be seated. The tables were set for two; each of us found ourselves placed vis-a-vis with one of our hosts, and each table had five other stalwarts nearby, unobtrusively watching. We had plenty of time to get tired of those women!

The breakfast was not profuse, but sufficient in amount and excellent in quality. We were all too good travelers to object to novelty, and this repast with its new but delicious fruit, its dish of large rich-flavored nuts, and its highly satisfactory little cakes was most agreeable. There was water to drink, and a hot beverage of a most pleasing quality, some preparation like cocoa.

And then and there, willy-nilly, before we had satisfied our appetites, our education began.

By each of our plates lay a little book, a real printed book, though different from ours both in paper and binding, as well, of course, as in type. We examined them curiously.

"Shades of Sauveur!" muttered Terry. "We're to learn the language!"

We were indeed to learn the language, and not only that, but to teach our own. There were blank books with parallel columns, neatly ruled, evidently prepared for the occasion, and in these, as fast as we learned and wrote down the name of anything, we were urged to write our own name for it by its side.

The book we had to study was evidently a schoolbook, one in which children learned to read, and we judged from this, and from their frequent consultation as to methods, that they had had no previous experience in the art of teaching foreigners their language, or of learning any other.

On the other hand, what they lacked in experience, they made up for in genius. Such subtle understanding, such instant recognition of our difficulties, and readiness to meet them, were a constant surprise to us.

Of course, we were willing to meet them halfway. It was wholly to our advantage to be able to understand and speak with them, and as to refusing to teach them—why should we? Later on we did try open rebellion, but only once.

That first meal was pleasant enough, each of us quietly studying his companion, Jeff with sincere admiration, Terry with that highly technical look of his, as of a past master—like a lion tamer, a serpent charmer, or some such professional. I myself was intensely interested.

It was evident that those sets of five were there to check any outbreak on our part. We had no weapons, and if we did try to do any damage, with a chair, say, why five to one was too many for us, even if they were women; that we had found out to our sorrow. It was not pleasant, having them always around, but we soon got used to it.

"It's better than being physically restrained ourselves," Jeff philosophically suggested when we were alone. "They've given us a room—with no great possibility of escape—and personal liberty—heavily chaperoned. It's better than we'd have been likely to get in a man-country."

"Man-Country! Do you really believe there are no men here, you innocent? Don't you know there must be?" demanded Terry.

"Ye—es," Jeff agreed. "Of course—and yet—"

"And yet—what! Come, you obdurate sentimentalist—what are you thinking about?"

"They may have some peculiar division of labor we've never heard of," I suggested. "The men may live in separate towns, or they may have subdued them—somehow—and keep them shut up. But there must be some."

"That last suggestion of yours is a nice one, Van," Terry protested. "Same as they've got us subdued and shut up! you make me shiver."

"Well, figure it out for yourself, anyway you please. We saw plenty of kids, the first day, and we've seen those girls—"

"Real girls!" Terry agreed, in immense relief. "Glad you mentioned 'em. I declare, if I thought there was nothing in the country but those grenadiers I'd jump out the window."

"Speaking of windows," I suggested, "let's examine ours."

We looked out of all the windows. The blinds opened easily enough, and there were no bars, but the prospect was not reassuring.

This was not the pink-walled town we had so rashly entered the day before. Our chamber was high up, in a projecting wing of a sort of castle, built out on a steep spur of rock. Immediately below us were gardens, fruitful and fragrant, but their high walls followed the edge of the cliff which dropped sheer down, we could not see how far. The distant sound of water suggested a river at the foot.

We could look out east, west, and south. To the southeastward stretched the open country, lying bright and fair in the morning light, but on either side, and evidently behind, rose great mountains.

"This thing is a regular fortress—and no women built it, I can tell you that," said Terry. We nodded agreeingly. "It's right up among the hills—they must have brought us a long way."

"We saw some kind of swift-moving vehicles the first day," Jeff reminded us. "If they've got motors, they ARE civilized."

"Civilized or not, we've got our work cut out for us to get away from here. I don't propose to make a rope of bedclothes and try those walls till I'm sure there is no better way."

We all concurred on this point, and returned to our discussion as to the women.

Jeff continued thoughtful. "All the same, there's something funny about it," he urged. "It isn't just that we don't see any men—but we don't see any signs of them. The—the—reaction of these women is different from any that I've ever met."

"There is something in what you say, Jeff," I agreed. "There is a different—atmosphere."

"They don't seem to notice our being men," he went on. "They treat us—well—just as they do one another. It's as if our being men was a minor incident."

I nodded. I'd noticed it myself. But Terry broke in rudely.

"Fiddlesticks!" he said. "It's because of their advanced age. They're all grandmas, I tell you—or ought to be. Great aunts, anyhow. Those girls were girls all right, weren't they?"

"Yes—" Jeff agreed, still slowly. "But they weren't afraid—they flew up that tree and hid, like schoolboys caught out of bounds—not like shy girls."

"And they ran like marathon winners—you'll admit that, Terry," he added.

Terry was moody as the days passed. He seemed to mind our confinement more than Jeff or I did; and he harped on Alima, and how near he'd come to catching her. "If I had—" he would say, rather savagely, "we'd have had a hostage and could have made terms."

But Jeff was getting on excellent terms with his tutor, and even his guards, and so was I. It interested me profoundly to note and study the subtle difference between these women and other women, and try to account for them. In the matter of personal appearance, there was a great difference. They all wore short hair, some few inches at most; some curly, some not; all light and clean and fresh-looking.

"If their hair was only long," Jeff would complain, "they would look so much more feminine."

I rather liked it myself, after I got used to it. Why we should so admire "a woman's crown of hair" and not admire a Chinaman's queue is hard to explain, except that we are so convinced that the long hair "belongs" to a woman. Whereas the "mane" in horses is on both, and in lions, buffalos, and such creatures only on the male. But I did miss it—at first.

Our time was quite pleasantly filled. We were free of the garden below our windows, quite long in its irregular rambling shape, bordering the cliff. The walls were perfectly smooth and high, ending in the masonry of the building; and as I studied the great stones I became convinced that the whole structure was extremely old. It was built like the pre-Incan architecture in Peru, of enormous monoliths, fitted as closely as mosaics.

"These folks have a history, that's sure," I told the others. "And SOME time they were fighters—else why a fortress?"

I said we were free of the garden, but not wholly alone in it. There was always a string of those uncomfortably strong women sitting about, always one of them watching us even if the others were reading, playing games, or busy at some kind of handiwork.

"When I see them knit," Terry said, "I can almost call them feminine."

"That doesn't prove anything," Jeff promptly replied. "Scotch shepherds knit—always knitting."

"When we get out—" Terry stretched himself and looked at the far peaks, "when we get out of this and get to where the real women are—the mothers, and the girls—"

"Well, what'll we do then?" I asked, rather gloomily. "How do you know we'll ever get out?"

This was an unpleasant idea, which we unanimously considered, returning with earnestness to our studies.

"If we are good boys and learn our lessons well," I suggested. "If we are quiet and respectful and polite and they are not afraid of us—then perhaps they will let us out. And anyway—when we do escape, it is of immense importance that we know the language."

Personally, I was tremendously interested in that language, and seeing they had books, was eager to get at them, to dig into their history, if they had one.

It was not hard to speak, smooth and pleasant to the ear, and so easy to read and write that I marveled at it. They had an absolutely phonetic system, the whole thing was as scientific as Esparanto yet bore all the marks of an old and rich civilization.

We were free to study as much as we wished, and were not left merely to wander in the garden for recreation but introduced to a great gymnasium, partly on the roof and partly in the story below. Here we learned real respect for our tall guards. No change of costume was needed for this work, save to lay off outer clothing. The first one was as perfect a garment for exercise as need be devised, absolutely free to move in, and, I had to admit, much better-looking than our usual one.

"Forty—over forty—some of 'em fifty, I bet—and look at 'em!" grumbled Terry in reluctant admiration.

There were no spectacular acrobatics, such as only the young can perform, but for all-around development they had a most excellent system. A good deal of music went with it, with posture dancing and, sometimes, gravely beautiful processional performances.

Jeff was much impressed by it. We did not know then how small a part of their physical culture methods this really was, but found it agreeable to watch, and to take part in.

Oh yes, we took part all right! It wasn't absolutely compulsory, but we thought it better to please.

Terry was the strongest of us, though I was wiry and had good staying power, and Jeff was a great sprinter and hurdler, but I can tell you those old ladies gave us cards and spades. They ran like deer, by which I mean that they ran not as if it was a performance, but as if it was their natural gait. We remembered those fleeting girls of our first bright adventure, and concluded that it was.

They leaped like deer, too, with a quick folding motion of the legs, drawn up and turned to one side with a sidelong twist of the body. I remembered the sprawling spread-eagle way in which some of the fellows used to come over the line—and tried to learn the trick. We did not easily catch up with these experts, however.

"Never thought I'd live to be bossed by a lot of elderly lady acrobats," Terry protested.

They had games, too, a good many of them, but we found them rather uninteresting at first. It was like two people playing solitaire to see who would get it first; more like a race or a—a competitive examination, than a real game with some fight in it.

I philosophized a bit over this and told Terry it argued against their having any men about. "There isn't a man-size game in the lot," I said.

"But they are interesting—I like them," Jeff objected, "and I'm sure they are educational."

"I'm sick and tired of being educated," Terry protested. "Fancy going to a dame school—at our age. I want to Get Out!"

But we could not get out, and we were being educated swiftly. Our special tutors rose rapidly in our esteem. They seemed of rather finer quality than the guards, though all were on terms of easy friendliness. Mine was named Somel, Jeff's Zava, and Terry's Moadine. We tried to generalize from the names, those of the guards, and of our three girls, but got nowhere.

"They sound well enough, and they're mostly short, but there's no similarity of termination—and no two alike. However, our acquaintance is limited as yet."

There were many things we meant to ask—as soon as we could talk well enough. Better teaching I never saw. From morning to night there was Somel, always on call except between two and four; always pleasant with a steady friendly kindness that I grew to enjoy very much. Jeff said Miss Zava—he would put on a title, though they apparently had none—was a darling, that she reminded him of his Aunt Esther at home; but Terry refused to be won, and rather jeered at his own companion, when we were alone.

"I'm sick of it!" he protested. "Sick of the whole thing. Here we are cooped up as helpless as a bunch of three-year-old orphans, and being taught what they think is necessary—whether we like it or not. Confound their old-maid impudence!"

Nevertheless we were taught. They brought in a raised map of their country, beautifully made, and increased our knowledge of geographical terms; but when we inquired for information as to the country outside, they smilingly shook their heads.

They brought pictures, not only the engravings in the books but colored studies of plants and trees and flowers and birds. They brought tools and various small objects—we had plenty of "material" in our school.

If it had not been for Terry we would have been much more contented, but as the weeks ran into months he grew more and more irritable.

"Don't act like a bear with a sore head," I begged him. "We're getting on finely. Every day we can understand them better, and pretty soon we can make a reasonable plea to be let out—"

"LET out!" he stormed. "LET out—like children kept after school. I want to Get Out, and I'm going to. I want to find the men of this place and fight!—or the girls—"

"Guess it's the girls you're most interested in," Jeff commented. "What are you going to fight WITH—your fists?"

"Yes—or sticks and stones—I'd just like to!" And Terry squared off and tapped Jeff softly on the jaw. "Just for instance," he said.

"Anyhow," he went on, "we could get back to our machine and clear out."

"If it's there," I cautiously suggested.

"Oh, don't croak, Van! If it isn't there, we'll find our way down somehow—the boat's there, I guess."

It was hard on Terry, so hard that he finally persuaded us to consider a plan of escape. It was difficult, it was highly dangerous, but he declared that he'd go alone if we wouldn't go with him, and of course we couldn't think of that.

It appeared he had made a pretty careful study of the environment. From our end window that faced the point of the promontory we could get a fair idea of the stretch of wall, and the drop below. Also from the roof we could make out more, and even, in one place, glimpse a sort of path below the wall.

"It's a question of three things," he said. "Ropes, agility, and not being seen."

"That's the hardest part," I urged, still hoping to dissuade him. "One or another pair of eyes is on us every minute except at night."

"Therefore we must do it at night," he answered. "That's easy."

"We've got to think that if they catch us we may not be so well treated afterward," said Jeff.

"That's the business risk we must take. I'm going—if I break my neck." There was no changing him.

The rope problem was not easy. Something strong enough to hold a man and long enough to let us down into the garden, and then down over the wall. There were plenty of strong ropes in the gymnasium—they seemed to love to swing and climb on them—but we were never there by ourselves.

We should have to piece it out from our bedding, rugs, and garments, and moreover, we should have to do it after we were shut in for the night, for every day the place was cleaned to perfection by two of our guardians.

We had no shears, no knives, but Terry was resourceful. "These Jennies have glass and china, you see. We'll break a glass from the bathroom and use that. 'Love will find out a way,'" he hummed. "When we're all out of the window, we'll stand three-man high and cut the rope as far up as we can reach, so as to have more for the wall. I know just where I saw that bit of path below, and there's a big tree there, too, or a vine or something—I saw the leaves."

It seemed a crazy risk to take, but this was, in a way, Terry's expedition, and we were all tired of our imprisonment.

So we waited for full moon, retired early, and spent an anxious hour or two in the unskilled manufacture of man-strong ropes.

To retire into the depths of the closet, muffle a glass in thick cloth, and break it without noise was not difficult, and broken glass will cut, though not as deftly as a pair of scissors.

The broad moonlight streamed in through four of our windows—we had not dared leave our lights on too long—and we worked hard and fast at our task of destruction.

Hangings, rugs, robes, towels, as well as bed-furniture—even the mattress covers—we left not one stitch upon another, as Jeff put it.

Then at an end window, as less liable to observation, we fastened one end of our cable, strongly, to the firm-set hinge of the inner blind, and dropped our coiled bundle of rope softly over.

"This part's easy enough—I'll come last, so as to cut the rope," said Terry.

So I slipped down first, and stood, well braced against the wall; then Jeff on my shoulders, then Terry, who shook us a little as he sawed through the cord above his head. Then I slowly dropped to the ground, Jeff following, and at last we all three stood safe in the garden, with most of our rope with us.

"Good-bye, Grandma!" whispered Terry, under his breath, and we crept softly toward the wall, taking advantage of the shadow of every bush and tree. He had been foresighted enough to mark the very spot, only a scratch of stone on stone, but we could see to read in that light. For anchorage there was a tough, fair-sized shrub close to the wall.

"Now I'll climb up on you two again and go over first," said Terry. "That'll hold the rope firm till you both get up on top. Then I'll go down to the end. If I can get off safely, you can see me and follow—or, say, I'll twitch it three times. If I find there's absolutely no footing—why I'll climb up again, that's all. I don't think they'll kill us."

From the top he reconnoitered carefully, waved his hand, and whispered, "OK," then slipped over. Jeff climbed up and I followed, and we rather shivered to see how far down that swaying, wavering figure dropped, hand under hand, till it disappeared in a mass of foliage far below.

Then there were three quick pulls, and Jeff and I, not without a joyous sense of recovered freedom, successfully followed our leader.

4. Our Venture

We were standing on a narrow, irregular, all too slanting little ledge, and should doubtless have ignominiously slipped off and broken our rash necks but for the vine. This was a thick-leaved, wide-spreading thing, a little like Amphelopsis.

"It's not QUITE vertical here, you see," said Terry, full of pride and enthusiasm. "This thing never would hold our direct weight, but I think if we sort of slide down on it, one at a time, sticking in with hands and feet, we'll reach that next ledge alive."

"As we do not wish to get up our rope again—and can't comfortably stay here—I approve," said Jeff solemnly.

Terry slid down first—said he'd show us how a Christian meets his death. Luck was with us. We had put on the thickest of those intermediate suits, leaving our tunics behind, and made this scramble quite successfully, though I got a pretty heavy fall just at the end, and was only kept on the second ledge by main force. The next stage was down a sort of "chimney"—a long irregular fissure; and so with scratches many and painful and bruises not a few, we finally reached the stream.

It was darker there, but we felt it highly necessary to put as much distance as possible behind us; so we waded, jumped, and clambered down that rocky riverbed, in the flickering black and white moonlight and leaf shadow, till growing daylight forced a halt.

We found a friendly nut-tree, those large, satisfying, soft-shelled nuts we already knew so well, and filled our pockets.

I see that I have not remarked that these women had pockets in surprising number and variety. They were in all their garments, and the middle one in particular was shingled with them. So we stocked up with nuts till we bulged like Prussian privates in marching order, drank all we could hold, and retired for the day.

It was not a very comfortable place, not at all easy to get at, just a sort of crevice high up along the steep bank, but it was well veiled with foliage and dry. After our exhaustive three- or four-hour scramble and the good breakfast food, we all lay down along that crack—heads and tails, as it were—and slept till the afternoon sun almost toasted our faces.

Terry poked a tentative foot against my head.

"How are you, Van? Alive yet?"

"Very much so," I told him. And Jeff was equally cheerful.

We had room to stretch, if not to turn around; but we could very carefully roll over, one at a time, behind the sheltering foliage.

It was no use to leave there by daylight. We could not see much of the country, but enough to know that we were now at the beginning of the cultivated area, and no doubt there would be an alarm sent out far and wide.

Terry chuckled softly to himself, lying there on that hot narrow little rim of rock. He dilated on the discomfiture of our guards and tutors, making many discourteous remarks.

I reminded him that we had still a long way to go before getting to the place where we'd left our machine, and no probability of finding it there; but he only kicked me, mildly, for a croaker.

"If you can't boost, don't knock," he protested. "I never said 'twould be a picnic. But I'd run away in the Antarctic ice fields rather than be a prisoner."

We soon dozed off again.

The long rest and penetrating dry heat were good for us, and that night we covered a considerable distance, keeping always in the rough forested belt of land which we knew bordered the whole country. Sometimes we were near the outer edge, and caught sudden glimpses of the tremendous depths beyond.

"This piece of geography stands up like a basalt column," Jeff said. "Nice time we'll have getting down if they have confiscated our machine!" For which suggestion he received summary chastisement.

What we could see inland was peaceable enough, but only moonlit glimpses; by daylight we lay very close. As Terry said, we did not wish to kill the old ladies—even if we could; and short of that they were perfectly competent to pick us up bodily and carry us back, if discovered. There was nothing for it but to lie low, and sneak out unseen if we could do it.

There wasn't much talking done. At night we had our marathon-obstacle race; we "stayed not for brake and we stopped not for stone," and swam whatever water was too deep to wade and could not be got around; but that was only necessary twice. By day, sleep, sound and sweet. Mighty lucky it was that we could live off the country as we did. Even that margin of forest seemed rich in foodstuffs.

But Jeff thoughtfully suggested that that very thing showed how careful we should have to be, as we might run into some stalwart group of gardeners or foresters or nut-gatherers at any minute. Careful we were, feeling pretty sure that if we did not make good this time we were not likely to have another opportunity; and at last we reached a point from which we could see, far below, the broad stretch of that still lake from which we had made our ascent.

"That looks pretty good to me!" said Terry, gazing down at it. "Now, if we can't find the 'plane, we know where to aim if we have to drop over this wall some other way."

The wall at that point was singularly uninviting. It rose so straight that we had to put our heads over to see the base, and the country below seemed to be a far-off marshy tangle of rank vegetation. We did not have to risk our necks to that extent, however, for at last, stealing along among the rocks and trees like so many creeping savages, we came to that flat space where we had landed; and there, in unbelievable good fortune, we found our machine.

"Covered, too, by jingo! Would you think they had that much sense?" cried Terry.

"If they had that much, they're likely to have more," I warned him, softly. "Bet you the thing's watched."

We reconnoitered as widely as we could in the failing moonlight—moons are of a painfully unreliable nature; but the growing dawn showed us the familiar shape, shrouded in some heavy cloth like canvas, and no slightest sign of any watchman near. We decided to make a quick dash as soon as the light was strong enough for accurate work.

"I don't care if the old thing'll go or not," Terry declared. "We can run her to the edge, get aboard, and just plane down—plop!—beside our boat there. Look there—see the boat!"

Sure enough—there was our motor, lying like a gray cocoon on the flat pale sheet of water.

Quietly but swiftly we rushed forward and began to tug at the fastenings of that cover.

"Confound the thing!" Terry cried in desperate impatience. "They've got it sewed up in a bag! And we've not a knife among us!"

Then, as we tugged and pulled at that tough cloth we heard a sound that made Terry lift his head like a war horse—the sound of an unmistakable giggle, yes—three giggles.

There they were—Celis, Alima, Ellador—looking just as they had when we first saw them, standing a little way off from us, as interested, as mischievous as three schoolboys.

"Hold on, Terry—hold on!" I warned. "That's too easy. Look out for a trap."

"Let us appeal to their kind hearts," Jeff urged. "I think they will help us. Perhaps they've got knives."

"It's no use rushing them, anyhow," I was absolutely holding on to Terry. "We know they can out-run and out-climb us."

He reluctantly admitted this; and after a brief parley among ourselves, we all advanced slowly toward them, holding out our hands in token of friendliness.

They stood their ground till we had come fairly near, and then indicated that we should stop. To make sure, we advanced a step or two and they promptly and swiftly withdrew. So we stopped at the distance specified. Then we used their language, as far as we were able, to explain our plight, telling how we were imprisoned, how we had escaped—a good deal of pantomime here and vivid interest on their part—how we had traveled by night and hidden by day, living on nuts—and here Terry pretended great hunger.

I know he could not have been hungry; we had found plenty to eat and had not been sparing in helping ourselves. But they seemed somewhat impressed; and after a murmured consultation they produced from their pockets certain little packages, and with the utmost ease and accuracy tossed them into our hands.

Jeff was most appreciative of this; and Terry made extravagant gestures of admiration, which seemed to set them off, boy-fashion, to show their skill. While we ate the excellent biscuits they had thrown us, and while Ellador kept a watchful eye on our movements, Celis ran off to some distance, and set up a sort of "duck-on-a-rock" arrangement, a big yellow nut on top of three balanced sticks; Alima, meanwhile, gathering stones.

They urged us to throw at it, and we did, but the thing was a long way off, and it was only after a number of failures, at which those elvish damsels laughed delightedly, that Jeff succeeded in bringing the whole structure to the ground. It took me still longer, and Terry, to his intense annoyance, came third.

Then Celis set up the little tripod again, and looked back at us, knocking it down, pointing at it, and shaking her short curls severely. "No," she said. "Bad—wrong!" We were quite able to follow her.

Then she set it up once more, put the fat nut on top, and returned to the others; and there those aggravating girls sat and took turns throwing little stones at that thing, while one stayed by as a setter-up; and they just popped that nut off, two times out of three, without upsetting the sticks. Pleased as Punch they were, too, and we pretended to be, but weren't.

We got very friendly over this game, but I told Terry we'd be sorry if we didn't get off while we could, and then we begged for knives. It was easy to show what we wanted to do, and they each proudly produced a sort of strong clasp-knife from their pockets.

"Yes," we said eagerly, "that's it! Please—" We had learned quite a bit of their language, you see. And we just begged for those knives, but they would not give them to us. If we came a step too near they backed off, standing light and eager for flight.

"It's no sort of use," I said. "Come on—let's get a sharp stone or something—we must get this thing off."

So we hunted about and found what edged fragments we could, and hacked away, but it was like trying to cut sailcloth with a clamshell.

Terry hacked and dug, but said to us under his breath. "Boys, we're in pretty good condition—let's make a life and death dash and get hold of those girls—we've got to."

They had drawn rather nearer to watch our efforts, and we did take them rather by surprise; also, as Terry said, our recent training had strengthened us in wind and limb, and for a few desperate moments those girls were scared and we almost triumphant.

But just as we stretched out our hands, the distance between us widened; they had got their pace apparently, and then, though we ran at our utmost speed, and much farther than I thought wise, they kept just out of reach all the time.

We stopped breathless, at last, at my repeated admonitions.

"This is stark foolishness," I urged. "They are doing it on purpose—come back or you'll be sorry."

We went back, much slower than we came, and in truth we were sorry.

As we reached our swaddled machine, and sought again to tear loose its covering, there rose up from all around the sturdy forms, the quiet determined faces we knew so well.

"Oh Lord!" groaned Terry. "The Colonels! It's all up—they're forty to one."

It was no use to fight. These women evidently relied on numbers, not so much as a drilled force but as a multitude actuated by a common impulse. They showed no sign of fear, and since we had no weapons whatever and there were at least a hundred of them, standing ten deep about us, we gave in as gracefully as we might.

Of course we looked for punishment—a closer imprisonment, solitary confinement maybe—but nothing of the kind happened. They treated us as truants only, and as if they quite understood our truancy.

Back we went, not under an anesthetic this time but skimming along in electric motors enough like ours to be quite recognizable, each of us in a separate vehicle with one able-bodied lady on either side and three facing him.

They were all pleasant enough, and talked to us as much as was possible with our limited powers. And though Terry was keenly mortified, and at first we all rather dreaded harsh treatment, I for one soon began to feel a sort of pleasant confidence and to enjoy the trip.

Here were my five familiar companions, all good-natured as could be, seeming to have no worse feeling than a mild triumph as of winning some simple game; and even that they politely suppressed.

This was a good opportunity to see the country, too, and the more I saw of it, the better I liked it. We went too swiftly for close observation, but I could appreciate perfect roads, as dustless as a swept floor; the shade of endless lines of trees; the ribbon of flowers that unrolled beneath them; and the rich comfortable country that stretched off and away, full of varied charm.

We rolled through many villages and towns, and I soon saw that the parklike beauty of our first-seen city was no exception. Our swift high-sweeping view from the 'plane had been most attractive, but lacked detail; and in that first day of struggle and capture, we noticed little. But now we were swept along at an easy rate of some thirty miles an hour and covered quite a good deal of ground.

We stopped for lunch in quite a sizable town, and here, rolling slowly through the streets, we saw more of the population. They had come out to look at us everywhere we had passed, but here were more; and when we went in to eat, in a big garden place with little shaded tables among the trees and flowers, many eyes were upon us. And everywhere, open country, village, or city—only women. Old women and young women and a great majority who seemed neither young nor old, but just women; young girls, also, though these, and the children, seeming to be in groups by themselves generally, were less in evidence. We caught many glimpses of girls and children in what seemed to be schools or in playgrounds, and so far as we could judge there were no boys. We all looked, carefully. Everyone gazed at us politely, kindly, and with eager interest. No one was impertinent. We could catch quite a bit of the talk now, and all they said seemed pleasant enough.

Well—before nightfall we were all safely back in our big room. The damage we had done was quite ignored; the beds as smooth and comfortable as before, new clothing and towels supplied. The only thing those women did was to illuminate the gardens at night, and to set an extra watch. But they called us to account next day. Our three tutors, who had not joined in the recapturing expedition, had been quite busy in preparing for us, and now made explanation.

They knew well we would make for our machine, and also that there was no other way of getting down—alive. So our flight had troubled no one; all they did was to call the inhabitants to keep an eye on our movements all along the edge of the forest between the two points. It appeared that many of those nights we had been seen, by careful ladies sitting snugly in big trees by the riverbed, or up among the rocks.

Terry looked immensely disgusted, but it struck me as extremely funny. Here we had been risking our lives, hiding and prowling like outlaws, living on nuts and fruit, getting wet and cold at night, and dry and hot by day, and all the while these estimable women had just been waiting for us to come out.

Now they began to explain, carefully using such words as we could understand. It appeared that we were considered as guests of the country—sort of public wards. Our first violence had made it necessary to keep us safeguarded for a while, but as soon as we learned the language—and would agree to do no harm—they would show us all about the land.

Jeff was eager to reassure them. Of course he did not tell on Terry, but he made it clear that he was ashamed of himself, and that he would now conform. As to the language—we all fell upon it with redoubled energy. They brought us books, in greater numbers, and I began to study them seriously.

"Pretty punk literature," Terry burst forth one day, when we were in the privacy of our own room. "Of course one expects to begin on child-stories, but I would like something more interesting now."

"Can't expect stirring romance and wild adventure without men, can you?" I asked. Nothing irritated Terry more than to have us assume that there were no men; but there were no signs of them in the books they gave us, or the pictures.

"Shut up!" he growled. "What infernal nonsense you talk! I'm going to ask 'em outright—we know enough now."

In truth we had been using our best efforts to master the language, and were able to read fluently and to discuss what we read with considerable ease.

That afternoon we were all sitting together on the roof—we three and the tutors gathered about a table, no guards about. We had been made to understand some time earlier that if we would agree to do no violence they would withdraw their constant attendance, and we promised most willingly.

So there we sat, at ease; all in similar dress; our hair, by now, as long as theirs, only our beards to distinguish us. We did not want those beards, but had so far been unable to induce them to give us any cutting instruments.

"Ladies," Terry began, out of a clear sky, as it were, "are there no men in this country?"

"Men?" Somel answered. "Like you?"

"Yes, men," Terry indicated his beard, and threw back his broad shoulders. "Men, real men."

"No," she answered quietly. "There are no men in this country. There has not been a man among us for two thousand years."

Her look was clear and truthful and she did not advance this astonishing statement as if it was astonishing, but quite as a matter of fact.

"But—the people—the children," he protested, not believing her in the least, but not wishing to say so.

"Oh yes," she smiled. "I do not wonder you are puzzled. We are mothers—all of us—but there are no fathers. We thought you would ask about that long ago—why have you not?" Her look was as frankly kind as always, her tone quite simple.

Terry explained that we had not felt sufficiently used to the language, making rather a mess of it, I thought, but Jeff was franker.

"Will you excuse us all," he said, "if we admit that we find it hard to believe? There is no such—possibility—in the rest of the world."

"Have you no kind of life where it is possible?" asked Zava.

"Why, yes—some low forms, of course."

"How low—or how high, rather?"

"Well—there are some rather high forms of insect life in which it occurs. Parthenogenesis, we call it—that means virgin birth."

She could not follow him.

"BIRTH, we know, of course; but what is VIRGIN?"

Terry looked uncomfortable, but Jeff met the question quite calmly. "Among mating animals, the term VIRGIN is applied to the female who has not mated," he answered.

"Oh, I see. And does it apply to the male also? Or is there a different term for him?"

He passed this over rather hurriedly, saying that the same term would apply, but was seldom used.

"No?" she said. "But one cannot mate without the other surely. Is not each then—virgin—before mating? And, tell me, have you any forms of life in which there is birth from a father only?"

"I know of none," he answered, and I inquired seriously.

"You ask us to believe that for two thousand years there have been only women here, and only girl babies born?"

"Exactly," answered Somel, nodding gravely. "Of course we know that among other animals it is not so, that there are fathers as well as mothers; and we see that you are fathers, that you come from a people who are of both kinds. We have been waiting, you see, for you to be able to speak freely with us, and teach us about your country and the rest of the world. You know so much, you see, and we know only our own land."

In the course of our previous studies we had been at some pains to tell them about the big world outside, to draw sketches, maps, to make a globe, even, out of a spherical fruit, and show the size and relation of the countries, and to tell of the numbers of their people. All this had been scant and in outline, but they quite understood.

I find I succeed very poorly in conveying the impression I would like to of these women. So far from being ignorant, they were deeply wise—that we realized more and more; and for clear reasoning, for real brain scope and power they were A No. 1, but there were a lot of things they did not know.

They had the evenest tempers, the most perfect patience and good nature—one of the things most impressive about them all was the absence of irritability. So far we had only this group to study, but afterward I found it a common trait.

We had gradually come to feel that we were in the hands of friends, and very capable ones at that—but we couldn't form any opinion yet of the general level of these women.

"We want you to teach us all you can," Somel went on, her firm shapely hands clasped on the table before her, her clear quiet eyes meeting ours frankly. "And we want to teach you what we have that is novel and useful. You can well imagine that it is a wonderful event to us, to have men among us—after two thousand years. And we want to know about your women."

What she said about our importance gave instant pleasure to Terry. I could see by the way he lifted his head that it pleased him. But when she spoke of our women—someway I had a queer little indescribable feeling, not like any feeling I ever had before when "women" were mentioned.

"Will you tell us how it came about?" Jeff pursued. "You said 'for two thousand years'—did you have men here before that?"

"Yes," answered Zava.

They were all quiet for a little.

"You should have our full history to read—do not be alarmed—it has been made clear and short. It took us a long time to learn how to write history. Oh, how I should love to read yours!"

She turned with flashing eager eyes, looking from one to the other of us.

"It would be so wonderful—would it not? To compare the history of two thousand years, to see what the differences are—between us, who are only mothers, and you, who are mothers and fathers, too. Of course we see, with our birds, that the father is as useful as the mother, almost. But among insects we find him of less importance, sometimes very little. Is it not so with you?"

"Oh, yes, birds and bugs," Terry said, "but not among animals—have you NO animals?"

"We have cats," she said. "The father is not very useful."

"Have you no cattle—sheep—horses?" I drew some rough outlines of these beasts and showed them to her.

"We had, in the very old days, these," said Somel, and sketched with swift sure touches a sort of sheep or llama, "and these"—dogs, of two or three kinds, "that that"—pointing to my absurd but recognizable horse.

"What became of them?" asked Jeff.

"We do not want them anymore. They took up too much room—we need all our land to feed our people. It is such a little country, you know."

"Whatever do you do without milk?" Terry demanded incredulously.

"MILK? We have milk in abundance—our own."

"But—but—I mean for cooking—for grown people," Terry blundered, while they looked amazed and a shade displeased.

Jeff came to the rescue. "We keep cattle for their milk, as well as for their meat," he explained. "Cow's milk is a staple article of diet. There is a great milk industry—to collect and distribute it."

Still they looked puzzled. I pointed to my outline of a cow. "The farmer milks the cow," I said, and sketched a milk pail, the stool, and in pantomime showed the man milking. "Then it is carried to the city and distributed by milkmen—everybody has it at the door in the morning."

"Has the cow no child?" asked Somel earnestly.

"Oh, yes, of course, a calf, that is."

"Is there milk for the calf and you, too?"

It took some time to make clear to those three sweet-faced women the process which robs the cow of her calf, and the calf of its true food; and the talk led us into a further discussion of the meat business. They heard it out, looking very white, and presently begged to be excused.

5. A Unique History

It is no use for me to try to piece out this account with adventures. If the people who read it are not interested in these amazing women and their history, they will not be interested at all.

As for us—three young men to a whole landful of women—what could we do? We did get away, as described, and were peacefully brought back again without, as Terry complained, even the satisfaction of hitting anybody.

There were no adventures because there was nothing to fight. There were no wild beasts in the country and very few tame ones. Of these I might as well stop to describe the one common pet of the country. Cats, of course. But such cats!

What do you suppose these Lady Burbanks had done with their cats? By the most prolonged and careful selection and exclusion they had developed a race of cats that did not sing! That's a fact. The most those poor dumb brutes could do was to make a kind of squeak when they were hungry or wanted the door open, and, of course, to purr, and make the various mother-noises to their kittens.

Moreover, they had ceased to kill birds. They were rigorously bred to destroy mice and moles and all such enemies of the food supply; but the birds were numerous and safe.

While we were discussing birds, Terry asked them if they used feathers for their hats, and they seemed amused at the idea. He made a few sketches of our women's hats, with plumes and quills and those various tickling things that stick out so far; and they were eagerly interested, as at everything about our women.

As for them, they said they only wore hats for shade when working in the sun; and those were big light straw hats, something like those used in China and Japan. In cold weather they wore caps or hoods.

"But for decorative purposes—don't you think they would be becoming?" pursued Terry, making as pretty a picture as he could of a lady with a plumed hat.

They by no means agreed to that, asking quite simply if the men wore the same kind. We hastened to assure her that they did not—drew for them our kind of headgear.

"And do no men wear feathers in their hats?"

"Only Indians," Jeff explained. "Savages, you know." And he sketched a war bonnet to show them.

"And soldiers," I added, drawing a military hat with plumes.

They never expressed horror or disapproval, nor indeed much surprise—just a keen interest. And the notes they made!—miles of them!

But to return to our pussycats. We were a good deal impressed by this achievement in breeding, and when they questioned us—I can tell you we were well pumped for information—we told of what had been done for dogs and horses and cattle, but that there was no effort applied to cats, except for show purposes.

I wish I could represent the kind, quiet, steady, ingenious way they questioned us. It was not just curiosity—they weren't a bit more curious about us than we were about them, if as much. But they were bent on understanding our kind of civilization, and their lines of interrogation would gradually surround us and drive us in till we found ourselves up against some admissions we did not want to make.

"Are all these breeds of dogs you have made useful?" they asked.

"Oh—useful! Why, the hunting dogs and watchdogs and sheepdogs are useful—and sleddogs of course!—and ratters, I suppose, but we don't keep dogs for their USEFULNESS. The dog is 'the friend of man,' we say—we love them."

That they understood. "We love our cats that way. They surely are our friends, and helpers, too. You can see how intelligent and affectionate they are."

It was a fact. I'd never seen such cats, except in a few rare instances. Big, handsome silky things, friendly with everyone and devotedly attached to their special owners.

"You must have a heartbreaking time drowning kittens," we suggested. But they said, "Oh, no! You see we care for them as you do for your valuable cattle. The fathers are few compared to the mothers, just a few very fine ones in each town; they live quite happily in walled gardens and the houses of their friends. But they only have a mating season once a year."

"Rather hard on Thomas, isn't it?" suggested Terry.

"Oh, no—truly! You see, it is many centuries that we have been breeding the kind of cats we wanted. They are healthy and happy and friendly, as you see. How do you manage with your dogs? Do you keep them in pairs, or segregate the fathers, or what?"

Then we explained that—well, that it wasn't a question of fathers exactly; that nobody wanted a—a mother dog; that, well, that practically all our dogs were males—there was only a very small percentage of females allowed to live.

Then Zava, observing Terry with her grave sweet smile, quoted back at him: "Rather hard on Thomas, isn't it? Do they enjoy it—living without mates? Are your dogs as uniformly healthy and sweet-tempered as our cats?"

Jeff laughed, eyeing Terry mischievously. As a matter of fact we began to feel Jeff something of a traitor—he so often flopped over and took their side of things; also his medical knowledge gave him a different point of view somehow.

"I'm sorry to admit," he told them, "that the dog, with us, is the most diseased of any animal—next to man. And as to temper—there are always some dogs who bite people—especially children."

That was pure malice. You see, children were the—the RAISON D'ETRE in this country. All our interlocutors sat up straight at once. They were still gentle, still restrained, but there was a note of deep amazement in their voices.

"Do we understand that you keep an animal—an unmated male animal—that bites children? About how many are there of them, please?"

"Thousands—in a large city," said Jeff, "and nearly every family has one in the country."

Terry broke in at this. "You must not imagine they are all dangerous—it's not one in a hundred that ever bites anybody. Why, they are the best friends of the children—a boy doesn't have half a chance that hasn't a dog to play with!"

"And the girls?" asked Somel.

"Oh—girls—why they like them too," he said, but his voice flatted a little. They always noticed little things like that, we found later.

Little by little they wrung from us the fact that the friend of man, in the city, was a prisoner; was taken out for his meager exercise on a leash; was liable not only to many diseases but to the one destroying horror of rabies; and, in many cases, for the safety of the citizens, had to go muzzled. Jeff maliciously added vivid instances he had known or read of injury and death from mad dogs.

They did not scold or fuss about it. Calm as judges, those women were. But they made notes; Moadine read them to us.

"Please tell me if I have the facts correct," she said. "In your country—and in others too?"

"Yes," we admitted, "in most civilized countries."

"In most civilized countries a kind of animal is kept which is no longer useful—"

"They are a protection," Terry insisted. "They bark if burglars try to get in."

Then she made notes of "burglars" and went on: "because of the love which people bear to this animal."

Zava interrupted here. "Is it the men or the women who love this animal so much?"

"Both!" insisted Terry.

"Equally?" she inquired.

And Jeff said, "Nonsense, Terry—you know men like dogs better than women do—as a whole."

"Because they love it so much—especially men. This animal is kept shut up, or chained."

"Why?" suddenly asked Somel. "We keep our father cats shut up because we do not want too much fathering; but they are not chained—they have large grounds to run in."

"A valuable dog would be stolen if he was let loose," I said. "We put collars on them, with the owner's name, in case they do stray. Besides, they get into fights—a valuable dog might easily be killed by a bigger one."

"I see," she said. "They fight when they meet—is that common?" We admitted that it was.

"They are kept shut up, or chained." She paused again, and asked, "Is not a dog fond of running? Are they not built for speed?" That we admitted, too, and Jeff, still malicious, enlightened them further.

"I've always thought it was a pathetic sight, both ways—to see a man or a woman taking a dog to walk—at the end of a string."

"Have you bred them to be as neat in their habits as cats are?" was the next question. And when Jeff told them of the effect of dogs on sidewalk merchandise and the streets generally, they found it hard to believe.

You see, their country was as neat as a Dutch kitchen, and as to sanitation—but I might as well start in now with as much as I can remember of the history of this amazing country before further description.

And I'll summarize here a bit as to our opportunities for learning it. I will not try to repeat the careful, detailed account I lost; I'll just say that we were kept in that fortress a good six months all told, and after that, three in a pleasant enough city where—to Terry's infinite disgust—there were only "Colonels" and little children—no young women whatever. Then we were under surveillance for three more—always with a tutor or a guard or both. But those months were pleasant because we were really getting acquainted with the girls. That was a chapter!—or will be—I will try to do justice to it.

We learned their language pretty thoroughly—had to; and they learned ours much more quickly and used it to hasten our own studies.

Jeff, who was never without reading matter of some sort, had two little books with him, a novel and a little anthology of verse; and I had one of those pocket encyclopedias—a fat little thing, bursting with facts. These were used in our education—and theirs. Then as soon as we were up to it, they furnished us with plenty of their own books, and I went in for the history part—I wanted to understand the genesis of this miracle of theirs.

And this is what happened, according to their records.

As to geography—at about the time of the Christian era this land had a free passage to the sea. I'm not saying where, for good reasons. But there was a fairly easy pass through that wall of mountains behind us, and there is no doubt in my mind that these people were of Aryan stock, and were once in contact with the best civilization of the old world. They were "white," but somewhat darker than our northern races because of their constant exposure to sun and air.

The country was far larger then, including much land beyond the pass, and a strip of coast. They had ships, commerce, an army, a king—for at that time they were what they so calmly called us—a bi-sexual race.

What happened to them first was merely a succession of historic misfortunes such as have befallen other nations often enough. They were decimated by war, driven up from their coastline till finally the reduced population, with many of the men killed in battle, occupied this hinterland, and defended it for years, in the mountain passes. Where it was open to any possible attack from below they strengthened the natural defenses so that it became unscalably secure, as we found it.

They were a polygamous people, and a slave-holding people, like all of their time; and during the generation or two of this struggle to defend their mountain home they built the fortresses, such as the one we were held in, and other of their oldest buildings, some still in use. Nothing but earthquakes could destroy such architecture—huge solid blocks, holding by their own weight. They must have had efficient workmen and enough of them in those days.

They made a brave fight for their existence, but no nation can stand up against what the steamship companies call "an act of God." While the whole fighting force was doing its best to defend their mountain pathway, there occurred a volcanic outburst, with some local tremors, and the result was the complete filling up of the pass—their only outlet. Instead of a passage, a new ridge, sheer and high, stood between them and the sea; they were walled in, and beneath that wall lay their whole little army. Very few men were left alive, save the slaves; and these now seized their opportunity, rose in revolt, killed their remaining masters even to the youngest boy, killed the old women too, and the mothers, intending to take possession of the country with the remaining young women and girls.

But this succession of misfortunes was too much for those infuriated virgins. There were many of them, and but few of these would-be masters, so the young women, instead of submitting, rose in sheer desperation and slew their brutal conquerors.

This sounds like Titus Andronicus, I know, but that is their account. I suppose they were about crazy—can you blame them?

There was literally no one left on this beautiful high garden land but a bunch of hysterical girls and some older slave women.

That was about two thousand years ago.

At first there was a period of sheer despair. The mountains towered between them and their old enemies, but also between them and escape.

There was no way up or down or out—they simply had to stay there. Some were for suicide, but not the majority. They must have been a plucky lot, as a whole, and they decided to live—as long as they did live. Of course they had hope, as youth must, that something would happen to change their fate.

So they set to work, to bury the dead, to plow and sow, to care for one another.

Speaking of burying the dead, I will set down while I think of it, that they had adopted cremation in about the thirteenth century, for the same reason that they had left off raising cattle—they could not spare the room. They were much surprised to learn that we were still burying—asked our reasons for it, and were much dissatisfied with what we gave. We told them of the belief in the resurrection of the body, and they asked if our God was not as well able to resurrect from ashes as from long corruption. We told them of how people thought it repugnant to have their loved ones burn, and they asked if it was less repugnant to have them decay. They were inconveniently reasonable, those women.

Well—that original bunch of girls set to work to clean up the place and make their living as best they could. Some of the remaining slave women rendered invaluable service, teaching such trades as they knew. They had such records as were then kept, all the tools and implements of the time, and a most fertile land to work in.

There were a handful of the younger matrons who had escaped slaughter, and a few babies were born after the cataclysm—but only two boys, and they both died.

For five or ten years they worked together, growing stronger and wiser and more and more mutually attached, and then the miracle happened—one of these young women bore a child. Of course they all thought there must be a man somewhere, but none was found. Then they decided it must be a direct gift from the gods, and placed the proud mother in the Temple of Maaia—their Goddess of Motherhood—under strict watch. And there, as years passed, this wonder-woman bore child after child, five of them—all girls.

I did my best, keenly interested as I have always been in sociology and social psychology, to reconstruct in my mind the real position of these ancient women. There were some five or six hundred of them, and they were harem-bred; yet for the few preceding generations they had been reared in the atmosphere of such heroic struggle that the stock must have been toughened somewhat. Left alone in that terrific orphanhood, they had clung together, supporting one another and their little sisters, and developing unknown powers in the stress of new necessity. To this pain-hardened and work-strengthened group, who had lost not only the love and care of parents, but the hope of ever having children of their own, there now dawned the new hope.

Here at last was Motherhood, and though it was not for all of them personally, it might—if the power was inherited—found here a new race.

It may be imagined how those five Daughters of Maaia, Children of the Temple, Mothers of the Future—they had all the titles that love and hope and reverence could give—were reared. The whole little nation of women surrounded them with loving service, and waited, between a boundless hope and an equally boundless despair, to see if they, too, would be mothers.

And they were! As fast as they reached the age of twenty-five they began bearing. Each of them, like her mother, bore five daughters. Presently there were twenty-five New Women, Mothers in their own right, and the whole spirit of the country changed from mourning and mere courageous resignation to proud joy. The older women, those who remembered men, died off; the youngest of all the first lot of course died too, after a while, and by that time there were left one hundred and fifty-five parthenogenetic women, founding a new race.

They inherited all that the devoted care of that declining band of original ones could leave them. Their little country was quite safe. Their farms and gardens were all in full production. Such industries as they had were in careful order. The records of their past were all preserved, and for years the older women had spent their time in the best teaching they were capable of, that they might leave to the little group of sisters and mothers all they possessed of skill and knowledge.

There you have the start of Herland! One family, all descended from one mother! She lived to a hundred years old; lived to see her hundred and twenty-five great-granddaughters born; lived as Queen-Priestess-Mother of them all; and died with a nobler pride and a fuller joy than perhaps any human soul has ever known—she alone had founded a new race!

The first five daughters had grown up in an atmosphere of holy calm, of awed watchful waiting, of breathless prayer. To them the longed-for motherhood was not only a personal joy, but a nation's hope. Their twenty-five daughters in turn, with a stronger hope, a richer, wider outlook, with the devoted love and care of all the surviving population, grew up as a holy sisterhood, their whole ardent youth looking forward to their great office. And at last they were left alone; the white-haired First Mother was gone, and this one family, five sisters, twenty-five first cousins, and a hundred and twenty-five second cousins, began a new race.

Here you have human beings, unquestionably, but what we were slow in understanding was how these ultra-women, inheriting only from women, had eliminated not only certain masculine characteristics, which of course we did not look for, but so much of what we had always thought essentially feminine.

The tradition of men as guardians and protectors had quite died out. These stalwart virgins had no men to fear and therefore no need of protection. As to wild beasts—there were none in their sheltered land.

The power of mother-love, that maternal instinct we so highly laud, was theirs of course, raised to its highest power; and a sister-love which, even while recognizing the actual relationship, we found it hard to credit.

Terry, incredulous, even contemptuous, when we were alone, refused to believe the story. "A lot of traditions as old as Herodotus—and about as trustworthy!" he said. "It's likely women—just a pack of women—would have hung together like that! We all know women can't organize—that they scrap like anything—are frightfully jealous."

"But these New Ladies didn't have anyone to be jealous of, remember," drawled Jeff.

"That's a likely story," Terry sneered.

"Why don't you invent a likelier one?" I asked him. "Here ARE the women—nothing but women, and you yourself admit there's no trace of a man in the country." This was after we had been about a good deal.

"I'll admit that," he growled. "And it's a big miss, too. There's not only no fun without 'em—no real sport—no competition; but these women aren't WOMANLY. You know they aren't."

That kind of talk always set Jeff going; and I gradually grew to side with him. "Then you don't call a breed of women whose one concern is motherhood—womanly?" he asked.

"Indeed I don't," snapped Terry. "What does a man care for motherhood—when he hasn't a ghost of a chance at fatherhood? And besides—what's the good of talking sentiment when we are just men together? What a man wants of women is a good deal more than all this 'motherhood'!"

We were as patient as possible with Terry. He had lived about nine months among the "Colonels" when he made that outburst; and with no chance at any more strenuous excitement than our gymnastics gave us—save for our escape fiasco. I don't suppose Terry had ever lived so long with neither Love, Combat, nor Danger to employ his superabundant energies, and he was irritable. Neither Jeff nor I found it so wearing. I was so much interested intellectually that our confinement did not wear on me; and as for Jeff, bless his heart!—he enjoyed the society of that tutor of his almost as much as if she had been a girl—I don't know but more.

As to Terry's criticism, it was true. These women, whose essential distinction of motherhood was the dominant note of their whole culture, were strikingly deficient in what we call "femininity." This led me very promptly to the conviction that those "feminine charms" we are so fond of are not feminine at all, but mere reflected masculinity—developed to please us because they had to please us, and in no way essential to the real fulfillment of their great process. But Terry came to no such conclusion.

"Just you wait till I get out!" he muttered.

Then we both cautioned him. "Look here, Terry, my boy! You be careful! They've been mighty good to us—but do you remember the anesthesia? If you do any mischief in this virgin land, beware of the vengeance of the Maiden Aunts! Come, be a man! It won't be forever."

To return to the history:

They began at once to plan and built for their children, all the strength and intelligence of the whole of them devoted to that one thing. Each girl, of course, was reared in full knowledge of her Crowning Office, and they had, even then, very high ideas of the molding powers of the mother, as well as those of education.

Such high ideals as they had! Beauty, Health, Strength, Intellect, Goodness—for those they prayed and worked.

They had no enemies; they themselves were all sisters and friends. The land was fair before them, and a great future began to form itself in their minds.

The religion they had to begin with was much like that of old Greece—a number of gods and goddesses; but they lost all interest in deities of war and plunder, and gradually centered on their Mother Goddess altogether. Then, as they grew more intelligent, this had turned into a sort of Maternal Pantheism.

Here was Mother Earth, bearing fruit. All that they ate was fruit of motherhood, from seed or egg or their product. By motherhood they were born and by motherhood they lived—life was, to them, just the long cycle of motherhood.

But very early they recognized the need of improvement as well as of mere repetition, and devoted their combined intelligence to that problem—how to make the best kind of people. First this was merely the hope of bearing better ones, and then they recognized that however the children differed at birth, the real growth lay later—through education.

Then things began to hum.

As I learned more and more to appreciate what these women had accomplished, the less proud I was of what we, with all our manhood, had done.

You see, they had had no wars. They had had no kings, and no priests, and no aristocracies. They were sisters, and as they grew, they grew together—not by competition, but by united action.

We tried to put in a good word for competition, and they were keenly interested. Indeed, we soon found from their earnest questions of us that they were prepared to believe our world must be better than theirs. They were not sure; they wanted to know; but there was no such arrogance about them as might have been expected.

We rather spread ourselves, telling of the advantages of competition: how it developed fine qualities; that without it there would be "no stimulus to industry." Terry was very strong on that point.

"No stimulus to industry," they repeated, with that puzzled look we had learned to know so well. "STIMULUS? TO INDUSTRY? But don't you LIKE to work?"

"No man would work unless he had to," Terry declared.

"Oh, no MAN! You mean that is one of your sex distinctions?"

"No, indeed!" he said hastily. "No one, I mean, man or woman, would work without incentive. Competition is the—the motor power, you see."

"It is not with us," they explained gently, "so it is hard for us to understand. Do you mean, for instance, that with you no mother would work for her children without the stimulus of competition?"

No, he admitted that he did not mean that. Mothers, he supposed, would of course work for their children in the home; but the world's work was different—that had to be done by men, and required the competitive element.

All our teachers were eagerly interested.

"We want so much to know—you have the whole world to tell us of, and we have only our little land! And there are two of you—the two sexes—to love and help one another. It must be a rich and wonderful world. Tell us—what is the work of the world, that men do—which we have not here?"

"Oh, everything," Terry said grandly. "The men do everything, with us." He squared his broad shoulders and lifted his chest. "We do not allow our women to work. Women are loved—idolized—honored—kept in the home to care for the children."

"What is 'the home'?" asked Somel a little wistfully.

But Zava begged: "Tell me first, do NO women work, really?"

"Why, yes," Terry admitted. "Some have to, of the poorer sort."

"About how many—in your country?"

"About seven or eight million," said Jeff, as mischievous as ever.

6. Comparisons Are Odious

I had always been proud of my country, of course. Everyone is. Compared with the other lands and other races I knew, the United States of America had always seemed to me, speaking modestly, as good as the best of them.

But just as a clear-eyed, intelligent, perfectly honest, and well-meaning child will frequently jar one's self-esteem by innocent questions, so did these women, without the slightest appearance of malice or satire, continually bring up points of discussion which we spent our best efforts in evading.

Now that we were fairly proficient in their language, had read a lot about their history, and had given them the general outlines of ours, they were able to press their questions closer.

So when Jeff admitted the number of "women wage earners" we had, they instantly asked for the total population, for the proportion of adult women, and found that there were but twenty million or so at the outside.

"Then at least a third of your women are—what is it you call them—wage earners? And they are all POOR. What is POOR, exactly?"

"Ours is the best country in the world as to poverty," Terry told them. "We do not have the wretched paupers and beggars of the older countries, I assure you. Why, European visitors tell us, we don't know what poverty is."

"Neither do we," answered Zava. "Won't you tell us?"

Terry put it up to me, saying I was the sociologist, and I explained that the laws of nature require a struggle for existence, and that in the struggle the fittest survive, and the unfit perish. In our economic struggle, I continued, there was always plenty of opportunity for the fittest to reach the top, which they did, in great numbers, particularly in our country; that where there was severe economic pressure the lowest classes of course felt it the worst, and that among the poorest of all the women were driven into the labor market by necessity.

They listened closely, with the usual note-taking.

"About one-third, then, belong to the poorest class," observed Moadine gravely. "And two-thirds are the ones who are—how was it you so beautifully put it?—'loved, honored, kept in the home to care for the children.' This inferior one-third have no children, I suppose?"

Jeff—he was getting as bad as they were—solemnly replied that, on the contrary, the poorer they were, the more children they had. That too, he explained, was a law of nature: "Reproduction is in inverse proportion to individuation."

"These 'laws of nature,'" Zava gently asked, "are they all the laws you have?"

"I should say not!" protested Terry. "We have systems of law that go back thousands and thousands of years—just as you do, no doubt," he finished politely.

"Oh no," Moadine told him. "We have no laws over a hundred years old, and most of them are under twenty. In a few weeks more," she continued, "we are going to have the pleasure of showing you over our little land and explaining everything you care to know about. We want you to see our people."

"And I assure you," Somel added, "that our people want to see you."

Terry brightened up immensely at this news, and reconciled himself to the renewed demands upon our capacity as teachers. It was lucky that we knew so little, really, and had no books to refer to, else, I fancy we might all be there yet, teaching those eager-minded women about the rest of the world.

As to geography, they had the tradition of the Great Sea, beyond the mountains; and they could see for themselves the endless thick-forested plains below them—that was all. But from the few records of their ancient condition—not "before the flood" with them, but before that mighty quake which had cut them off so completely—they were aware that there were other peoples and other countries.

In geology they were quite ignorant.

As to anthropology, they had those same remnants of information about other peoples, and the knowledge of the savagery of the occupants of those dim forests below. Nevertheless, they had inferred (marvelously keen on inference and deduction their minds were!) the existence and development of civilization in other places, much as we infer it on other planets.

When our biplane came whirring over their heads in that first scouting flight of ours, they had instantly accepted it as proof of the high development of Some Where Else, and had prepared to receive us as cautiously and eagerly as we might prepare to welcome visitors who came "by meteor" from Mars.

Of history—outside their own—they knew nothing, of course, save for their ancient traditions.

Of astronomy they had a fair working knowledge—that is a very old science; and with it, a surprising range and facility in mathematics.

Physiology they were quite familiar with. Indeed, when it came to the simpler and more concrete sciences, wherein the subject matter was at hand and they had but to exercise their minds upon it, the results were surprising. They had worked out a chemistry, a botany, a physics, with all the blends where a science touches an art, or merges into an industry, to such fullness of knowledge as made us feel like schoolchildren.

Also we found this out—as soon as we were free of the country, and by further study and question—that what one knew, all knew, to a very considerable extent.

I talked later with little mountain girls from the fir-dark valleys away up at their highest part, and with sunburned plains-women and agile foresters, all over the country, as well as those in the towns, and everywhere there was the same high level of intelligence. Some knew far more than others about one thing—they were specialized, of course; but all of them knew more about everything—that is, about everything the country was acquainted with—than is the case with us.

We boast a good deal of our "high level of general intelligence" and our "compulsory public education," but in proportion to their opportunities they were far better educated than our people.

With what we told them, from what sketches and models we were able to prepare, they constructed a sort of working outline to fill in as they learned more.

A big globe was made, and our uncertain maps, helped out by those in that precious yearbook thing I had, were tentatively indicated upon it.

They sat in eager groups, masses of them who came for the purpose, and listened while Jeff roughly ran over the geologic history of the earth, and showed them their own land in relation to the others. Out of that same pocket reference book of mine came facts and figures which were seized upon and placed in right relation with unerring acumen.

Even Terry grew interested in this work. "If we can keep this up, they'll be having us lecture to all the girls' schools and colleges—how about that?" he suggested to us. "Don't know as I'd object to being an Authority to such audiences."

They did, in fact, urge us to give public lectures later, but not to the hearers or with the purpose we expected.

What they were doing with us was like—like—well, say like Napoleon extracting military information from a few illiterate peasants. They knew just what to ask, and just what use to make of it; they had mechanical appliances for disseminating information almost equal to ours at home; and by the time we were led forth to lecture, our audiences had thoroughly mastered a well-arranged digest of all we had previously given to our teachers, and were prepared with such notes and questions as might have intimidated a university professor.

They were not audiences of girls, either. It was some time before we were allowed to meet the young women.

"Do you mind telling what you intend to do with us?" Terry burst forth one day, facing the calm and friendly Moadine with that funny half-blustering air of his. At first he used to storm and flourish quite a good deal, but nothing seemed to amuse them more; they would gather around and watch him as if it was an exhibition, politely, but with evident interest. So he learned to check himself, and was almost reasonable in his bearing—but not quite.

She announced smoothly and evenly: "Not in the least. I thought it was quite plain. We are trying to learn of you all we can, and to teach you what you are willing to learn of our country."

"Is that all?" he insisted.

She smiled a quiet enigmatic smile. "That depends."

"Depends on what?"

"Mainly on yourselves," she replied.

"Why do you keep us shut up so closely?"

"Because we do not feel quite safe in allowing you at large where there are so many young women."

Terry was really pleased at that. He had thought as much, inwardly; but he pushed the question. "Why should you be afraid? We are gentlemen."

She smiled that little smile again, and asked: "Are 'gentlemen' always safe?"

"You surely do not think that any of us," he said it with a good deal of emphasis on the "us," "would hurt your young girls?"

"Oh no," she said quickly, in real surprise. "The danger is quite the other way. They might hurt you. If, by any accident, you did harm any one of us, you would have to face a million mothers."

He looked so amazed and outraged that Jeff and I laughed outright, but she went on gently.

"I do not think you quite understand yet. You are but men, three men, in a country where the whole population are mothers—or are going to be. Motherhood means to us something which I cannot yet discover in any of the countries of which you tell us. You have spoken"—she turned to Jeff, "of Human Brotherhood as a great idea among you, but even that I judge is far from a practical expression?"

Jeff nodded rather sadly. "Very far—" he said.

"Here we have Human Motherhood—in full working use," she went on. "Nothing else except the literal sisterhood of our origin, and the far higher and deeper union of our social growth.

"The children in this country are the one center and focus of all our thoughts. Every step of our advance is always considered in its effect on them—on the race. You see, we are MOTHERS," she repeated, as if in that she had said it all.

"I don't see how that fact—which is shared by all women—constitutes any risk to us," Terry persisted. "You mean they would defend their children from attack. Of course. Any mothers would. But we are not savages, my dear lady; we are not going to hurt any mother's child."

They looked at one another and shook their heads a little, but Zava turned to Jeff and urged him to make us see—said he seemed to understand more fully than we did. And he tried.

I can see it now, or at least much more of it, but it has taken me a long time, and a good deal of honest intellectual effort.

What they call Motherhood was like this:

They began with a really high degree of social development, something like that of Ancient Egypt or Greece. Then they suffered the loss of everything masculine, and supposed at first that all human power and safety had gone too. Then they developed this virgin birth capacity. Then, since the prosperity of their children depended on it, the fullest and subtlest coordination began to be practiced.

I remember how long Terry balked at the evident unanimity of these women—the most conspicuous feature of their whole culture. "It's impossible!" he would insist. "Women cannot cooperate—it's against nature."

When we urged the obvious facts he would say: "Fiddlesticks!" or "Hang your facts—I tell you it can't be done!" And we never succeeded in shutting him up till Jeff dragged in the hymenoptera.

"'Go to the ant, thou sluggard'—and learn something," he said triumphantly. "Don't they cooperate pretty well? You can't beat it. This place is just like an enormous anthill—you know an anthill is nothing but a nursery. And how about bees? Don't they manage to cooperate and love one another? as that precious Constable had it. Just show me a combination of male creatures, bird, bug, or beast, that works as well, will you? Or one of our masculine countries where the people work together as well as they do here! I tell you, women are the natural cooperators, not men!"

Terry had to learn a good many things he did not want to. To go back to my little analysis of what happened:

They developed all this close inter-service in the interests of their children. To do the best work they had to specialize, of course; the children needed spinners and weavers, farmers and gardeners, carpenters and masons, as well as mothers.

Then came the filling up of the place. When a population multiplies by five every thirty years it soon reaches the limits of a country, especially a small one like this. They very soon eliminated all the grazing cattle—sheep were the last to go, I believe. Also, they worked out a system of intensive agriculture surpassing anything I ever heard of, with the very forests all reset with fruit- or nut-bearing trees.

Do what they would, however, there soon came a time when they were confronted with the problem of "the pressure of population" in an acute form. There was really crowding, and with it, unavoidably, a decline in standards.

And how did those women meet it?

Not by a "struggle for existence" which would result in an everlasting writhing mass of underbred people trying to get ahead of one another—some few on top, temporarily, many constantly crushed out underneath, a hopeless substratum of paupers and degenerates, and no serenity or peace for anyone, no possibility for really noble qualities among the people at large.

Neither did they start off on predatory excursions to get more land from somebody else, or to get more food from somebody else, to maintain their struggling mass.

Not at all. They sat down in council together and thought it out. Very clear, strong thinkers they were. They said: "With our best endeavors this country will support about so many people, with the standard of peace, comfort, health, beauty, and progress we demand. Very well. That is all the people we will make."

There you have it. You see, they were Mothers, not in our sense of helpless involuntary fecundity, forced to fill and overfill the land, every land, and then see their children suffer, sin, and die, fighting horribly with one another; but in the sense of Conscious Makers of People. Mother-love with them was not a brute passion, a mere "instinct," a wholly personal feeling; it was—a religion.

It included that limitless feeling of sisterhood, that wide unity in service, which was so difficult for us to grasp. And it was National, Racial, Human—oh, I don't know how to say it.

We are used to seeing what we call "a mother" completely wrapped up in her own pink bundle of fascinating babyhood, and taking but the faintest theoretic interest in anybody else's bundle, to say nothing of the common needs of ALL the bundles. But these women were working all together at the grandest of tasks—they were Making People—and they made them well.

There followed a period of "negative eugenics" which must have been an appalling sacrifice. We are commonly willing to "lay down our lives" for our country, but they had to forego motherhood for their country—and it was precisely the hardest thing for them to do.

When I got this far in my reading I went to Somel for more light. We were as friendly by that time as I had ever been in my life with any woman. A mighty comfortable soul she was, giving one the nice smooth mother-feeling a man likes in a woman, and yet giving also the clear intelligence and dependableness I used to assume to be masculine qualities. We had talked volumes already.

"See here," said I. "Here was this dreadful period when they got far too thick, and decided to limit the population. We have a lot of talk about that among us, but your position is so different that I'd like to know a little more about it.

"I understand that you make Motherhood the highest social service—a sacrament, really; that it is only undertaken once, by the majority of the population; that those held unfit are not allowed even that; and that to be encouraged to bear more than one child is the very highest reward and honor in the power of the state."

(She interpolated here that the nearest approach to an aristocracy they had was to come of a line of "Over Mothers"—those who had been so honored.)

"But what I do not understand, naturally, is how you prevent it. I gathered that each woman had five. You have no tyrannical husbands to hold in check—and you surely do not destroy the unborn—"

The look of ghastly horror she gave me I shall never forget. She started from her chair, pale, her eyes blazing.

"Destroy the unborn—!" she said in a hard whisper. "Do men do that in your country?"

"Men!" I began to answer, rather hotly, and then saw the gulf before me. None of us wanted these women to think that OUR women, of whom we boasted so proudly, were in any way inferior to them. I am ashamed to say that I equivocated. I told her of certain criminal types of women—perverts, or crazy, who had been known to commit infanticide. I told her, truly enough, that there was much in our land which was open to criticism, but that I hated to dwell on our defects until they understood us and our conditions better.

And, making a wide detour, I scrambled back to my question of how they limited the population.

As for Somel, she seemed sorry, a little ashamed even, of her too clearly expressed amazement. As I look back now, knowing them better, I am more and more and more amazed as I appreciate the exquisite courtesy with which they had received over and over again statements and admissions on our part which must have revolted them to the soul.

She explained to me, with sweet seriousness, that as I had supposed, at first each woman bore five children; and that, in their eager desire to build up a nation, they had gone on in that way for a few centuries, till they were confronted with the absolute need of a limit. This fact was equally plain to all—all were equally interested.

They were now as anxious to check their wonderful power as they had been to develop it; and for some generations gave the matter their most earnest thought and study.

"We were living on rations before we worked it out," she said. "But we did work it out. You see, before a child comes to one of us there is a period of utter exaltation—the whole being is uplifted and filled with a concentrated desire for that child. We learned to look forward to that period with the greatest caution. Often our young women, those to whom motherhood had not yet come, would voluntarily defer it. When that deep inner demand for a child began to be felt she would deliberately engage in the most active work, physical and mental; and even more important, would solace her longing by the direct care and service of the babies we already had."

She paused. Her wise sweet face grew deeply, reverently tender.

"We soon grew to see that mother-love has more than one channel of expression. I think the reason our children are so—so fully loved, by all of us, is that we never—any of us—have enough of our own."

This seemed to me infinitely pathetic, and I said so. "We have much that is bitter and hard in our life at home," I told her, "but this seems to me piteous beyond words—a whole nation of starving mothers!"

But she smiled her deep contented smile, and said I quite misunderstood.

"We each go without a certain range of personal joy," she said, "but remember—we each have a million children to love and serve—OUR children."

It was beyond me. To hear a lot of women talk about "our children"! But I suppose that is the way the ants and bees would talk—do talk, maybe.

That was what they did, anyhow.

When a woman chose to be a mother, she allowed the child-longing to grow within her till it worked its natural miracle. When she did not so choose she put the whole thing out of her mind, and fed her heart with the other babies.

Let me see—with us, children—minors, that is—constitute about three-fifths of the population; with them only about one-third, or less. And precious—! No sole heir to an empire's throne, no solitary millionaire baby, no only child of middle-aged parents, could compare as an idol with these Herland children.

But before I start on that subject I must finish up that little analysis I was trying to make.

They did effectually and permanently limit the population in numbers, so that the country furnished plenty for the fullest, richest life for all of them: plenty of everything, including room, air, solitude even.

And then they set to work to improve that population in quality—since they were restricted in quantity. This they had been at work on, uninterruptedly, for some fifteen hundred years. Do you wonder they were nice people?

Physiology, hygiene, sanitation, physical culture—all that line of work had been perfected long since. Sickness was almost wholly unknown among them, so much so that a previously high development in what we call the "science of medicine" had become practically a lost art. They were a clean-bred, vigorous lot, having the best of care, the most perfect living conditions always.

When it came to psychology—there was no one thing which left us so dumbfounded, so really awed, as the everyday working knowledge—and practice—they had in this line. As we learned more and more of it, we learned to appreciate the exquisite mastery with which we ourselves, strangers of alien race, of unknown opposite sex, had been understood and provided for from the first.

With this wide, deep, thorough knowledge, they had met and solved the problems of education in ways some of which I hope to make clear later. Those nation-loved children of theirs compared with the average in our country as the most perfectly cultivated, richly developed roses compare with—tumbleweeds. Yet they did not SEEM "cultivated" at all—it had all become a natural condition.

And this people, steadily developing in mental capacity, in will power, in social devotion, had been playing with the arts and sciences—as far as they knew them—for a good many centuries now with inevitable success.

Into this quiet lovely land, among these wise, sweet, strong women, we, in our easy assumption of superiority, had suddenly arrived; and now, tamed and trained to a degree they considered safe, we were at last brought out to see the country, to know the people.

7. Our Growing Modesty

Being at last considered sufficiently tamed and trained to be trusted with scissors, we barbered ourselves as best we could. A close-trimmed beard is certainly more comfortable than a full one. Razors, naturally, they could not supply.

"With so many old women you'd think there'd be some razors," sneered Terry. Whereat Jeff pointed out that he never before had seen such complete absence of facial hair on women.

"Looks to me as if the absence of men made them more feminine in that regard, anyhow," he suggested.

"Well, it's the only one then," Terry reluctantly agreed. "A less feminine lot I never saw. A child apiece doesn't seem to be enough to develop what I call motherliness."

Terry's idea of motherliness was the usual one, involving a baby in arms, or "a little flock about her knees," and the complete absorption of the mother in said baby or flock. A motherliness which dominated society, which influenced every art and industry, which absolutely protected all childhood, and gave to it the most perfect care and training, did not seem motherly—to Terry.

We had become well used to the clothes. They were quite as comfortable as our own—in some ways more so—and undeniably better looking. As to pockets, they left nothing to be desired. That second garment was fairly quilted with pockets. They were most ingeniously arranged, so as to be convenient to the hand and not inconvenient to the body, and were so placed as at once to strengthen the garment and add decorative lines of stitching.

In this, as in so many other points we had now to observe, there was shown the action of a practical intelligence, coupled with fine artistic feeling, and, apparently, untrammeled by any injurious influences.

Our first step of comparative freedom was a personally conducted tour of the country. No pentagonal bodyguard now! Only our special tutors, and we got on famously with them. Jeff said he loved Zava like an aunt—"only jollier than any aunt I ever saw"; Somel and I were as chummy as could be—the best of friends; but it was funny to watch Terry and Moadine. She was patient with him, and courteous, but it was like the patience and courtesy of some great man, say a skilled, experienced diplomat, with a schoolgirl. Her grave acquiescence with his most preposterous expression of feeling; her genial laughter, not only with, but, I often felt, at him—though impeccably polite; her innocent questions, which almost invariably led him to say more than he intended—Jeff and I found it all amusing to watch.

He never seemed to recognize that quiet background of superiority. When she dropped an argument he always thought he had silenced her; when she laughed he thought it tribute to his wit.

I hated to admit to myself how much Terry had sunk in my esteem. Jeff felt it too, I am sure; but neither of us admitted it to the other. At home we had measured him with other men, and, though we knew his failings, he was by no means an unusual type. We knew his virtues too, and they had always seemed more prominent than the faults. Measured among women—our women at home, I mean—he had always stood high. He was visibly popular. Even where his habits were known, there was no discrimination against him; in some cases his reputation for what was felicitously termed "gaiety" seemed a special charm.

But here, against the calm wisdom and quiet restrained humor of these women, with only that blessed Jeff and my inconspicuous self to compare with, Terry did stand out rather strong.

As "a man among men," he didn't; as a man among—I shall have to say, "females," he didn't; his intense masculinity seemed only fit complement to their intense femininity. But here he was all out of drawing.

Moadine was a big woman, with a balanced strength that seldom showed. Her eye was as quietly watchful as a fencer's. She maintained a pleasant relation with her charge, but I doubt if many, even in that country, could have done as well.

He called her "Maud," amongst ourselves, and said she was "a good old soul, but a little slow"; wherein he was quite wrong. Needless to say, he called Jeff's teacher "Java," and sometimes "Mocha," or plain "Coffee"; when specially mischievous, "Chicory," and even "Postum." But Somel rather escaped this form of humor, save for a rather forced "Some 'ell."

"Don't you people have but one name?" he asked one day, after we had been introduced to a whole group of them, all with pleasant, few-syllabled strange names, like the ones we knew.

"Oh yes," Moadine told him. "A good many of us have another, as we get on in life—a descriptive one. That is the name we earn. Sometimes even that is changed, or added to, in an unusually rich life. Such as our present Land Mother—what you call president or king, I believe. She was called Mera, even as a child; that means 'thinker.' Later there was added Du—Du-Mera—the wise thinker, and now we all know her as O-du-mera—great and wise thinker. You shall meet her."

"No surnames at all then?" pursued Terry, with his somewhat patronizing air. "No family name?"

"Why no," she said. "Why should we? We are all descended from a common source—all one 'family' in reality. You see, our comparatively brief and limited history gives us that advantage at least."

"But does not each mother want her own child to bear her name?" I asked.

"No—why should she? The child has its own."

"Why for—for identification—so people will know whose child she is."

"We keep the most careful records," said Somel. "Each one of us has our exact line of descent all the way back to our dear First Mother. There are many reasons for doing that. But as to everyone knowing which child belongs to which mother—why should she?"

Here, as in so many other instances, we were led to feel the difference between the purely maternal and the paternal attitude of mind. The element of personal pride seemed strangely lacking.

"How about your other works?" asked Jeff. "Don't you sign your names to them—books and statues and so on?"

"Yes, surely, we are all glad and proud to. Not only books and statues, but all kinds of work. You will find little names on the houses, on the furniture, on the dishes sometimes. Because otherwise one is likely to forget, and we want to know to whom to be grateful."

"You speak as if it were done for the convenience of the consumer—not the pride of the producer," I suggested.

"It's both," said Somel. "We have pride enough in our work."

"Then why not in your children?" urged Jeff.

"But we have! We're magnificently proud of them," she insisted.

"Then why not sign 'em?" said Terry triumphantly.

Moadine turned to him with her slightly quizzical smile. "Because the finished product is not a private one. When they are babies, we do speak of them, at times, as 'Essa's Lato,' or 'Novine's Amel'; but that is merely descriptive and conversational. In the records, of course, the child stands in her own line of mothers; but in dealing with it personally it is Lato, or Amel, without dragging in its ancestors."

"But have you names enough to give a new one to each child?"

"Assuredly we have, for each living generation."

Then they asked about our methods, and found first that "we" did so and so, and then that other nations did differently. Upon which they wanted to know which method has been proved best—and we had to admit that so far as we knew there had been no attempt at comparison, each people pursuing its own custom in the fond conviction of superiority, and either despising or quite ignoring the others.

With these women the most salient quality in all their institutions was reasonableness. When I dug into the records to follow out any line of development, that was the most astonishing thing—the conscious effort to make it better.

They had early observed the value of certain improvements, had easily inferred that there was room for more, and took the greatest pains to develop two kinds of minds—the critic and inventor. Those who showed an early tendency to observe, to discriminate, to suggest, were given special training for that function; and some of their highest officials spent their time in the most careful study of one or another branch of work, with a view to its further improvement.

In each generation there was sure to arrive some new mind to detect faults and show need of alterations; and the whole corps of inventors was at hand to apply their special faculty at the point criticized, and offer suggestions.

We had learned by this time not to open a discussion on any of their characteristics without first priming ourselves to answer questions about our own methods; so I kept rather quiet on this matter of conscious improvement. We were not prepared to show our way was better.

There was growing in our minds, at least in Jeff's and mine, a keen appreciation of the advantages of this strange country and its management. Terry remained critical. We laid most of it to his nerves. He certainly was irritable.

The most conspicuous feature of the whole land was the perfection of its food supply. We had begun to notice from that very first walk in the forest, the first partial view from our 'plane. Now we were taken to see this mighty garden, and shown its methods of culture.

The country was about the size of Holland, some ten or twelve thousand square miles. One could lose a good many Hollands along the forest-smothered flanks of those mighty mountains. They had a population of about three million—not a large one, but quality is something. Three million is quite enough to allow for considerable variation, and these people varied more widely than we could at first account for.

Terry had insisted that if they were parthenogenetic they'd be as alike as so many ants or aphids; he urged their visible differences as proof that there must be men—somewhere.

But when we asked them, in our later, more intimate conversations, how they accounted for so much divergence without cross-fertilization, they attributed it partly to the careful education, which followed each slight tendency to differ, and partly to the law of mutation. This they had found in their work with plants, and fully proven in their own case.

Physically they were more alike than we, as they lacked all morbid or excessive types. They were tall, strong, healthy, and beautiful as a race, but differed individually in a wide range of feature, coloring, and expression.

"But surely the most important growth is in mind—and in the things we make," urged Somel. "Do you find your physical variation accompanied by a proportionate variation in ideas, feelings, and products? Or, among people who look more alike, do you find their internal life and their work as similar?"

We were rather doubtful on this point, and inclined to hold that there was more chance of improvement in greater physical variation.

"It certainly should be," Zava admitted. "We have always thought it a grave initial misfortune to have lost half our little world. Perhaps that is one reason why we have so striven for conscious improvement."

"But acquired traits are not transmissible," Terry declared. "Weissman has proved that."

They never disputed our absolute statements, only made notes of them.

"If that is so, then our improvement must be due either to mutation, or solely to education," she gravely pursued. "We certainly have improved. It may be that all these higher qualities were latent in the original mother, that careful education is bringing them out, and that our personal differences depend on slight variations in prenatal condition."

"I think it is more in your accumulated culture," Jeff suggested. "And in the amazing psychic growth you have made. We know very little about methods of real soul culture—and you seem to know a great deal."

Be that as it might, they certainly presented a higher level of active intelligence, and of behavior, than we had so far really grasped. Having known in our lives several people who showed the same delicate courtesy and were equally pleasant to live with, at least when they wore their "company manners," we had assumed that our companions were a carefully chosen few. Later we were more and more impressed that all this gentle breeding was breeding; that they were born to it, reared in it, that it was as natural and universal with them as the gentleness of doves or the alleged wisdom of serpents.

As for the intelligence, I confess that this was the most impressive and, to me, most mortifying, of any single feature of Herland. We soon ceased to comment on this or other matters which to them were such obvious commonplaces as to call forth embarrassing questions about our own conditions.

This was nowhere better shown than in that matter of food supply, which I will now attempt to describe.

Having improved their agriculture to the highest point, and carefully estimated the number of persons who could comfortably live on their square miles; having then limited their population to that number, one would think that was all there was to be done. But they had not thought so. To them the country was a unit—it was theirs. They themselves were a unit, a conscious group; they thought in terms of the community. As such, their time-sense was not limited to the hopes and ambitions of an individual life. Therefore, they habitually considered and carried out plans for improvement which might cover centuries.

I had never seen, had scarcely imagined, human beings undertaking such a work as the deliberate replanting of an entire forest area with different kinds of trees. Yet this seemed to them the simplest common sense, like a man's plowing up an inferior lawn and reseeding it. Now every tree bore fruit—edible fruit, that is. In the case of one tree, in which they took especial pride, it had originally no fruit at all—that is, none humanly edible—yet was so beautiful that they wished to keep it. For nine hundred years they had experimented, and now showed us this particularly lovely graceful tree, with a profuse crop of nutritious seeds.

They had early decided that trees were the best food plants, requiring far less labor in tilling the soil, and bearing a larger amount of food for the same ground space; also doing much to preserve and enrich the soil.

Due regard had been paid to seasonable crops, and their fruit and nuts, grains and berries, kept on almost the year through.

On the higher part of the country, near the backing wall of mountains, they had a real winter with snow. Toward the south-eastern point, where there was a large valley with a lake whose outlet was subterranean, the climate was like that of California, and citrus fruits, figs, and olives grew abundantly.

What impressed me particularly was their scheme of fertilization. Here was this little shut-in piece of land where one would have thought an ordinary people would have been starved out long ago or reduced to an annual struggle for life. These careful culturists had worked out a perfect scheme of refeeding the soil with all that came out of it. All the scraps and leavings of their food, plant waste from lumber work or textile industry, all the solid matter from the sewage, properly treated and combined—everything which came from the earth went back to it.

The practical result was like that in any healthy forest; an increasingly valuable soil was being built, instead of the progressive impoverishment so often seen in the rest of the world.

When this first burst upon us we made such approving comments that they were surprised that such obvious common sense should be praised; asked what our methods were; and we had some difficulty in—well, in diverting them, by referring to the extent of our own land, and the—admitted—carelessness with which we had skimmed the cream of it.

At least we thought we had diverted them. Later I found that besides keeping a careful and accurate account of all we told them, they had a sort of skeleton chart, on which the things we said and the things we palpably avoided saying were all set down and studied. It really was child's play for those profound educators to work out a painfully accurate estimate of our conditions—in some lines. When a given line of observation seemed to lead to some very dreadful inference they always gave us the benefit of the doubt, leaving it open to further knowledge. Some of the things we had grown to accept as perfectly natural, or as belonging to our human limitations, they literally could not have believed; and, as I have said, we had all of us joined in a tacit endeavor to conceal much of the social status at home.

"Confound their grandmotherly minds!" Terry said. "Of course they can't understand a Man's World! They aren't human—they're just a pack of Fe-Fe-Females!" This was after he had to admit their parthenogenesis.

"I wish our grandfatherly minds had managed as well," said Jeff. "Do you really think it's to our credit that we have muddled along with all our poverty and disease and the like? They have peace and plenty, wealth and beauty, goodness and intellect. Pretty good people, I think!"

"You'll find they have their faults too," Terry insisted; and partly in self-defense, we all three began to look for those faults of theirs. We had been very strong on this subject before we got there—in those baseless speculations of ours.

"Suppose there is a country of women only," Jeff had put it, over and over. "What'll they be like?"

And we had been cocksure as to the inevitable limitations, the faults and vices, of a lot of women. We had expected them to be given over to what we called "feminine vanity"—"frills and furbelows," and we found they had evolved a costume more perfect than the Chinese dress, richly beautiful when so desired, always useful, of unfailing dignity and good taste.

We had expected a dull submissive monotony, and found a daring social inventiveness far beyond our own, and a mechanical and scientific development fully equal to ours.

We had expected pettiness, and found a social consciousness besides which our nations looked like quarreling children—feebleminded ones at that.

We had expected jealousy, and found a broad sisterly affection, a fair-minded intelligence, to which we could produce no parallel.

We had expected hysteria, and found a standard of health and vigor, a calmness of temper, to which the habit of profanity, for instance, was impossible to explain—we tried it.

All these things even Terry had to admit, but he still insisted that we should find out the other side pretty soon.

"It stands to reason, doesn't it?" he argued. "The whole thing's deuced unnatural—I'd say impossible if we weren't in it. And an unnatural condition's sure to have unnatural results. You'll find some awful characteristics—see if you don't! For instance—we don't know yet what they do with their criminals—their defectives—their aged. You notice we haven't seen any! There's got to be something!"

I was inclined to believe that there had to be something, so I took the bull by the horns—the cow, I should say!—and asked Somel.

"I want to find some flaw in all this perfection," I told her flatly. "It simply isn't possible that three million people have no faults. We are trying our best to understand and learn—would you mind helping us by saying what, to your minds, are the worst qualities of this unique civilization of yours?"

We were sitting together in a shaded arbor, in one of those eating-gardens of theirs. The delicious food had been eaten, a plate of fruit still before us. We could look out on one side over a stretch of open country, quietly rich and lovely; on the other, the garden, with tables here and there, far apart enough for privacy. Let me say right here that with all their careful "balance of population" there was no crowding in this country. There was room, space, a sunny breezy freedom everywhere.

Somel set her chin upon her hand, her elbow on the low wall beside her, and looked off over the fair land.

"Of course we have faults—all of us," she said. "In one way you might say that we have more than we used to—that is, our standard of perfection seems to get farther and farther away. But we are not discouraged, because our records do show gain—considerable gain.

"When we began—even with the start of one particularly noble mother—we inherited the characteristics of a long race-record behind her. And they cropped out from time to time—alarmingly. But it is—yes, quite six hundred years since we have had what you call a 'criminal.'

"We have, of course, made it our first business to train out, to breed out, when possible, the lowest types."

"Breed out?" I asked. "How could you—with parthenogenesis?"

"If the girl showing the bad qualities had still the power to appreciate social duty, we appealed to her, by that, to renounce motherhood. Some of the few worst types were, fortunately, unable to reproduce. But if the fault was in a disproportionate egotism—then the girl was sure she had the right to have children, even that hers would be better than others."

"I can see that," I said. "And then she would be likely to rear them in the same spirit."

"That we never allowed," answered Somel quietly.

"Allowed?" I queried. "Allowed a mother to rear her own children?"

"Certainly not," said Somel, "unless she was fit for that supreme task."

This was rather a blow to my previous convictions.

"But I thought motherhood was for each of you—"

"Motherhood—yes, that is, maternity, to bear a child. But education is our highest art, only allowed to our highest artists."

"Education?" I was puzzled again. "I don't mean education. I mean by motherhood not only child-bearing, but the care of babies."

"The care of babies involves education, and is entrusted only to the most fit," she repeated.

"Then you separate mother and child!" I cried in cold horror, something of Terry's feeling creeping over me, that there must be something wrong among these many virtues.

"Not usually," she patiently explained. "You see, almost every woman values her maternity above everything else. Each girl holds it close and dear, an exquisite joy, a crowning honor, the most intimate, most personal, most precious thing. That is, the child-rearing has come to be with us a culture so profoundly studied, practiced with such subtlety and skill, that the more we love our children the less we are willing to trust that process to unskilled hands—even our own."

"But a mother's love—" I ventured.

She studied my face, trying to work out a means of clear explanation.

"You told us about your dentists," she said, at length, "those quaintly specialized persons who spend their lives filling little holes in other persons' teeth—even in children's teeth sometimes."

"Yes?" I said, not getting her drift.

"Does mother-love urge mothers—with you—to fill their own children's teeth? Or to wish to?"

"Why no—of course not," I protested. "But that is a highly specialized craft. Surely the care of babies is open to any woman—any mother!"

"We do not think so," she gently replied. "Those of us who are the most highly competent fulfill that office; and a majority of our girls eagerly try for it—I assure you we have the very best."

"But the poor mother—bereaved of her baby—"

"Oh no!" she earnestly assured me. "Not in the least bereaved. It is her baby still—it is with her—she has not lost it. But she is not the only one to care for it. There are others whom she knows to be wiser. She knows it because she has studied as they did, practiced as they did, and honors their real superiority. For the child's sake, she is glad to have for it this highest care."

I was unconvinced. Besides, this was only hearsay; I had yet to see the motherhood of Herland.

8. The Girls of Herland

At last Terry's ambition was realized. We were invited, always courteously and with free choice on our part, to address general audiences and classes of girls.

I remember the first time—and how careful we were about our clothes, and our amateur barbering. Terry, in particular, was fussy to a degree about the cut of his beard, and so critical of our combined efforts, that we handed him the shears and told him to please himself. We began to rather prize those beards of ours; they were almost our sole distinction among those tall and sturdy women, with their cropped hair and sexless costume. Being offered a wide selection of garments, we had chosen according to our personal taste, and were surprised to find, on meeting large audiences, that we were the most highly decorated, especially Terry.

He was a very impressive figure, his strong features softened by the somewhat longer hair—though he made me trim it as closely as I knew how; and he wore his richly embroidered tunic with its broad, loose girdle with quite a Henry V air. Jeff looked more like—well, like a Huguenot Lover; and I don't know what I looked like, only that I felt very comfortable. When I got back to our own padded armor and its starched borders I realized with acute regret how comfortable were those Herland clothes.

We scanned that audience, looking for the three bright faces we knew; but they were not to be seen. Just a multitude of girls: quiet, eager, watchful, all eyes and ears to listen and learn.

We had been urged to give, as fully as we cared to, a sort of synopsis of world history, in brief, and to answer questions.

"We are so utterly ignorant, you see," Moadine had explained to us. "We know nothing but such science as we have worked out for ourselves, just the brain work of one small half-country; and you, we gather, have helped one another all over the globe, sharing your discoveries, pooling your progress. How wonderful, how supremely beautiful your civilization must be!"

Somel gave a further suggestion.

"You do not have to begin all over again, as you did with us. We have made a sort of digest of what we have learned from you, and it has been eagerly absorbed, all over the country. Perhaps you would like to see our outline?"

We were eager to see it, and deeply impressed. To us, at first, these women, unavoidably ignorant of what to us was the basic commonplace of knowledge, had seemed on the plane of children, or of savages. What we had been forced to admit, with growing acquaintance, was that they were ignorant as Plato and Aristotle were, but with a highly developed mentality quite comparable to that of Ancient Greece.

Far be it from me to lumber these pages with an account of what we so imperfectly strove to teach them. The memorable fact is what they taught us, or some faint glimpse of it. And at present, our major interest was not at all in the subject matter of our talk, but in the audience.

Girls—hundreds of them—eager, bright-eyed, attentive young faces; crowding questions, and, I regret to say, an increasing inability on our part to answer them effectively.

Our special guides, who were on the platform with us, and sometimes aided in clarifying a question or, oftener, an answer, noticed this effect, and closed the formal lecture part of the evening rather shortly.

"Our young women will be glad to meet you," Somel suggested, "to talk with you more personally, if you are willing?"

Willing! We were impatient and said as much, at which I saw a flickering little smile cross Moadine's face. Even then, with all those eager young things waiting to talk to us, a sudden question crossed my mind: "What was their point of view? What did they think of us?" We learned that later.

Terry plunged in among those young creatures with a sort of rapture, somewhat as a glad swimmer takes to the sea. Jeff, with a rapt look on his high-bred face, approached as to a sacrament. But I was a little chilled by that last thought of mine, and kept my eyes open. I found time to watch Jeff, even while I was surrounded by an eager group of questioners—as we all were—and saw how his worshipping eyes, his grave courtesy, pleased and drew some of them; while others, rather stronger spirits they looked to be, drew away from his group to Terry's or mine.

I watched Terry with special interest, knowing how he had longed for this time, and how irresistible he had always been at home. And I could see, just in snatches, of course, how his suave and masterful approach seemed to irritate them; his too-intimate glances were vaguely resented, his compliments puzzled and annoyed. Sometimes a girl would flush, not with drooped eyelids and inviting timidity, but with anger and a quick lift of the head. Girl after girl turned on her heel and left him, till he had but a small ring of questioners, and they, visibly, were the least "girlish" of the lot.

I saw him looking pleased at first, as if he thought he was making a strong impression; but, finally, casting a look at Jeff, or me, he seemed less pleased—and less.

As for me, I was most agreeably surprised. At home I never was "popular." I had my girl friends, good ones, but they were friends—nothing else. Also they were of somewhat the same clan, not popular in the sense of swarming admirers. But here, to my astonishment, I found my crowd was the largest.

I have to generalize, of course, rather telescoping many impressions; but the first evening was a good sample of the impression we made. Jeff had a following, if I may call it that, of the more sentimental—though that's not the word I want. The less practical, perhaps; the girls who were artists of some sort, ethicists, teachers—that kind.

Terry was reduced to a rather combative group: keen, logical, inquiring minds, not overly sensitive, the very kind he liked least; while, as for me—I became quite cocky over my general popularity.

Terry was furious about it. We could hardly blame him.

"Girls!" he burst forth, when that evening was over and we were by ourselves once more. "Call those GIRLS!"

"Most delightful girls, I call them," said Jeff, his blue eyes dreamily contented.

"What do YOU call them?" I mildly inquired.

"Boys! Nothing but boys, most of 'em. A standoffish, disagreeable lot at that. Critical, impertinent youngsters. No girls at all."

He was angry and severe, not a little jealous, too, I think. Afterward, when he found out just what it was they did not like, he changed his manner somewhat and got on better. He had to. For, in spite of his criticism, they were girls, and, furthermore, all the girls there were! Always excepting our three!—with whom we presently renewed our acquaintance.

When it came to courtship, which it soon did, I can of course best describe my own—and am least inclined to. But of Jeff I heard somewhat; he was inclined to dwell reverently and admiringly, at some length, on the exalted sentiment and measureless perfection of his Celis; and Terry—Terry made so many false starts and met so many rebuffs, that by the time he really settled down to win Alima, he was considerably wiser. At that, it was not smooth sailing. They broke and quarreled, over and over; he would rush off to console himself with some other fair one—the other fair one would have none of him—and he would drift back to Alima, becoming more and more devoted each time.

She never gave an inch. A big, handsome creature, rather exceptionally strong even in that race of strong women, with a proud head and sweeping level brows that lined across above her dark eager eyes like the wide wings of a soaring hawk.

I was good friends with all three of them but best of all with Ellador, long before that feeling changed, for both of us.

From her, and from Somel, who talked very freely with me, I learned at last something of the viewpoint of Herland toward its visitors.

Here they were, isolated, happy, contented, when the booming buzz of our biplane tore the air above them.

Everybody heard it—saw it—for miles and miles, word flashed all over the country, and a council was held in every town and village.

And this was their rapid determination:

"From another country. Probably men. Evidently highly civilized. Doubtless possessed of much valuable knowledge. May be dangerous. Catch them if possible; tame and train them if necessary This may be a chance to re-establish a bi-sexual state for our people."

They were not afraid of us—three million highly intelligent women—or two million, counting only grown-ups—were not likely to be afraid of three young men. We thought of them as "Women," and therefore timid; but it was two thousand years since they had had anything to be afraid of, and certainly more than one thousand since they had outgrown the feeling.

We thought—at least Terry did—that we could have our pick of them. They thought—very cautiously and farsightedly—of picking us, if it seemed wise.

All that time we were in training they studied us, analyzed us, prepared reports about us, and this information was widely disseminated all about the land.

Not a girl in that country had not been learning for months as much as could be gathered about our country, our culture, our personal characters. No wonder their questions were hard to answer. But I am sorry to say, when we were at last brought out and—exhibited (I hate to call it that, but that's what it was), there was no rush of takers. Here was poor old Terry fondly imagining that at last he was free to stray in "a rosebud garden of girls"—and behold! the rosebuds were all with keen appraising eye, studying us.

They were interested, profoundly interested, but it was not the kind of interest we were looking for.

To get an idea of their attitude you have to hold in mind their extremely high sense of solidarity. They were not each choosing a lover; they hadn't the faintest idea of love—sex-love, that is. These girls—to each of whom motherhood was a lodestar, and that motherhood exalted above a mere personal function, looked forward to as the highest social service, as the sacrament of a lifetime—were now confronted with an opportunity to make the great step of changing their whole status, of reverting to their earlier bi-sexual order of nature.

Beside this underlying consideration there was the limitless interest and curiosity in our civilization, purely impersonal, and held by an order of mind beside which we were like—schoolboys.

It was small wonder that our lectures were not a success; and none at all that our, or at least Terry's, advances were so ill received. The reason for my own comparative success was at first far from pleasing to my pride.

"We like you the best," Somel told me, "because you seem more like us."

"More like a lot of women!" I thought to myself disgustedly, and then remembered how little like "women," in our derogatory sense, they were. She was smiling at me, reading my thought.

"We can quite see that we do not seem like—women—to you. Of course, in a bi-sexual race the distinctive feature of each sex must be intensified. But surely there are characteristics enough which belong to People, aren't there? That's what I mean about you being more like us—more like People. We feel at ease with you."

Jeff's difficulty was his exalted gallantry. He idealized women, and was always looking for a chance to "protect" or to "serve" them. These needed neither protection nor service. They were living in peace and power and plenty; we were their guests, their prisoners, absolutely dependent.

Of course we could promise whatsoever we might of advantages, if they would come to our country; but the more we knew of theirs, the less we boasted.

Terry's jewels and trinkets they prized as curios; handed them about, asking questions as to workmanship, not in the least as to value; and discussed not ownership, but which museum to put them in.

When a man has nothing to give a woman, is dependent wholly on his personal attraction, his courtship is under limitations.

They were considering these two things: the advisability of making the Great Change; and the degree of personal adaptability which would best serve that end.

Here we had the advantage of our small personal experience with those three fleet forest girls; and that served to draw us together.

As for Ellador: Suppose you come to a strange land and find it pleasant enough—just a little more than ordinarily pleasant—and then you find rich farmland, and then gardens, gorgeous gardens, and then palaces full of rare and curious treasures—incalculable, inexhaustible, and then—mountains—like the Himalayas, and then the sea.

I liked her that day she balanced on the branch before me and named the trio. I thought of her most. Afterward I turned to her like a friend when we met for the third time, and continued the acquaintance. While Jeff's ultra-devotion rather puzzled Celis, really put off their day of happiness, while Terry and Alima quarreled and parted, re-met and re-parted, Ellador and I grew to be close friends.

We talked and talked. We took long walks together. She showed me things, explained them, interpreted much that I had not understood. Through her sympathetic intelligence I became more and more comprehending of the spirit of the people of Herland, more and more appreciative of its marvelous inner growth as well as outer perfection.

I ceased to feel a stranger, a prisoner. There was a sense of understanding, of identity, of purpose. We discussed—everything. And, as I traveled farther and farther, exploring the rich, sweet soul of her, my sense of pleasant friendship became but a broad foundation for such height, such breadth, such interlocked combination of feeling as left me fairly blinded with the wonder of it.

As I've said, I had never cared very much for women, nor they for me—not Terry-fashion. But this one—

At first I never even thought of her "in that way," as the girls have it. I had not come to the country with any Turkish-harem intentions, and I was no woman-worshipper like Jeff. I just liked that girl "as a friend," as we say. That friendship grew like a tree. She was SUCH a good sport! We did all kinds of things together. She taught me games and I taught her games, and we raced and rowed and had all manner of fun, as well as higher comradeship.

Then, as I got on farther, the palace and treasures and snowy mountain ranges opened up. I had never known there could be such a human being. So—great. I don't mean talented. She was a forester—one of the best—but it was not that gift I mean. When I say GREAT, I mean great—big, all through. If I had known more of those women, as intimately, I should not have found her so unique; but even among them she was noble. Her mother was an Over Mother—and her grandmother, too, I heard later.

So she told me more and more of her beautiful land; and I told her as much, yes, more than I wanted to, about mine; and we became inseparable. Then this deeper recognition came and grew. I felt my own soul rise and lift its wings, as it were. Life got bigger. It seemed as if I understood—as I never had before—as if I could Do things—as if I too could grow—if she would help me. And then It came—to both of us, all at once.

A still day—on the edge of the world, their world. The two of us, gazing out over the far dim forestland below, talking of heaven and earth and human life, and of my land and other lands and what they needed and what I hoped to do for them—

"If you will help me," I said.

She turned to me, with that high, sweet look of hers, and then, as her eyes rested in mine and her hands too—then suddenly there blazed out between us a farther glory, instant, overwhelming—quite beyond any words of mine to tell.

Celis was a blue-and-gold-and-rose person; Alma, black-and-white-and-red, a blazing beauty. Ellador was brown: hair dark and soft, like a seal coat; clear brown skin with a healthy red in it; brown eyes—all the way from topaz to black velvet they seemed to range—splendid girls, all of them.

They had seen us first of all, far down in the lake below, and flashed the tidings across the land even before our first exploring flight. They had watched our landing, flitted through the forest with us, hidden in that tree and—I shrewdly suspect—giggled on purpose.

They had kept watch over our hooded machine, taking turns at it; and when our escape was announced, had followed along-side for a day or two, and been there at the last, as described. They felt a special claim on us—called us "their men"—and when we were at liberty to study the land and people, and be studied by them, their claim was recognized by the wise leaders.

But I felt, we all did, that we should have chosen them among millions, unerringly.

And yet "the path of true love never did run smooth"; this period of courtship was full of the most unsuspected pitfalls.

Writing this as late as I do, after manifold experiences both in Herland and, later, in my own land, I can now understand and philosophize about what was then a continual astonishment and often a temporary tragedy.

The "long suit" in most courtships is sex attraction, of course. Then gradually develops such comradeship as the two temperaments allow. Then, after marriage, there is either the establishment of a slow-growing, widely based friendship, the deepest, tenderest, sweetest of relations, all lit and warmed by the recurrent flame of love; or else that process is reversed, love cools and fades, no friendship grows, the whole relation turns from beauty to ashes.

Here everything was different. There was no sex-feeling to appeal to, or practically none. Two thousand years' disuse had left very little of the instinct; also we must remember that those who had at times manifested it as atavistic exceptions were often, by that very fact, denied motherhood.

Yet while the mother process remains, the inherent ground for sex-distinction remains also; and who shall say what long-forgotten feeling, vague and nameless, was stirred in some of these mother hearts by our arrival?

What left us even more at sea in our approach was the lack of any sex-tradition. There was no accepted standard of what was "manly" and what was "womanly."

When Jeff said, taking the fruit basket from his adored one, "A woman should not carry anything," Celis said, "Why?" with the frankest amazement. He could not look that fleet-footed, deep-chested young forester in the face and say, "Because she is weaker." She wasn't. One does not call a race horse weak because it is visibly not a cart horse.

He said, rather lamely, that women were not built for heavy work.

She looked out across the fields to where some women were working, building a new bit of wall out of large stones; looked back at the nearest town with its woman-built houses; down at the smooth, hard road we were walking on; and then at the little basket he had taken from her.

"I don't understand," she said quite sweetly. "Are the women in your country so weak that they could not carry such a thing as that?"

"It is a convention," he said. "We assume that motherhood is a sufficient burden—that men should carry all the others."

"What a beautiful feeling!" she said, her blue eyes shining.

"Does it work?" asked Alima, in her keen, swift way. "Do all men in all countries carry everything? Or is it only in yours?"

"Don't be so literal," Terry begged lazily. "Why aren't you willing to be worshipped and waited on? We like to do it."

"You don't like to have us do it to you," she answered.

"That's different," he said, annoyed; and when she said, "Why is it?" he quite sulked, referring her to me, saying, "Van's the philosopher."

Ellador and I talked it all out together, so that we had an easier experience of it when the real miracle time came. Also, between us, we made things clearer to Jeff and Celis. But Terry would not listen to reason.

He was madly in love with Alima. He wanted to take her by storm, and nearly lost her forever.

You see, if a man loves a girl who is in the first place young and inexperienced; who in the second place is educated with a background of caveman tradition, a middle-ground of poetry and romance, and a foreground of unspoken hope and interest all centering upon the one Event; and who has, furthermore, absolutely no other hope or interest worthy of the name—why, it is a comparatively easy matter to sweep her off her feet with a dashing attack. Terry was a past master in this process. He tried it here, and Alima was so affronted, so repelled, that it was weeks before he got near enough to try again.

The more coldly she denied him, the hotter his determination; he was not used to real refusal. The approach of flattery she dismissed with laughter, gifts and such "attentions" we could not bring to bear, pathos and complaint of cruelty stirred only a reasoning inquiry. It took Terry a long time.

I doubt if she ever accepted her strange lover as fully as did Celis and Ellador theirs. He had hurt and offended her too often; there were reservations.

But I think Alima retained some faint vestige of long-descended feeling which made Terry more possible to her than to others; and that she had made up her mind to the experiment and hated to renounce it.

However it came about, we all three at length achieved full understanding, and solemnly faced what was to them a step of measureless importance, a grave question as well as a great happiness; to us a strange, new joy.

Of marriage as a ceremony they knew nothing. Jeff was for bringing them to our country for the religious and the civil ceremony, but neither Celis nor the others would consent.

"We can't expect them to want to go with us—yet," said Terry sagely. "Wait a bit, boys. We've got to take 'em on their own terms—if at all." This, in rueful reminiscence of his repeated failures.

"But our time's coming," he added cheerfully. "These women have never been mastered, you see—" This, as one who had made a discovery.

"You'd better not try to do any mastering if you value your chances," I told him seriously; but he only laughed, and said, "Every man to his trade!"

We couldn't do anything with him. He had to take his own medicine.

If the lack of tradition of courtship left us much at sea in our wooing, we found ourselves still more bewildered by lack of tradition of matrimony.

And here again, I have to draw on later experience, and as deep an acquaintance with their culture as I could achieve, to explain the gulfs of difference between us.

Two thousand years of one continuous culture with no men. Back of that, only traditions of the harem. They had no exact analogue for our word HOME, any more than they had for our Roman-based FAMILY.

They loved one another with a practically universal affection, rising to exquisite and unbroken friendships, and broadening to a devotion to their country and people for which our word PATRIOTISM is no definition at all.

Patriotism, red hot, is compatible with the existence of a neglect of national interests, a dishonesty, a cold indifference to the suffering of millions. Patriotism is largely pride, and very largely combativeness. Patriotism generally has a chip on its shoulder.

This country had no other country to measure itself by—save the few poor savages far below, with whom they had no contact.

They loved their country because it was their nursery, playground, and workshop—theirs and their children's. They were proud of it as a workshop, proud of their record of ever-increasing efficiency; they had made a pleasant garden of it, a very practical little heaven; but most of all they valued it—and here it is hard for us to understand them—as a cultural environment for their children.

That, of course, is the keynote of the whole distinction—their children.

From those first breathlessly guarded, half-adored race mothers, all up the ascending line, they had this dominant thought of building up a great race through the children.

All the surrendering devotion our women have put into their private families, these women put into their country and race. All the loyalty and service men expect of wives, they gave, not singly to men, but collectively to one another.

And the mother instinct, with us so painfully intense, so thwarted by conditions, so concentrated in personal devotion to a few, so bitterly hurt by death, disease, or barrenness, and even by the mere growth of the children, leaving the mother alone in her empty nest—all this feeling with them flowed out in a strong, wide current, unbroken through the generations, deepening and widening through the years, including every child in all the land.

With their united power and wisdom, they had studied and overcome the "diseases of childhood"—their children had none.

They had faced the problems of education and so solved them that their children grew up as naturally as young trees; learning through every sense; taught continuously but unconsciously—never knowing they were being educated.

In fact, they did not use the word as we do. Their idea of education was the special training they took, when half grown up, under experts. Then the eager young minds fairly flung themselves on their chosen subjects, and acquired with an ease, a breadth, a grasp, at which I never ceased to wonder.

But the babies and little children never felt the pressure of that "forcible feeding" of the mind that we call "education." Of this, more later.

9. Our Relations and Theirs

What I'm trying to show here is that with these women the whole relationship of life counted in a glad, eager growing-up to join the ranks of workers in the line best loved; a deep, tender reverence for one's own mother—too deep for them to speak of freely—and beyond that, the whole, free, wide range of sisterhood, the splendid service of the country, and friendships.

To these women we came, filled with the ideas, convictions, traditions, of our culture, and undertook to rouse in them the emotions which—to us—seemed proper.

However much, or little, of true sex-feeling there was between us, it phrased itself in their minds in terms of friendship, the one purely personal love they knew, and of ultimate parentage. Visibly we were not mothers, nor children, nor compatriots; so, if they loved us, we must be friends.

That we should pair off together in our courting days was natural to them; that we three should remain much together, as they did themselves, was also natural. We had as yet no work, so we hung about them in their forest tasks; that was natural, too.

But when we began to talk about each couple having "homes" of our own, they could not understand it.

"Our work takes us all around the country," explained Celis. "We cannot live in one place all the time."

"We are together now," urged Alima, looking proudly at Terry's stalwart nearness. (This was one of the times when they were "on," though presently "off" again.)

"It's not the same thing at all," he insisted. "A man wants a home of his own, with his wife and family in it."

"Staying in it? All the time?" asked Ellador. "Not imprisoned, surely!"

"Of course not! Living there—naturally," he answered.

"What does she do there—all the time?" Alima demanded. "What is her work?"

Then Terry patiently explained again that our women did not work—with reservations.

"But what do they do—if they have no work?" she persisted.

"They take care of the home—and the children."

"At the same time?" asked Ellador.

"Why yes. The children play about, and the mother has charge of it all. There are servants, of course."

It seemed so obvious, so natural to Terry, that he always grew impatient; but the girls were honestly anxious to understand.

"How many children do your women have?" Alima had her notebook out now, and a rather firm set of lip. Terry began to dodge.

"There is no set number, my dear," he explained. "Some have more, some have less."

"Some have none at all," I put in mischievously.

They pounced on this admission and soon wrung from us the general fact that those women who had the most children had the least servants, and those who had the most servants had the least children.

"There!" triumphed Alima. "One or two or no children, and three or four servants. Now what do those women DO?"

We explained as best we might. We talked of "social duties," disingenuously banking on their not interpreting the words as we did; we talked of hospitality, entertainment, and various "interests." All the time we knew that to these large-minded women whose whole mental outlook was so collective, the limitations of a wholly personal life were inconceivable.

"We cannot really understand it," Ellador concluded. "We are only half a people. We have our woman-ways and they have their man-ways and their both-ways. We have worked out a system of living which is, of course, limited. They must have a broader, richer, better one. I should like to see it."

"You shall, dearest," I whispered.

"There's nothing to smoke," complained Terry. He was in the midst of a prolonged quarrel with Alima, and needed a sedative. "There's nothing to drink. These blessed women have no pleasant vices. I wish we could get out of here!"

This wish was vain. We were always under a certain degree of watchfulness. When Terry burst forth to tramp the streets at night he always found a "Colonel" here or there; and when, on an occasion of fierce though temporary despair, he had plunged to the cliff edge with some vague view to escape, he found several of them close by. We were free—but there was a string to it.

"They've no unpleasant ones, either," Jeff reminded him.

"Wish they had!" Terry persisted. "They've neither the vices of men, nor the virtues of women—they're neuters!"

"You know better than that. Don't talk nonsense," said I, severely.

I was thinking of Ellador's eyes when they gave me a certain look, a look she did not at all realize.

Jeff was equally incensed. "I don't know what 'virtues of women' you miss. Seems to me they have all of them."

"They've no modesty," snapped Terry. "No patience, no submissiveness, none of that natural yielding which is woman's greatest charm."

I shook my head pityingly. "Go and apologize and make friends again, Terry. You've got a grouch, that's all. These women have the virtue of humanity, with less of its faults than any folks I ever saw. As for patience—they'd have pitched us over the cliffs the first day we lit among 'em, if they hadn't that."

"There are no—distractions," he grumbled. "Nowhere a man can go and cut loose a bit. It's an everlasting parlor and nursery."

"And workshop," I added. "And school, and office, and laboratory, and studio, and theater, and—home."

"HOME!" he sneered. "There isn't a home in the whole pitiful place."

"There isn't anything else, and you know it," Jeff retorted hotly. "I never saw, I never dreamed of, such universal peace and good will and mutual affection."

"Oh, well, of course, if you like a perpetual Sunday school, it's all very well. But I like Something Doing. Here it's all done."

There was something to this criticism. The years of pioneering lay far behind them. Theirs was a civilization in which the initial difficulties had long since been overcome. The untroubled peace, the unmeasured plenty, the steady health, the large good will and smooth management which ordered everything, left nothing to overcome. It was like a pleasant family in an old established, perfectly run country place.

I liked it because of my eager and continued interest in the sociological achievements involved. Jeff liked it as he would have liked such a family and such a place anywhere.

Terry did not like it because he found nothing to oppose, to struggle with, to conquer.

"Life is a struggle, has to be," he insisted. "If there is no struggle, there is no life—that's all."

"You're talking nonsense—masculine nonsense," the peaceful Jeff replied. He was certainly a warm defender of Herland. "Ants don't raise their myriads by a struggle, do they? Or the bees?"

"Oh, if you go back to insects—and want to live in an anthill—! I tell you the higher grades of life are reached only through struggle—combat. There's no Drama here. Look at their plays! They make me sick."

He rather had us there. The drama of the country was—to our taste—rather flat. You see, they lacked the sex motive and, with it, jealousy. They had no interplay of warring nations, no aristocracy and its ambitions, no wealth and poverty opposition.

I see I have said little about the economics of the place; it should have come before, but I'll go on about the drama now.

They had their own kind. There was a most impressive array of pageantry, of processions, a sort of grand ritual, with their arts and their religion broadly blended. The very babies joined in it. To see one of their great annual festivals, with the massed and marching stateliness of those great mothers, the young women brave and noble, beautiful and strong; and then the children, taking part as naturally as ours would frolic round a Christmas tree—it was overpowering in the impression of joyous, triumphant life.

They had begun at a period when the drama, the dance, music, religion, and education were all very close together; and instead of developing them in detached lines, they had kept the connection. Let me try again to give, if I can, a faint sense of the difference in the life view—the background and basis on which their culture rested.

Ellador told me a lot about it. She took me to see the children, the growing girls, the special teachers. She picked out books for me to read. She always seemed to understand just what I wanted to know, and how to give it to me.

While Terry and Alima struck sparks and parted—he always madly drawn to her and she to him—she must have been, or she'd never have stood the way he behaved—Ellador and I had already a deep, restful feeling, as if we'd always had one another. Jeff and Celis were happy; there was no question of that; but it didn't seem to me as if they had the good times we did.

Well, here is the Herland child facing life—as Ellador tried to show it to me. From the first memory, they knew Peace, Beauty, Order, Safety, Love, Wisdom, Justice, Patience, and Plenty. By "plenty" I mean that the babies grew up in an environment which met their needs, just as young fawns might grow up in dewy forest glades and brook-fed meadows. And they enjoyed it as frankly and utterly as the fawns would.

They found themselves in a big bright lovely world, full of the most interesting and enchanting things to learn about and to do. The people everywhere were friendly and polite. No Herland child ever met the overbearing rudeness we so commonly show to children. They were People, too, from the first; the most precious part of the nation.

In each step of the rich experience of living, they found the instance they were studying widen out into contact with an endless range of common interests. The things they learned were RELATED, from the first; related to one another, and to the national prosperity.

"It was a butterfly that made me a forester," said Ellador. "I was about eleven years old, and I found a big purple-and-green butterfly on a low flower. I caught it, very carefully, by the closed wings, as I had been told to do, and carried it to the nearest insect teacher"—I made a note there to ask her what on earth an insect teacher was—"to ask her its name. She took it from me with a little cry of delight. 'Oh, you blessed child,' she said. 'Do you like obernuts?' Of course I liked obernuts, and said so. It is our best food-nut, you know. 'This is a female of the obernut moth,' she told me. 'They are almost gone. We have been trying to exterminate them for centuries. If you had not caught this one, it might have laid eggs enough to raise worms enough to destroy thousands of our nut trees—thousands of bushels of nuts—and make years and years of trouble for us.'

"Everybody congratulated me. The children all over the country were told to watch for that moth, if there were any more. I was shown the history of the creature, and an account of the damage it used to do and of how long and hard our foremothers had worked to save that tree for us. I grew a foot, it seemed to me, and determined then and there to be a forester."

This is but an instance; she showed me many. The big difference was that whereas our children grow up in private homes and families, with every effort made to protect and seclude them from a dangerous world, here they grew up in a wide, friendly world, and knew it for theirs, from the first.

Their child-literature was a wonderful thing. I could have spent years following the delicate subtleties, the smooth simplicities with which they had bent that great art to the service of the child mind.

We have two life cycles: the man's and the woman's. To the man there is growth, struggle, conquest, the establishment of his family, and as much further success in gain or ambition as he can achieve.

To the woman, growth, the securing of a husband, the subordinate activities of family life, and afterward such "social" or charitable interests as her position allows.

Here was but one cycle, and that a large one.

The child entered upon a broad open field of life, in which motherhood was the one great personal contribution to the national life, and all the rest the individual share in their common activities. Every girl I talked to, at any age above babyhood, had her cheerful determination as to what she was going to be when she grew up.

What Terry meant by saying they had no "modesty" was that this great life-view had no shady places; they had a high sense of personal decorum, but no shame—no knowledge of anything to be ashamed of.

Even their shortcomings and misdeeds in childhood never were presented to them as sins; merely as errors and misplays—as in a game. Some of them, who were palpably less agreeable than others or who had a real weakness or fault, were treated with cheerful allowance, as a friendly group at whist would treat a poor player.

Their religion, you see, was maternal; and their ethics, based on the full perception of evolution, showed the principle of growth and the beauty of wise culture. They had no theory of the essential opposition of good and evil; life to them was growth; their pleasure was in growing, and their duty also.

With this background, with their sublimated mother-love, expressed in terms of widest social activity, every phase of their work was modified by its effect on the national growth. The language itself they had deliberately clarified, simplified, made easy and beautiful, for the sake of the children.

This seemed to us a wholly incredible thing: first, that any nation should have the foresight, the strength, and the persistence to plan and fulfill such a task; and second, that women should have had so much initiative. We have assumed, as a matter of course, that women had none; that only the man, with his natural energy and impatience of restriction, would ever invent anything.

Here we found that the pressure of life upon the environment develops in the human mind its inventive reactions, regardless of sex; and further, that a fully awakened motherhood plans and works without limit, for the good of the child.

That the children might be most nobly born, and reared in an environment calculated to allow the richest, freest growth, they had deliberately remodeled and improved the whole state.

I do not mean in the least that they stopped at that, any more than a child stops at childhood. The most impressive part of their whole culture beyond this perfect system of child-rearing was the range of interests and associations open to them all, for life. But in the field of literature I was most struck, at first, by the child-motive.

They had the same gradation of simple repetitive verse and story that we are familiar with, and the most exquisite, imaginative tales; but where, with us, these are the dribbled remnants of ancient folk myths and primitive lullabies, theirs were the exquisite work of great artists; not only simple and unfailing in appeal to the child-mind, but TRUE, true to the living world about them.

To sit in one of their nurseries for a day was to change one's views forever as to babyhood. The youngest ones, rosy fatlings in their mothers' arms, or sleeping lightly in the flower-sweet air, seemed natural enough, save that they never cried. I never heard a child cry in Herland, save once or twice at a bad fall; and then people ran to help, as we would at a scream of agony from a grown person.

Each mother had her year of glory; the time to love and learn, living closely with her child, nursing it proudly, often for two years or more. This perhaps was one reason for their wonderful vigor.

But after the baby-year the mother was not so constantly in attendance, unless, indeed, her work was among the little ones. She was never far off, however, and her attitude toward the co-mothers, whose proud child-service was direct and continuous, was lovely to see.

As for the babies—a group of those naked darlings playing on short velvet grass, clean-swept; or rugs as soft; or in shallow pools of bright water; tumbling over with bubbling joyous baby laughter—it was a view of infant happiness such as I had never dreamed.

The babies were reared in the warmer part of the country, and gradually acclimated to the cooler heights as they grew older.

Sturdy children of ten and twelve played in the snow as joyfully as ours do; there were continuous excursions of them, from one part of the land to another, so that to each child the whole country might be home.

It was all theirs, waiting for them to learn, to love, to use, to serve; as our own little boys plan to be "a big soldier," or "a cowboy," or whatever pleases their fancy; and our little girls plan for the kind of home they mean to have, or how many children; these planned, freely and gaily with much happy chattering, of what they would do for the country when they were grown.

It was the eager happiness of the children and young people which first made me see the folly of that common notion of ours—that if life was smooth and happy, people would not enjoy it.

As I studied these youngsters, vigorous, joyous, eager little creatures, and their voracious appetite for life, it shook my previous ideas so thoroughly that they have never been re-established. The steady level of good health gave them all that natural stimulus we used to call "animal spirits"—an odd contradiction in terms. They found themselves in an immediate environment which was agreeable and interesting, and before them stretched the years of learning and discovery, the fascinating, endless process of education.

As I looked into these methods and compared them with our own, my strange uncomfortable sense of race-humility grew apace.

Ellador could not understand my astonishment. She explained things kindly and sweetly, but with some amazement that they needed explaining, and with sudden questions as to how we did it that left me meeker than ever.

I betook myself to Somel one day, carefully not taking Ellador. I did not mind seeming foolish to Somel—she was used to it.

"I want a chapter of explanation," I told her. "You know my stupidities by heart, and I do not want to show them to Ellador—she thinks me so wise!"

She smiled delightedly. "It is beautiful to see," she told me, "this new wonderful love between you. The whole country is interested, you know—how can we help it!"

I had not thought of that. We say: "All the world loves a lover," but to have a couple of million people watching one's courtship—and that a difficult one—was rather embarrassing.

"Tell me about your theory of education," I said. "Make it short and easy. And, to show you what puzzles me, I'll tell you that in our theory great stress is laid on the forced exertion of the child's mind; we think it is good for him to overcome obstacles."

"Of course it is," she unexpectedly agreed. "All our children do that—they love to."

That puzzled me again. If they loved to do it, how could it be educational?

"Our theory is this," she went on carefully. "Here is a young human being. The mind is as natural a thing as the body, a thing that grows, a thing to use and enjoy. We seek to nourish, to stimulate, to exercise the mind of a child as we do the body. There are the two main divisions in education—you have those of course?—the things it is necessary to know, and the things it is necessary to do."

"To do? Mental exercises, you mean?"

"Yes. Our general plan is this: In the matter of feeding the mind, of furnishing information, we use our best powers to meet the natural appetite of a healthy young brain; not to overfeed it, to provide such amount and variety of impressions as seem most welcome to each child. That is the easiest part. The other division is in arranging a properly graduated series of exercises which will best develop each mind; the common faculties we all have, and most carefully, the especial faculties some of us have. You do this also, do you not?"

"In a way," I said rather lamely. "We have not so subtle and highly developed a system as you, not approaching it; but tell me more. As to the information—how do you manage? It appears that all of you know pretty much everything—is that right?"

This she laughingly disclaimed. "By no means. We are, as you soon found out, extremely limited in knowledge. I wish you could realize what a ferment the country is in over the new things you have told us; the passionate eagerness among thousands of us to go to your country and learn—learn—learn! But what we do know is readily divisible into common knowledge and special knowledge. The common knowledge we have long since learned to feed into the minds of our little ones with no waste of time or strength; the special knowledge is open to all, as they desire it. Some of us specialize in one line only. But most take up several—some for their regular work, some to grow with."

"To grow with?"

"Yes. When one settles too close in one kind of work there is a tendency to atrophy in the disused portions of the brain. We like to keep on learning, always."

"What do you study?"

"As much as we know of the different sciences. We have, within our limits, a good deal of knowledge of anatomy, physiology, nutrition—all that pertains to a full and beautiful personal life. We have our botany and chemistry, and so on—very rudimentary, but interesting; our own history, with its accumulating psychology."

"You put psychology with history—not with personal life?"

"Of course. It is ours; it is among and between us, and it changes with the succeeding and improving generations. We are at work, slowly and carefully, developing our whole people along these lines. It is glorious work—splendid! To see the thousands of babies improving, showing stronger clearer minds, sweeter dispositions, higher capacities—don't you find it so in your country?"

This I evaded flatly. I remembered the cheerless claim that the human mind was no better than in its earliest period of savagery, only better informed—a statement I had never believed.

"We try most earnestly for two powers," Somel continued. "The two that seem to us basically necessary for all noble life: a clear, far-reaching judgment, and a strong well-used will. We spend our best efforts, all through childhood and youth, in developing these faculties, individual judgment and will."

"As part of your system of education, you mean?"

"Exactly. As the most valuable part. With the babies, as you may have noticed, we first provide an environment which feeds the mind without tiring it; all manner of simple and interesting things to do, as soon as they are old enough to do them; physical properties, of course, come first. But as early as possible, going very carefully, not to tax the mind, we provide choices, simple choices, with very obvious causes and consequences. You've noticed the games?"

I had. The children seemed always playing something; or else, sometimes, engaged in peaceful researches of their own. I had wondered at first when they went to school, but soon found that they never did—to their knowledge. It was all education but no schooling.

"We have been working for some sixteen hundred years, devising better and better games for children," continued Somel.

I sat aghast. "Devising games?" I protested. "Making up new ones, you mean?"

"Exactly," she answered. "Don't you?"

Then I remembered the kindergarten, and the "material" devised by Signora Montessori, and guardedly replied: "To some extent." But most of our games, I told her, were very old—came down from child to child, along the ages, from the remote past.

"And what is their effect?" she asked. "Do they develop the faculties you wish to encourage?"

Again I remembered the claims made by the advocates of "sports," and again replied guardedly that that was, in part, the theory.

"But do the children LIKE it?" I asked. "Having things made up and set before them that way? Don't they want the old games?"

"You can see the children," she answered. "Are yours more contented—more interested—happier?"

Then I thought, as in truth I never had thought before, of the dull, bored children I had seen, whining; "What can I do now?"; of the little groups and gangs hanging about; of the value of some one strong spirit who possessed initiative and would "start something"; of the children's parties and the onerous duties of the older people set to "amuse the children"; also of that troubled ocean of misdirected activity we call "mischief," the foolish, destructive, sometimes evil things done by unoccupied children.

"No," said I grimly. "I don't think they are."

The Herland child was born not only into a world carefully prepared, full of the most fascinating materials and opportunities to learn, but into the society of plentiful numbers of teachers, teachers born and trained, whose business it was to accompany the children along that, to us, impossible thing—the royal road to learning.

There was no mystery in their methods. Being adapted to children it was at least comprehensible to adults. I spent many days with the little ones, sometimes with Ellador, sometimes without, and began to feel a crushing pity for my own childhood, and for all others that I had known.

The houses and gardens planned for babies had in them nothing to hurt—no stairs, no corners, no small loose objects to swallow, no fire—just a babies' paradise. They were taught, as rapidly as feasible, to use and control their own bodies, and never did I see such sure-footed, steady-handed, clear-headed little things. It was a joy to watch a row of toddlers learning to walk, not only on a level floor, but, a little later, on a sort of rubber rail raised an inch or two above the soft turf or heavy rugs, and falling off with shrieks of infant joy, to rush back to the end of the line and try again. Surely we have noticed how children love to get up on something and walk along it! But we have never thought to provide that simple and inexhaustible form of amusement and physical education for the young.

Water they had, of course, and could swim even before they walked. If I feared at first the effects of a too intensive system of culture, that fear was dissipated by seeing the long sunny days of pure physical merriment and natural sleep in which these heavenly babies passed their first years. They never knew they were being educated. They did not dream that in this association of hilarious experiment and achievement they were laying the foundation for that close beautiful group feeling into which they grew so firmly with the years. This was education for citizenship.

10. Their Religions and Our Marriages

It took me a long time, as a man, a foreigner, and a species of Christian—I was that as much as anything—to get any clear understanding of the religion of Herland.

Its deification of motherhood was obvious enough; but there was far more to it than that; or, at least, than my first interpretation of that.

I think it was only as I grew to love Ellador more than I believed anyone could love anybody, as I grew faintly to appreciate her inner attitude and state of mind, that I began to get some glimpses of this faith of theirs.

When I asked her about it, she tried at first to tell me, and then, seeing me flounder, asked for more information about ours. She soon found that we had many, that they varied widely, but had some points in common. A clear methodical luminous mind had my Ellador, not only reasonable, but swiftly perceptive.

She made a sort of chart, superimposing the different religions as I described them, with a pin run through them all, as it were; their common basis being a Dominant Power or Powers, and some Special Behavior, mostly taboos, to please or placate. There were some common features in certain groups of religions, but the one always present was this Power, and the things which must be done or not done because of it. It was not hard to trace our human imagery of the Divine Force up through successive stages of bloodthirsty, sensual, proud, and cruel gods of early times to the conception of a Common Father with its corollary of a Common Brotherhood.

This pleased her very much, and when I expatiated on the Omniscience, Omnipotence, Omnipresence, and so on, of our God, and of the loving kindness taught by his Son, she was much impressed.

The story of the Virgin birth naturally did not astonish her, but she was greatly puzzled by the Sacrifice, and still more by the Devil, and the theory of Damnation.

When in an inadvertent moment I said that certain sects had believed in infant damnation—and explained it—she sat very still indeed.

"They believed that God was Love—and Wisdom—and Power?"

"Yes—all of that."

Her eyes grew large, her face ghastly pale.

"And yet that such a God could put little new babies to burn—for eternity?" She fell into a sudden shuddering and left me, running swiftly to the nearest temple.

Every smallest village had its temple, and in those gracious retreats sat wise and noble women, quietly busy at some work of their own until they were wanted, always ready to give comfort, light, or help, to any applicant.

Ellador told me afterward how easily this grief of hers was assuaged, and seemed ashamed of not having helped herself out of it.

"You see, we are not accustomed to horrible ideas," she said, coming back to me rather apologetically. "We haven't any. And when we get a thing like that into our minds it's like—oh, like red pepper in your eyes. So I just ran to her, blinded and almost screaming, and she took it out so quickly—so easily!"

"How?" I asked, very curious.

"'Why, you blessed child,' she said, 'you've got the wrong idea altogether. You do not have to think that there ever was such a God—for there wasn't. Or such a happening—for there wasn't. Nor even that this hideous false idea was believed by anybody. But only this—that people who are utterly ignorant will believe anything—which you certainly knew before.'"

"Anyhow," pursued Ellador, "she turned pale for a minute when I first said it."

This was a lesson to me. No wonder this whole nation of women was peaceful and sweet in expression—they had no horrible ideas.

"Surely you had some when you began," I suggested.

"Oh, yes, no doubt. But as soon as our religion grew to any height at all we left them out, of course."

From this, as from many other things, I grew to see what I finally put in words.

"Have you no respect for the past? For what was thought and believed by your foremothers?"

"Why, no," she said. "Why should we? They are all gone. They knew less than we do. If we are not beyond them, we are unworthy of them—and unworthy of the children who must go beyond us."

This set me thinking in good earnest. I had always imagined—simply from hearing it said, I suppose—that women were by nature conservative. Yet these women, quite unassisted by any masculine spirit of enterprise, had ignored their past and built daringly for the future.

Ellador watched me think. She seemed to know pretty much what was going on in my mind.

"It's because we began in a new way, I suppose. All our folks were swept away at once, and then, after that time of despair, came those wonder children—the first. And then the whole breathless hope of us was for THEIR children—if they should have them. And they did! Then there was the period of pride and triumph till we grew too numerous; and after that, when it all came down to one child apiece, we began to really work—to make better ones."

"But how does this account for such a radical difference in your religion?" I persisted.

She said she couldn't talk about the difference very intelligently, not being familiar with other religions, but that theirs seemed simple enough. Their great Mother Spirit was to them what their own motherhood was—only magnified beyond human limits. That meant that they felt beneath and behind them an upholding, unfailing, serviceable love—perhaps it was really the accumulated mother-love of the race they felt—but it was a Power.

"Just what is your theory of worship?" I asked her.

"Worship? What is that?"

I found it singularly difficult to explain. This Divine Love which they felt so strongly did not seem to ask anything of them—"any more than our mothers do," she said.

"But surely your mothers expect honor, reverence, obedience, from you. You have to do things for your mothers, surely?"

"Oh, no," she insisted, smiling, shaking her soft brown hair. "We do things FROM our mothers—not FOR them. We don't have to do things FOR them—they don't need it, you know. But we have to live on—splendidly—because of them; and that's the way we feel about God."

I meditated again. I thought of that God of Battles of ours, that Jealous God, that Vengeance-is-mine God. I thought of our world-nightmare—Hell.

"You have no theory of eternal punishment then, I take it?"

Ellador laughed. Her eyes were as bright as stars, and there were tears in them, too. She was so sorry for me.

"How could we?" she asked, fairly enough. "We have no punishments in life, you see, so we don't imagine them after death."

"Have you NO punishments? Neither for children nor criminals—such mild criminals as you have?" I urged.

"Do you punish a person for a broken leg or a fever? We have preventive measures, and cures; sometimes we have to 'send the patient to bed,' as it were; but that's not a punishment—it's only part of the treatment," she explained.

Then studying my point of view more closely, she added: "You see, we recognize, in our human motherhood, a great tender limitless uplifting force—patience and wisdom and all subtlety of delicate method. We credit God—our idea of God—with all that and more. Our mothers are not angry with us—why should God be?"

"Does God mean a person to you?"

This she thought over a little. "Why—in trying to get close to it in our minds we personify the idea, naturally; but we certainly do not assume a Big Woman somewhere, who is God. What we call God is a Pervading Power, you know, an Indwelling Spirit, something inside of us that we want more of. Is your God a Big Man?" she asked innocently.

"Why—yes, to most of us, I think. Of course we call it an Indwelling Spirit just as you do, but we insist that it is Him, a Person, and a Man—with whiskers."

"Whiskers? Oh yes—because you have them! Or do you wear them because He does?"

"On the contrary, we shave them off—because it seems cleaner and more comfortable."

"Does He wear clothes—in your idea, I mean?"

I was thinking over the pictures of God I had seen—rash advances of the devout mind of man, representing his Omnipotent Deity as an old man in a flowing robe, flowing hair, flowing beard, and in the light of her perfectly frank and innocent questions this concept seemed rather unsatisfying.

I explained that the God of the Christian world was really the ancient Hebrew God, and that we had simply taken over the patriarchal idea—that ancient one which quite inevitably clothed its thought of God with the attributes of the patriarchal ruler, the grandfather.

"I see," she said eagerly, after I had explained the genesis and development of our religious ideals. "They lived in separate groups, with a male head, and he was probably a little—domineering?"

"No doubt of that," I agreed.

"And we live together without any 'head,' in that sense—just our chosen leaders—that DOES make a difference."

"Your difference is deeper than that," I assured her. "It is in your common motherhood. Your children grow up in a world where everybody loves them. They find life made rich and happy for them by the diffused love and wisdom of all mothers. So it is easy for you to think of God in the terms of a similar diffused and competent love. I think you are far nearer right than we are."

"What I cannot understand," she pursued carefully, "is your preservation of such a very ancient state of mind. This patriarchal idea you tell me is thousands of years old?"

"Oh yes—four, five, six thousand—every so many."

"And you have made wonderful progress in those years—in other things?"

"We certainly have. But religion is different. You see, our religions come from behind us, and are initiated by some great teacher who is dead. He is supposed to have known the whole thing and taught it, finally. All we have to do is believe—and obey."

"Who was the great Hebrew teacher?"

"Oh—there it was different. The Hebrew religion is an accumulation of extremely ancient traditions, some far older than their people, and grew by accretion down the ages. We consider it inspired—'the Word of God.'"

"How do you know it is?"

"Because it says so."

"Does it say so in as many words? Who wrote that in?"

I began to try to recall some text that did say so, and could not bring it to mind.

"Apart from that," she pursued, "what I cannot understand is why you keep these early religious ideas so long. You have changed all your others, haven't you?"

"Pretty generally," I agreed. "But this we call 'revealed religion,' and think it is final. But tell me more about these little temples of yours," I urged. "And these Temple Mothers you run to."

Then she gave me an extended lesson in applied religion, which I will endeavor to concentrate.

They developed their central theory of a Loving Power, and assumed that its relation to them was motherly—that it desired their welfare and especially their development. Their relation to it, similarly, was filial, a loving appreciation and a glad fulfillment of its high purposes. Then, being nothing if not practical, they set their keen and active minds to discover the kind of conduct expected of them. This worked out in a most admirable system of ethics. The principle of Love was universally recognized—and used.

Patience, gentleness, courtesy, all that we call "good breeding," was part of their code of conduct. But where they went far beyond us was in the special application of religious feeling to every field of life. They had no ritual, no little set of performances called "divine service," save those religious pageants I have spoken of, and those were as much educational as religious, and as much social as either. But they had a clear established connection between everything they did—and God. Their cleanliness, their health, their exquisite order, the rich peaceful beauty of the whole land, the happiness of the children, and above all the constant progress they made—all this was their religion.

They applied their minds to the thought of God, and worked out the theory that such an inner power demanded outward expression. They lived as if God was real and at work within them.

As for those little temples everywhere—some of the women were more skilled, more temperamentally inclined, in this direction, than others. These, whatever their work might be, gave certain hours to the Temple Service, which meant being there with all their love and wisdom and trained thought, to smooth out rough places for anyone who needed it. Sometimes it was a real grief, very rarely a quarrel, most often a perplexity; even in Herland the human soul had its hours of darkness. But all through the country their best and wisest were ready to give help.

If the difficulty was unusually profound, the applicant was directed to someone more specially experienced in that line of thought.

Here was a religion which gave to the searching mind a rational basis in life, the concept of an immense Loving Power working steadily out through them, toward good. It gave to the "soul" that sense of contact with the inmost force, of perception of the uttermost purpose, which we always crave. It gave to the "heart" the blessed feeling of being loved, loved and UNDERSTOOD. It gave clear, simple, rational directions as to how we should live—and why. And for ritual it gave first those triumphant group demonstrations, when with a union of all the arts, the revivifying combination of great multitudes moved rhythmically with march and dance, song and music, among their own noblest products and the open beauty of their groves and hills. Second, it gave these numerous little centers of wisdom where the least wise could go to the most wise and be helped.

"It is beautiful!" I cried enthusiastically. "It is the most practical, comforting, progressive religion I ever heard of. You DO love one another—you DO bear one another's burdens—you DO realize that a little child is a type of the kingdom of heaven. You are more Christian than any people I ever saw. But—how about death? And the life everlasting? What does your religion teach about eternity?"

"Nothing," said Ellador. "What is eternity?"

What indeed? I tried, for the first time in my life, to get a real hold on the idea.

"It is—never stopping."

"Never stopping?" She looked puzzled.

"Yes, life, going on forever."

"Oh—we see that, of course. Life does go on forever, all about us."

"But eternal life goes on WITHOUT DYING."

"The same person?"

"Yes, the same person, unending, immortal." I was pleased to think that I had something to teach from our religion, which theirs had never promulgated.

"Here?" asked Ellador. "Never to die—here?" I could see her practical mind heaping up the people, and hurriedly reassured her.

"Oh no, indeed, not here—hereafter. We must die here, of course, but then we 'enter into eternal life.' The soul lives forever."

"How do you know?" she inquired.

"I won't attempt to prove it to you," I hastily continued. "Let us assume it to be so. How does this idea strike you?"

Again she smiled at me, that adorable, dimpling, tender, mischievous, motherly smile of hers. "Shall I be quite, quite honest?"

"You couldn't be anything else," I said, half gladly and half a little sorry. The transparent honesty of these women was a never-ending astonishment to me.

"It seems to me a singularly foolish idea," she said calmly. "And if true, most disagreeable."

Now I had always accepted the doctrine of personal immortality as a thing established. The efforts of inquiring spiritualists, always seeking to woo their beloved ghosts back again, never seemed to me necessary. I don't say I had ever seriously and courageously discussed the subject with myself even; I had simply assumed it to be a fact. And here was the girl I loved, this creature whose character constantly revealed new heights and ranges far beyond my own, this superwoman of a superland, saying she thought immortality foolish! She meant it, too.

"What do you WANT it for?" she asked.

"How can you NOT want it!" I protested. "Do you want to go out like a candle? Don't you want to go on and on—growing and—and—being happy, forever?"

"Why, no," she said. "I don't in the least. I want my child—and my child's child—to go on—and they will. Why should I want to?"

"But it means Heaven!" I insisted. "Peace and Beauty and Comfort and Love—with God." I had never been so eloquent on the subject of religion. She could be horrified at Damnation, and question the justice of Salvation, but Immortality—that was surely a noble faith.

"Why, Van," she said, holding out her hands to me. "Why Van—darling!

How splendid of you to feel it so keenly. That's what we all want, of course—Peace and Beauty, and Comfort and Love—with God! And Progress too, remember; Growth, always and always. That is what our religion teaches us to want and to work for, and we do!"

"But that is HERE," I said, "only for this life on earth."

"Well? And do not you in your country, with your beautiful religion of love and service have it here, too—for this life—on earth?"

None of us were willing to tell the women of Herland about the evils of our own beloved land. It was all very well for us to assume them to be necessary and essential, and to criticize—strictly among ourselves—their all-too-perfect civilization, but when it came to telling them about the failures and wastes of our own, we never could bring ourselves to do it.

Moreover, we sought to avoid too much discussion, and to press the subject of our approaching marriages.

Jeff was the determined one on this score.

"Of course they haven't any marriage ceremony or service, but we can make it a sort of Quaker wedding, and have it in the temple—it is the least we can do for them."

It was. There was so little, after all, that we could do for them. Here we were, penniless guests and strangers, with no chance even to use our strength and courage—nothing to defend them from or protect them against.

"We can at least give them our names," Jeff insisted.

They were very sweet about it, quite willing to do whatever we asked, to please us. As to the names, Alima, frank soul that she was, asked what good it would do.

Terry, always irritating her, said it was a sign of possession. "You are going to be Mrs. Nicholson," he said. "Mrs. T. O. Nicholson. That shows everyone that you are my wife."

"What is a 'wife' exactly?" she demanded, a dangerous gleam in her eye.

"A wife is the woman who belongs to a man," he began.

But Jeff took it up eagerly: "And a husband is the man who belongs to a woman. It is because we are monogamous, you know. And marriage is the ceremony, civil and religious, that joins the two together—'until death do us part,'" he finished, looking at Celis with unutterable devotion.

"What makes us all feel foolish," I told the girls, "is that here we have nothing to give you—except, of course, our names."

"Do your women have no names before they are married?" Celis suddenly demanded.

"Why, yes," Jeff explained. "They have their maiden names—their father's names, that is."

"And what becomes of them?" asked Alima.

"They change them for their husbands', my dear," Terry answered her.

"Change them? Do the husbands then take the wives' 'maiden names'?"

"Oh, no," he laughed. "The man keeps his own and gives it to her, too."

"Then she just loses hers and takes a new one—how unpleasant! We won't do that!" Alima said decidedly.

Terry was good-humored about it. "I don't care what you do or don't do so long as we have that wedding pretty soon," he said, reaching a strong brown hand after Alima's, quite as brown and nearly as strong.

"As to giving us things—of course we can see that you'd like to, but we are glad you can't," Celis continued. "You see, we love you just for yourselves—we wouldn't want you to—to pay anything. Isn't it enough to know that you are loved personally—and just as men?"

Enough or not, that was the way we were married. We had a great triple wedding in the biggest temple of all, and it looked as if most of the nation was present. It was very solemn and very beautiful. Someone had written a new song for the occasion, nobly beautiful, about the New Hope for their people—the New Tie with other lands—Brotherhood as well as Sisterhood, and, with evident awe, Fatherhood.

Terry was always restive under their talk of fatherhood. "Anybody'd think we were High Priests of—of Philoprogenitiveness!" he protested. "These women think of NOTHING but children, seems to me! We'll teach 'em!"

He was so certain of what he was going to teach, and Alima so uncertain in her moods of reception, that Jeff and I feared the worst. We tried to caution him—much good that did. The big handsome fellow drew himself up to his full height, lifted that great chest of his, and laughed.

"There are three separate marriages," he said. "I won't interfere with yours—nor you with mine."

So the great day came, and the countless crowds of women, and we three bridegrooms without any supporting "best men," or any other men to back us up, felt strangely small as we came forward.

Somel and Zava and Moadine were on hand; we were thankful to have them, too—they seemed almost like relatives.

There was a splendid procession, wreathing dances, the new anthem I spoke of, and the whole great place pulsed with feeling—the deep awe, the sweet hope, the wondering expectation of a new miracle.

"There has been nothing like this in the country since our Motherhood began!" Somel said softly to me, while we watched the symbolic marches. "You see, it is the dawn of a new era. You don't know how much you mean to us. It is not only Fatherhood—that marvelous dual parentage to which we are strangers—the miracle of union in life-giving—but it is Brotherhood. You are the rest of the world. You join us to our kind—to all the strange lands and peoples we have never seen. We hope to know them—to love and help them—and to learn of them. Ah! You cannot know!"

Thousands of voices rose in the soaring climax of that great Hymn of The Coming Life. By the great Altar of Motherhood, with its crown of fruit and flowers, stood a new one, crowned as well. Before the Great Over Mother of the Land and her ring of High Temple Counsellors, before that vast multitude of calm-faced mothers and holy-eyed maidens, came forward our own three chosen ones, and we, three men alone in all that land, joined hands with them and made our marriage vows.

11. Our Difficulties

We say, "Marriage is a lottery"; also "Marriages are made in Heaven"—but this is not so widely accepted as the other.

We have a well-founded theory that it is best to marry "in one's class," and certain well-grounded suspicions of international marriages, which seem to persist in the interests of social progress, rather than in those of the contracting parties.

But no combination of alien races, of color, of caste, or creed, was ever so basically difficult to establish as that between us, three modern American men, and these three women of Herland.

It is all very well to say that we should have been frank about it beforehand. We had been frank. We had discussed—at least Ellador and I had—the conditions of The Great Adventure, and thought the path was clear before us. But there are some things one takes for granted, supposes are mutually understood, and to which both parties may repeatedly refer without ever meaning the same thing.

The differences in the education of the average man and woman are great enough, but the trouble they make is not mostly for the man; he generally carries out his own views of the case. The woman may have imagined the conditions of married life to be different; but what she imagined, was ignorant of, or might have preferred, did not seriously matter.

I can see clearly and speak calmly about this now, writing after a lapse of years, years full of growth and education, but at the time it was rather hard sledding for all of us—especially for Terry. Poor Terry! You see, in any other imaginable marriage among the peoples of the earth, whether the woman were black, red, yellow, brown, or white; whether she were ignorant or educated, submissive or rebellious, she would have behind her the marriage tradition of our general history. This tradition relates the woman to the man. He goes on with his business, and she adapts herself to him and to it. Even in citizenship, by some strange hocus-pocus, that fact of birth and geography was waved aside, and the woman automatically acquired the nationality of her husband.

Well—here were we, three aliens in this land of women. It was small in area, and the external differences were not so great as to astound us. We did not yet appreciate the differences between the race-mind of this people and ours.

In the first place, they were a "pure stock" of two thousand uninterrupted years. Where we have some long connected lines of thought and feeling, together with a wide range of differences, often irreconcilable, these people were smoothly and firmly agreed on most of the basic principles of their life; and not only agreed in principle, but accustomed for these sixty-odd generations to act on those principles.

This is one thing which we did not understand—had made no allowance for. When in our pre-marital discussions one of those dear girls had said: "We understand it thus and thus," or "We hold such and such to be true," we men, in our own deep-seated convictions of the power of love, and our easy views about beliefs and principles, fondly imagined that we could convince them otherwise. What we imagined, before marriage, did not matter any more than what an average innocent young girl imagines. We found the facts to be different.

It was not that they did not love us; they did, deeply and warmly. But there are you again—what they meant by "love" and what we meant by "love" were so different.

Perhaps it seems rather cold-blooded to say "we" and "they," as if we were not separate couples, with our separate joys and sorrows, but our positions as aliens drove us together constantly. The whole strange experience had made our friendship more close and intimate than it would ever have become in a free and easy lifetime among our own people. Also, as men, with our masculine tradition of far more than two thousand years, we were a unit, small but firm, against this far larger unit of feminine tradition.

I think I can make clear the points of difference without a too painful explicitness. The more external disagreement was in the matter of "the home," and the housekeeping duties and pleasures we, by instinct and long education, supposed to be inherently appropriate to women.

I will give two illustrations, one away up, and the other away down, to show how completely disappointed we were in this regard.

For the lower one, try to imagine a male ant, coming from some state of existence where ants live in pairs, endeavoring to set up housekeeping with a female ant from a highly developed anthill. This female ant might regard him with intense personal affection, but her ideas of parentage and economic management would be on a very different scale from his. Now, of course, if she was a stray female in a country of pairing ants, he might have had his way with her; but if he was a stray male in an anthill—!

For the higher one, try to imagine a devoted and impassioned man trying to set up housekeeping with a lady angel, a real wings-and-harp-and-halo angel, accustomed to fulfilling divine missions all over interstellar space. This angel might love the man with an affection quite beyond his power of return or even of appreciation, but her ideas of service and duty would be on a very different scale from his. Of course, if she was a stray angel in a country of men, he might have had his way with her; but if he was a stray man among angels—!

Terry, at his worst, in a black fury for which, as a man, I must have some sympathy, preferred the ant simile. More of Terry and his special troubles later. It was hard on Terry.

Jeff—well, Jeff always had a streak that was too good for this world! He's the kind that would have made a saintly priest in parentagearlier times. He accepted the angel theory, swallowed it whole, tried to force it on us—with varying effect. He so worshipped Celis, and not only Celis, but what she represented; he had become so deeply convinced of the almost supernatural advantages of this country and people, that he took his medicine like a—I cannot say "like a man," but more as if he wasn't one.

Don't misunderstand me for a moment. Dear old Jeff was no milksop or molly-coddle either. He was a strong, brave, efficient man, and an excellent fighter when fighting was necessary. But there was always this angel streak in him. It was rather a wonder, Terry being so different, that he really loved Jeff as he did; but it happens so sometimes, in spite of the difference—perhaps because of it.

As for me, I stood between. I was no such gay Lothario as Terry, and no such Galahad as Jeff. But for all my limitations I think I had the habit of using my brains in regard to behavior rather more frequently than either of them. I had to use brain-power now, I can tell you.

The big point at issue between us and our wives was, as may easily be imagined, in the very nature of the relation.

"Wives! Don't talk to me about wives!" stormed Terry. "They don't know what the word means."

Which is exactly the fact—they didn't. How could they? Back in their prehistoric records of polygamy and slavery there were no ideals of wifehood as we know it, and since then no possibility of forming such.

"The only thing they can think of about a man is FATHERHOOD!" said Terry in high scorn. "FATHERHOOD! As if a man was always wanting to be a FATHER!"

This also was correct. They had their long, wide, deep, rich experience of Motherhood, and their only perception of the value of a male creature as such was for Fatherhood.

Aside from that, of course, was the whole range of personal love, love which as Jeff earnestly phrased it "passeth the love of women!" It did, too. I can give no idea—either now, after long and happy experience of it, or as it seemed then, in the first measureless wonder—of the beauty and power of the love they gave us.

Even Alima—who had a more stormy temperament than either of the others, and who, heaven knows, had far more provocation—even Alima was patience and tenderness and wisdom personified to the man she loved, until he—but I haven't got to that yet.

These, as Terry put it, "alleged or so-called wives" of ours, went right on with their profession as foresters. We, having no special learnings, had long since qualified as assistants. We had to do something, if only to pass the time, and it had to be work—we couldn't be playing forever.

This kept us out of doors with those dear girls, and more or less together—too much together sometimes.

These people had, it now became clear to us, the highest, keenest, most delicate sense of personal privacy, but not the faintest idea of that SOLITUDE A DEUX we are so fond of. They had, every one of them, the "two rooms and a bath" theory realized. From earliest childhood each had a separate bedroom with toilet conveniences, and one of the marks of coming of age was the addition of an outer room in which to receive friends.

Long since we had been given our own two rooms apiece, and as being of a different sex and race, these were in a separate house. It seemed to be recognized that we should breathe easier if able to free our minds in real seclusion.

For food we either went to any convenient eating-house, ordered a meal brought in, or took it with us to the woods, always and equally good. All this we had become used to and enjoyed—in our courting days.

After marriage there arose in us a somewhat unexpected urge of feeling that called for a separate house; but this feeling found no response in the hearts of those fair ladies.

"We ARE alone, dear," Ellador explained to me with gentle patience. "We are alone in these great forests; we may go and eat in any little summer-house—just we two, or have a separate table anywhere—or even have a separate meal in our own rooms. How could we be aloner?"

This was all very true. We had our pleasant mutual solitude about our work, and our pleasant evening talks in their apartments or ours; we had, as it were, all the pleasures of courtship carried right on; but we had no sense of—perhaps it may be called possession.

"Might as well not be married at all," growled Terry. "They only got up that ceremony to please us—please Jeff, mostly. They've no real idea of being married."

I tried my best to get Ellador's point of view, and naturally I tried to give her mine. Of course, what we, as men, wanted to make them see was that there were other, and as we proudly said "higher," uses in this relation than what Terry called "mere parentage." In the highest terms I knew I tried to explain this to Ellador.

"Anything higher than for mutual love to hope to give life, as we did?" she said. "How is it higher?"

"It develops love," I explained. "All the power of beautiful permanent mated love comes through this higher development."

"Are you sure?" she asked gently. "How do you know that it was so developed? There are some birds who love each other so that they mope and pine if separated, and never pair again if one dies, but they never mate except in the mating season. Among your people do you find high and lasting affection appearing in proportion to this indulgence?"

It is a very awkward thing, sometimes, to have a logical mind.

Of course I knew about those monogamous birds and beasts too, that mate for life and show every sign of mutual affection, without ever having stretched the sex relationship beyond its original range. But what of it?

"Those are lower forms of life!" I protested. "They have no capacity for faithful and affectionate, and apparently happy—but oh, my dear! my dear!—what can they know of such a love as draws us together? Why, to touch you—to be near you—to come closer and closer—to lose myself in you—surely you feel it too, do you not?"

I came nearer. I seized her hands.

Her eyes were on mine, tender radiant, but steady and strong. There was something so powerful, so large and changeless, in those eyes that I could not sweep her off her feet by my own emotion as I had unconsciously assumed would be the case.

It made me feel as, one might imagine, a man might feel who loved a goddess—not a Venus, though! She did not resent my attitude, did not repel it, did not in the least fear it, evidently. There was not a shade of that timid withdrawal or pretty resistance which are so—provocative.

"You see, dearest," she said, "you have to be patient with us. We are not like the women of your country. We are Mothers, and we are People, but we have not specialized in this line."

"We" and "we" and "we"—it was so hard to get her to be personal. And, as I thought that, I suddenly remembered how we were always criticizing OUR women for BEING so personal.

Then I did my earnest best to picture to her the sweet intense joy of married lovers, and the result in higher stimulus to all creative work.

"Do you mean," she asked quite calmly, as if I was not holding her cool firm hands in my hot and rather quivering ones, "that with you, when people marry, they go right on doing this in season and out of season, with no thought of children at all?"

"They do," I said, with some bitterness. "They are not mere parents. They are men and women, and they love each other."

"How long?" asked Ellador, rather unexpectedly.

"How long?" I repeated, a little dashed. "Why as long as they live."

"There is something very beautiful in the idea," she admitted, still as if she were discussing life on Mars. "This climactic expression, which, in all the other life-forms, has but the one purpose, has with you become specialized to higher, purer, nobler uses. It has—I judge from what you tell me—the most ennobling effect on character. People marry, not only for parentage, but for this exquisite interchange—and, as a result, you have a world full of continuous lovers, ardent, happy, mutually devoted, always living on that high tide of supreme emotion which we had supposed to belong only to one season and one use. And you say it has other results, stimulating all high creative work. That must mean floods, oceans of such work, blossoming from this intense happiness of every married pair! It is a beautiful idea!"

She was silent, thinking.

So was I.

She slipped one hand free, and was stroking my hair with it in a gentle motherly way. I bowed my hot head on her shoulder and felt a dim sense of peace, a restfulness which was very pleasant.

"You must take me there someday, darling," she was saying. "It is not only that I love you so much, I want to see your country—your people—your mother—" she paused reverently. "Oh, how I shall love your mother!"

I had not been in love many times—my experience did not compare with Terry's. But such as I had was so different from this that I was perplexed, and full of mixed feelings: partly a growing sense of common ground between us, a pleasant rested calm feeling, which I had imagined could only be attained in one way; and partly a bewildered resentment because what I found was not what I had looked for.

It was their confounded psychology! Here they were with this profound highly developed system of education so bred into them that even if they were not teachers by profession they all had a general proficiency in it—it was second nature to them.

And no child, stormily demanding a cookie "between meals," was ever more subtly diverted into an interest in house-building than was I when I found an apparently imperative demand had disappeared without my noticing it.

And all the time those tender mother eyes, those keen scientific eyes, noting every condition and circumstance, and learning how to "take time by the forelock" and avoid discussion before occasion arose.

I was amazed at the results. I found that much, very much, of what I had honestly supposed to be a physiological necessity was a psychological necessity—or so believed. I found, after my ideas of what was essential had changed, that my feelings changed also. And more than all, I found this—a factor of enormous weight—these women were not provocative. That made an immense difference.

The thing that Terry had so complained of when we first came—that they weren't "feminine," they lacked "charm," now became a great comfort. Their vigorous beauty was an aesthetic pleasure, not an irritant. Their dress and ornaments had not a touch of the "come-and-find-me" element.

Even with my own Ellador, my wife, who had for a time unveiled a woman's heart and faced the strange new hope and joy of dual parentage, she afterward withdrew again into the same good comrade she had been at first. They were women, PLUS, and so much plus that when they did not choose to let the womanness appear, you could not find it anywhere.

I don't say it was easy for me; it wasn't. But when I made appeal to her sympathies I came up against another immovable wall. She was sorry, honestly sorry, for my distresses, and made all manner of thoughtful suggestions, often quite useful, as well as the wise foresight I have mentioned above, which often saved all difficulty before it arose; but her sympathy did not alter her convictions.

"If I thought it was really right and necessary, I could perhaps bring myself to it, for your sake, dear; but I do not want to—not at all. You would not have a mere submission, would you? That is not the kind of high romantic love you spoke of, surely? It is a pity, of course, that you should have to adjust your highly specialized faculties to our unspecialized ones."

Confound it! I hadn't married the nation, and I told her so. But she only smiled at her own limitations and explained that she had to "think in we's."

Confound it again! Here I'd have all my energies focused on one wish, and before I knew it she'd have them dissipated in one direction or another, some subject of discussion that began just at the point I was talking about and ended miles away.

It must not be imagined that I was just repelled, ignored, left to cherish a grievance. Not at all. My happiness was in the hands of a larger, sweeter womanhood than I had ever imagined. Before our marriage my own ardor had perhaps blinded me to much of this. I was madly in love with not so much what was there as with what I supposed to be there. Now I found an endlessly beautiful undiscovered country to explore, and in it the sweetest wisdom and understanding. It was as if I had come to some new place and people, with a desire to eat at all hours, and no other interests in particular; and as if my hosts, instead of merely saying, "You shall not eat," had presently aroused in me a lively desire for music, for pictures, for games, for exercise, for playing in the water, for running some ingenious machine; and, in the multitude of my satisfactions, I forgot the one point which was not satisfied, and got along very well until mealtime.

One of the cleverest and most ingenious of these tricks was only clear to me many years after, when we were so wholly at one on this subject that I could laugh at my own predicament then. It was this: You see, with us, women are kept as different as possible and as feminine as possible. We men have our own world, with only men in it; we get tired of our ultra-maleness and turn gladly to the ultra-femaleness. Also, in keeping our women as feminine as possible, we see to it that when we turn to them we find the thing we want always in evidence. Well, the atmosphere of this place was anything but seductive. The very numbers of these human women, always in human relation, made them anything but alluring. When, in spite of this, my hereditary instincts and race-traditions made me long for the feminine response in Ellador, instead of withdrawing so that I should want her more, she deliberately gave me a little too much of her society.—always de-feminized, as it were. It was awfully funny, really.

Here was I, with an Ideal in mind, for which I hotly longed, and here was she, deliberately obtruding in the foreground of my consciousness a Fact—a fact which I coolly enjoyed, but which actually interfered with what I wanted. I see now clearly enough why a certain kind of man, like Sir Almroth Wright, resents the professional development of women. It gets in the way of the sex ideal; it temporarily covers and excludes femininity.

Of course, in this case, I was so fond of Ellador my friend, of Ellador my professional companion, that I necessarily enjoyed her society on any terms. Only—when I had had her with me in her de-feminine capacity for a sixteen-hour day, I could go to my own room and sleep without dreaming about her.

The witch! If ever anybody worked to woo and win and hold a human soul, she did, great superwoman that she was. I couldn't then half comprehend the skill of it, the wonder. But this I soon began to find: that under all our cultivated attitude of mind toward women, there is an older, deeper, more "natural" feeling, the restful reverence which looks up to the Mother sex.

So we grew together in friendship and happiness, Ellador and I, and so did Jeff and Celis.

When it comes to Terry's part of it, and Alima's, I'm sorry—and I'm ashamed. Of course I blame her somewhat. She wasn't as fine a psychologist as Ellador, and what's more, I think she had a far-descended atavistic trace of more marked femaleness, never apparent till Terry called it out. But when all is said, it doesn't excuse him. I hadn't realized to the full Terry's character—I couldn't, being a man.

The position was the same as with us, of course, only with these distinctions. Alima, a shade more alluring, and several shades less able as a practical psychologist; Terry, a hundredfold more demanding—and proportionately less reasonable.

Things grew strained very soon between them. I fancy at first, when they were together, in her great hope of parentage and his keen joy of conquest—that Terry was inconsiderate. In fact, I know it, from things he said.

"You needn't talk to me," he snapped at Jeff one day, just before our weddings. "There never was a woman yet that did not enjoy being MASTERED. All your pretty talk doesn't amount to a hill o'beans—I KNOW." And Terry would hum:

I've taken my fun where I found it.
I've rogued and I've ranged in my time,

and

The things that I learned from the yellow and black,
They 'ave helped me a 'eap with the white.

Jeff turned sharply and left him at the time. I was a bit disquieted myself.

Poor old Terry! The things he'd learned didn't help him a heap in Herland. His idea was to take—he thought that was the way. He thought, he honestly believed, that women like it. Not the women of Herland! Not Alima!

I can see her now—one day in the very first week of their marriage, setting forth to her day's work with long determined strides and hard-set mouth, and sticking close to Ellador. She didn't wish to be alone with Terry—you could see that.

But the more she kept away from him, the more he wanted her—naturally.

He made a tremendous row about their separate establishments, tried to keep her in his rooms, tried to stay in hers. But there she drew the line sharply.

He came away one night, and stamped up and down the moonlit road, swearing under his breath. I was taking a walk that night too, but I wasn't in his state of mind. To hear him rage you'd not have believed that he loved Alima at all—you'd have thought that she was some quarry he was pursuing, something to catch and conquer.

I think that, owing to all those differences I spoke of, they soon lost the common ground they had at first, and were unable to meet sanely and dispassionately. I fancy too—this is pure conjecture—that he had succeeded in driving Alima beyond her best judgment, her real conscience, and that after that her own sense of shame, the reaction of the thing, made her bitter perhaps.

They quarreled, really quarreled, and after making it up once or twice, they seemed to come to a real break—she would not be alone with him at all. And perhaps she was a bit nervous, I don't know, but she got Moadine to come and stay next door to her. Also, she had a sturdy assistant detailed to accompany her in her work.

Terry had his own ideas, as I've tried to show. I daresay he thought he had a right to do as he did. Perhaps he even convinced himself that it would be better for her. Anyhow, he hid himself in her bedroom one night...

The women of Herland have no fear of men. Why should they have? They are not timid in any sense. They are not weak; and they all have strong trained athletic bodies. Othello could not have extinguished Alima with a pillow, as if she were a mouse.

Terry put in practice his pet conviction that a woman loves to be mastered, and by sheer brute force, in all the pride and passion of his intense masculinity, he tried to master this woman.

It did not work. I got a pretty clear account of it later from Ellador, but what we heard at the time was the noise of a tremendous struggle, and Alima calling to Moadine. Moadine was close by and came at once; one or two more strong grave women followed.

Terry dashed about like a madman; he would cheerfully have killed them—he told me that, himself—but he couldn't. When he swung a chair over his head one sprang in the air and caught it, two threw themselves bodily upon him and forced him to the floor; it was only the work of a few moments to have him tied hand and foot, and then, in sheer pity for his futile rage, to anesthetize him.

Alima was in a cold fury. She wanted him killed—actually.

There was a trial before the local Over Mother, and this woman, who did not enjoy being mastered, stated her case.

In a court in our country he would have been held quite "within his rights," of course. But this was not our country; it was theirs. They seemed to measure the enormity of the offense by its effect upon a possible fatherhood, and he scorned even to reply to this way of putting it.

He did let himself go once, and explained in definite terms that they were incapable of understanding a man's needs, a man's desires, a man's point of view. He called them neuters, epicenes, bloodless, sexless creatures. He said they could of course kill him—as so many insects could—but that he despised them nonetheless.

And all those stern grave mothers did not seem to mind his despising them, not in the least.

It was a long trial, and many interesting points were brought out as to their views of our habits, and after a while Terry had his sentence. He waited, grim and defiant. The sentence was: "You must go home!"

12. Expelled

We had all meant to go home again. Indeed we had NOT meant—not by any means—to stay as long as we had. But when it came to being turned out, dismissed, sent away for bad conduct, we none of us really liked it.

Terry said he did. He professed great scorn of the penalty and the trial, as well as all the other characteristics of "this miserable half-country." But he knew, and we knew, that in any "whole" country we should never have been as forgivingly treated as we had been here.

"If the people had come after us according to the directions we left, there'd have been quite a different story!" said Terry. We found out later why no reserve party had arrived. All our careful directions had been destroyed in a fire. We might have all died there and no one at home have ever known our whereabouts.

Terry was under guard now, all the time, known as unsafe, convicted of what was to them an unpardonable sin.

He laughed at their chill horror. "Parcel of old maids!" he called them. "They're all old maids—children or not. They don't know the first thing about Sex."

When Terry said SEX, sex with a very large S, he meant the male sex, naturally; its special values, its profound conviction of being "the life force," its cheerful ignoring of the true life process, and its interpretation of the other sex solely from its own point of view.

I had learned to see these things very differently since living with Ellador; and as for Jeff, he was so thoroughly Herlandized that he wasn't fair to Terry, who fretted sharply in his new restraint.

Moadine, grave and strong, as sadly patient as a mother with a degenerate child, kept steady watch on him, with enough other women close at hand to prevent an outbreak. He had no weapons, and well knew that all his strength was of small avail against those grim, quiet women.

We were allowed to visit him freely, but he had only his room, and a small high-walled garden to walk in, while the preparations for our departure were under way.

Three of us were to go: Terry, because he must; I, because two were safer for our flyer, and the long boat trip to the coast; Ellador, because she would not let me go without her.

If Jeff had elected to return, Celis would have gone too—they were the most absorbed of lovers; but Jeff had no desire that way.

"Why should I want to go back to all our noise and dirt, our vice and crime, our disease and degeneracy?" he demanded of me privately. We never spoke like that before the women. "I wouldn't take Celis there for anything on earth!" he protested. "She'd die! She'd die of horror and shame to see our slums and hospitals. How can you risk it with Ellador? You'd better break it to her gently before she really makes up her mind."

Jeff was right. I ought to have told her more fully than I did, of all the things we had to be ashamed of. But it is very hard to bridge the gulf of as deep a difference as existed between our life and theirs. I tried to.

"Look here, my dear," I said to her. "If you are really going to my country with me, you've got to be prepared for a good many shocks. It's not as beautiful as this—the cities, I mean, the civilized parts—of course the wild country is."

"I shall enjoy it all," she said, her eyes starry with hope. "I understand it's not like ours. I can see how monotonous our quiet life must seem to you, how much more stirring yours must be. It must be like the biological change you told me about when the second sex was introduced—a far greater movement, constant change, with new possibilities of growth."

I had told her of the later biological theories of sex, and she was deeply convinced of the superior advantages of having two, the superiority of a world with men in it.

"We have done what we could alone; perhaps we have some things better in a quiet way, but you have the whole world—all the people of the different nations—all the long rich history behind you—all the wonderful new knowledge. Oh, I just can't wait to see it!"

What could I do? I told her in so many words that we had our unsolved problems, that we had dishonesty and corruption, vice and crime, disease and insanity, prisons and hospitals; and it made no more impression on her than it would to tell a South Sea Islander about the temperature of the Arctic Circle. She could intellectually see that it was bad to have those things; but she could not FEEL it.

We had quite easily come to accept the Herland life as normal, because it was normal—none of us make any outcry over mere health and peace and happy industry. And the abnormal, to which we are all so sadly well acclimated, she had never seen.

The two things she cared most to hear about, and wanted most to see, were these: the beautiful relation of marriage and the lovely women who were mothers and nothing else; beyond these her keen, active mind hungered eagerly for the world life.

"I'm almost as anxious to go as you are yourself," she insisted, "and you must be desperately homesick."

I assured her that no one could be homesick in such a paradise as theirs, but she would have none of it.

"Oh, yes—I know. It's like those little tropical islands you've told me about, shining like jewels in the big blue sea—I can't wait to see the sea! The little island may be as perfect as a garden, but you always want to get back to your own big country, don't you? Even if it is bad in some ways?"

Ellador was more than willing. But the nearer it came to our really going, and to my having to take her back to our "civilization," after the clean peace and beauty of theirs, the more I began to dread it, and the more I tried to explain.

Of course I had been homesick at first, while we were prisoners, before I had Ellador. And of course I had, at first, rather idealized my country and its ways, in describing it. Also, I had always accepted certain evils as integral parts of our civilization and never dwelt on them at all. Even when I tried to tell her the worst, I never remembered some things—which, when she came to see them, impressed her at once, as they had never impressed me. Now, in my efforts at explanation, I began to see both ways more keenly than I had before; to see the painful defects of my own land, the marvelous gains of this.

In missing men we three visitors had naturally missed the larger part of life, and had unconsciously assumed that they must miss it too. It took me a long time to realize—Terry never did realize—how little it meant to them. When we say MEN, MAN, MANLY, MANHOOD, and all the other masculine derivatives, we have in the background of our minds a huge vague crowded picture of the world and all its activities. To grow up and "be a man," to "act like a man"—the meaning and connotation is wide indeed. That vast background is full of marching columns of men, of changing lines of men, of long processions of men; of men steering their ships into new seas, exploring unknown mountains, breaking horses, herding cattle, ploughing and sowing and reaping, toiling at the forge and furnace, digging in the mine, building roads and bridges and high cathedrals, managing great businesses, teaching in all the colleges, preaching in all the churches; of men everywhere, doing everything—"the world."

And when we say WOMEN, we think FEMALE—the sex.

But to these women, in the unbroken sweep of this two-thousand-year-old feminine civilization, the word WOMAN called up all that big background, so far as they had gone in social development; and the word MAN meant to them only MALE—the sex.

Of course we could TELL them that in our world men did everything; but that did not alter the background of their minds. That man, "the male," did all these things was to them a statement, making no more change in the point of view than was made in ours when we first faced the astounding fact—to us—that in Herland women were "the world."

We had been living there more than a year. We had learned their limited history, with its straight, smooth, upreaching lines, reaching higher and going faster up to the smooth comfort of their present life. We had learned a little of their psychology, a much wider field than the history, but here we could not follow so readily. We were now well used to seeing women not as females but as people; people of all sorts, doing every kind of work.

This outbreak of Terry's, and the strong reaction against it, gave us a new light on their genuine femininity. This was given me with great clearness by both Ellador and Somel. The feeling was the same—sick revulsion and horror, such as would be felt at some climactic blasphemy.

They had no faintest approach to such a thing in their minds, knowing nothing of the custom of marital indulgence among us. To them the one high purpose of motherhood had been for so long the governing law of life, and the contribution of the father, though known to them, so distinctly another method to the same end, that they could not, with all their effort, get the point of view of the male creature whose desires quite ignore parentage and seek only for what we euphoniously term "the joys of love."

When I tried to tell Ellador that women too felt so, with us, she drew away from me, and tried hard to grasp intellectually what she could in no way sympathize with.

"You mean—that with you—love between man and woman expresses itself in that way—without regard to motherhood? To parentage, I mean," she added carefully.

"Yes, surely. It is love we think of—the deep sweet love between two. Of course we want children, and children come—but that is not what we think about."

"But—but—it seems so against nature!" she said. "None of the creatures we know do that. Do other animals—in your country?"

"We are not animals!" I replied with some sharpness. "At least we are something more—something higher. This is a far nobler and more beautiful relation, as I have explained before. Your view seems to us rather—shall I say, practical? Prosaic? Merely a means to an end! With us—oh, my dear girl—cannot you see? Cannot you feel? It is the last, sweetest, highest consummation of mutual love."

She was impressed visibly. She trembled in my arms, as I held her close, kissing her hungrily. But there rose in her eyes that look I knew so well, that remote clear look as if she had gone far away even though I held her beautiful body so close, and was now on some snowy mountain regarding me from a distance.

"I feel it quite clearly," she said to me. "It gives me a deep sympathy with what you feel, no doubt more strongly still. But what I feel, even what you feel, dearest, does not convince me that it is right. Until I am sure of that, of course I cannot do as you wish."

Ellador, at times like this, always reminded me of Epictetus. "I will put you in prison!" said his master. "My body, you mean," replied Epictetus calmly. "I will cut your head off," said his master. "Have I said that my head could not be cut off?" A difficult person, Epictetus.

What is this miracle by which a woman, even in your arms, may withdraw herself, utterly disappear till what you hold is as inaccessible as the face of a cliff?

"Be patient with me, dear," she urged sweetly. "I know it is hard for you. And I begin to see—a little—how Terry was so driven to crime."

"Oh, come, that's a pretty hard word for it. After all, Alima was his wife, you know," I urged, feeling at the moment a sudden burst of sympathy for poor Terry. For a man of his temperament—and habits—it must have been an unbearable situation.

But Ellador, for all her wide intellectual grasp, and the broad sympathy in which their religion trained them, could not make allowance for such—to her—sacrilegious brutality.

It was the more difficult to explain to her, because we three, in our constant talks and lectures about the rest of the world, had naturally avoided the seamy side; not so much from a desire to deceive, but from wishing to put the best foot foremost for our civilization, in the face of the beauty and comfort of theirs. Also, we really thought some things were right, or at least unavoidable, which we could readily see would be repugnant to them, and therefore did not discuss. Again there was much of our world's life which we, being used to it, had not noticed as anything worth describing. And still further, there was about these women a colossal innocence upon which many of the things we did say had made no impression whatever.

I am thus explicit about it because it shows how unexpectedly strong was the impression made upon Ellador when she at last entered our civilization.

She urged me to be patient, and I was patient. You see, I loved her so much that even the restrictions she so firmly established left me much happiness. We were lovers, and there is surely delight enough in that.

Do not imagine that these young women utterly refused "the Great New Hope," as they called it, that of dual parentage. For that they had agreed to marry us, though the marrying part of it was a concession to our prejudices rather than theirs. To them the process was the holy thing—and they meant to keep it holy.

But so far only Celis, her blue eyes swimming in happy tears, her heart lifted with that tide of race-motherhood which was their supreme passion, could with ineffable joy and pride announce that she was to be a mother. "The New Motherhood" they called it, and the whole country knew. There was no pleasure, no service, no honor in all the land that Celis might not have had. Almost like the breathless reverence with which, two thousand years ago, that dwindling band of women had watched the miracle of virgin birth, was the deep awe and warm expectancy with which they greeted this new miracle of union.

All mothers in that land were holy. To them, for long ages, the approach to motherhood has been by the most intense and exquisite love and longing, by the Supreme Desire, the overmastering demand for a child. Every thought they held in connection with the processes of maternity was open to the day, simple yet sacred. Every woman of them placed motherhood not only higher than other duties, but so far higher that there were no other duties, one might almost say. All their wide mutual love, all the subtle interplay of mutual friendship and service, the urge of progressive thought and invention, the deepest religious emotion, every feeling and every act was related to this great central Power, to the River of Life pouring through them, which made them the bearers of the very Spirit of God.

Of all this I learned more and more—from their books, from talk, especially from Ellador. She was at first, for a brief moment, envious of her friend—a thought she put away from her at once and forever.

"It is better," she said to me. "It is much better that it has not come to me yet—to us, that is. For if I am to go with you to your country, we may have 'adventures by sea and land,' as you say [and as in truth we did], and it might not be at all safe for a baby. So we won't try again, dear, till it is safe—will we?"

This was a hard saying for a very loving husband.

"Unless," she went on, "if one is coming, you will leave me behind. You can come back, you know—and I shall have the child."

Then that deep ancient chill of male jealousy of even his own progeny touched my heart.

"I'd rather have you, Ellador, than all the children in the world. I'd rather have you with me—on your own terms—than not to have you."

This was a very stupid saying. Of course I would! For if she wasn't there I should want all of her and have none of her. But if she went along as a sort of sublimated sister—only much closer and warmer than that, really—why I should have all of her but that one thing. And I was beginning to find that Ellador's friendship, Ellador's comradeship, Ellador's sisterly affection, Ellador's perfectly sincere love—none the less deep that she held it back on a definite line of reserve—were enough to live on very happily.

I find it quite beyond me to describe what this woman was to me. We talk fine things about women, but in our hearts we know that they are very limited beings—most of them. We honor them for their functional powers, even while we dishonor them by our use of it; we honor them for their carefully enforced virtue, even while we show by our own conduct how little we think of that virtue; we value them, sincerely, for the perverted maternal activities which make our wives the most comfortable of servants, bound to us for life with the wages wholly at our own decision, their whole business, outside of the temporary duties of such motherhood as they may achieve, to meet our needs in every way. Oh, we value them, all right, "in their place," which place is the home, where they perform that mixture of duties so ably described by Mrs. Josephine Dodge Daskam Bacon, in which the services of "a mistress" are carefully specified. She is a very clear writer, Mrs. J. D. D. Bacon, and understands her subject—from her own point of view. But—that combination of industries, while convenient, and in a way economical, does not arouse the kind of emotion commanded by the women of Herland. These were women one had to love "up," very high up, instead of down. They were not pets. They were not servants. They were not timid, inexperienced, weak.

After I got over the jar to my pride (which Jeff, I truly think, never felt—he was a born worshipper, and which Terry never got over—he was quite clear in his ideas of "the position of women"), I found that loving "up" was a very good sensation after all. It gave me a queer feeling, way down deep, as of the stirring of some ancient dim prehistoric consciousness, a feeling that they were right somehow—that this was the way to feel. It was like—coming home to mother. I don't mean the underflannels-and-doughnuts mother, the fussy person that waits on you and spoils you and doesn't really know you. I mean the feeling that a very little child would have, who had been lost—for ever so long. It was a sense of getting home; of being clean and rested; of safety and yet freedom; of love that was always there, warm like sunshine in May, not hot like a stove or a featherbed—a love that didn't irritate and didn't smother.

I looked at Ellador as if I hadn't seen her before. "If you won't go," I said, "I'll get Terry to the coast and come back alone. You can let me down a rope. And if you will go—why you blessed wonder-woman—I would rather live with you all my life—like this—than to have any other woman I ever saw, or any number of them, to do as I like with. Will you come?"

She was keen for coming. So the plans went on. She'd have liked to wait for that Marvel of Celis's, but Terry had no such desire. He was crazy to be out of it all. It made him sick, he said, SICK; this everlasting mother-mother-mothering. I don't think Terry had what the phrenologists call "the lump of philoprogenitiveness" at all well developed.

"Morbid one-sided cripples," he called them, even when from his window he could see their splendid vigor and beauty; even while Moadine, as patient and friendly as if she had never helped Alima to hold and bind him, sat there in the room, the picture of wisdom and serene strength. "Sexless, epicene, undeveloped neuters!" he went on bitterly. He sounded like Sir Almwroth Wright.

Well—it was hard. He was madly in love with Alima, really; more so than he had ever been before, and their tempestuous courtship, quarrels, and reconciliations had fanned the flame. And then when he sought by that supreme conquest which seems so natural a thing to that type of man, to force her to love him as her master—to have the sturdy athletic furious woman rise up and master him—she and her friends—it was no wonder he raged.

Come to think of it, I do not recall a similar case in all history or fiction. Women have killed themselves rather than submit to outrage; they have killed the outrager; they have escaped; or they have submitted—sometimes seeming to get on very well with the victor afterward. There was that adventure of "false Sextus," for instance, who "found Lucrese combing the fleece, under the midnight lamp." He threatened, as I remember, that if she did not submit he would slay her, slay a slave and place him beside her and say he found him there. A poor device, it always seemed to me. If Mr. Lucretius had asked him how he came to be in his wife's bedroom overlooking her morals, what could he have said? But the point is Lucrese submitted, and Alima didn't.

"She kicked me," confided the embittered prisoner—he had to talk to someone. "I was doubled up with the pain, of course, and she jumped on me and yelled for this old harpy [Moadine couldn't hear him] and they had me trussed up in no time. I believe Alima could have done it alone," he added with reluctant admiration. "She's as strong as a horse. And of course a man's helpless when you hit him like that. No woman with a shade of decency—"

I had to grin at that, and even Terry did, sourly. He wasn't given to reasoning, but it did strike him that an assault like his rather waived considerations of decency.

"I'd give a year of my life to have her alone again," he said slowly, his hands clenched till the knuckles were white.

But he never did. She left our end of the country entirely, went up into the fir-forest on the highest slopes, and stayed there. Before we left he quite desperately longed to see her, but she would not come and he could not go. They watched him like lynxes. (Do lynxes watch any better than mousing cats, I wonder!)

Well—we had to get the flyer in order, and be sure there was enough fuel left, though Terry said we could glide all right, down to that lake, once we got started. We'd have gone gladly in a week's time, of course, but there was a great to-do all over the country about Ellador's leaving them. She had interviews with some of the leading ethicists—wise women with still eyes, and with the best of the teachers. There was a stir, a thrill, a deep excitement everywhere.

Our teaching about the rest of the world has given them all a sense of isolation, of remoteness, of being a little outlying sample of a country, overlooked and forgotten among the family of nations. We had called it "the family of nations," and they liked the phrase immensely.

They were deeply aroused on the subject of evolution; indeed, the whole field of natural science drew them irresistibly. Any number of them would have risked everything to go to the strange unknown lands and study; but we could take only one, and it had to be Ellador, naturally.

We planned greatly about coming back, about establishing a connecting route by water; about penetrating those vast forests and civilizing—or exterminating—the dangerous savages. That is, we men talked of that last—not with the women. They had a definite aversion to killing things.

But meanwhile there was high council being held among the wisest of them all. The students and thinkers who had been gathering facts from us all this time, collating and relating them, and making inferences, laid the result of their labors before the council.

Little had we thought that our careful efforts at concealment had been so easily seen through, with never a word to show us that they saw. They had followed up words of ours on the science of optics, asked innocent questions about glasses and the like, and were aware of the defective eyesight so common among us.

With the lightest touch, different women asking different questions at different times, and putting all our answers together like a picture puzzle, they had figured out a sort of skeleton chart as to the prevalence of disease among us. Even more subtly with no show of horror or condemnation, they had gathered something—far from the truth, but something pretty clear—about poverty, vice, and crime. They even had a goodly number of our dangers all itemized, from asking us about insurance and innocent things like that.

They were well posted as to the different races, beginning with their poison-arrow natives down below and widening out to the broad racial divisions we had told them about. Never a shocked expression of the face or exclamation of revolt had warned us; they had been extracting the evidence without our knowing it all this time, and now were studying with the most devout earnestness the matter they had prepared.

The result was rather distressing to us. They first explained the matter fully to Ellador, as she was the one who purposed visiting the Rest of the World. To Celis they said nothing. She must not be in any way distressed, while the whole nation waited on her Great Work.

Finally Jeff and I were called in. Somel and Zava were there, and Ellador, with many others that we knew.

They had a great globe, quite fairly mapped out from the small section maps in that compendium of ours. They had the different peoples of the earth roughly outlined, and their status in civilization indicated. They had charts and figures and estimates, based on the facts in that traitorous little book and what they had learned from us.

Somel explained: "We find that in all your historic period, so much longer than ours, that with all the interplay of services, the exchange of inventions and discoveries, and the wonderful progress we so admire, that in this widespread Other World of yours, there is still much disease, often contagious."

We admitted this at once.

"Also there is still, in varying degree, ignorance, with prejudice and unbridled emotion."

This too was admitted.

"We find also that in spite of the advance of democracy and the increase of wealth, that there is still unrest and sometimes combat."

Yes, yes, we admitted it all. We were used to these things and saw no reason for so much seriousness.

"All things considered," they said, and they did not say a hundredth part of the things they were considering, "we are unwilling to expose our country to free communication with the rest of the world—as yet. If Ellador comes back, and we approve her report, it may be done later—but not yet.

"So we have this to ask of you gentlemen [they knew that word was held a title of honor with us], that you promise not in any way to betray the location of this country until permission—after Ellador's return."

Jeff was perfectly satisfied. He thought they were quite right. He always did. I never saw an alien become naturalized more quickly than that man in Herland.

I studied it awhile, thinking of the time they'd have if some of our contagions got loose there, and concluded they were right. So I agreed.

Terry was the obstacle. "Indeed I won't!" he protested. "The first thing I'll do is to get an expedition fixed up to force an entrance into Ma-land."

"Then," they said quite calmly, "he must remain an absolute prisoner, always."

"Anesthesia would be kinder," urged Moadine.

"And safer," added Zava.

"He will promise, I think," said Ellador.

And he did. With which agreement we at last left Herland.

THE MAN-MADE WORLD

I. AS TO HUMANNESS.

Let us begin, inoffensively, with sheep. The sheep is a beast with which we are all familiar, being much used in religious imagery; the common stock of painters; a staple article of diet; one of our main sources of clothing; and an everyday symbol of bashfulness and stupidity.

In some grazing regions the sheep is an object of terror, destroying grass, bush and forest by omnipresent nibbling; on the great plains, sheep-keeping frequently results in insanity, owing to the loneliness of the shepherd, and the monotonous appearance and behavior of the sheep.

By the poet, young sheep are preferred, the lamb gambolling gaily; unless it be in hymns, where "all we like sheep" are repeatedly described, and much stress is laid upon the straying propensities of the animal.

To the scientific mind there is special interest in the sequacity of sheep, their habit of following one another with automatic imitation. This instinct, we are told, has been developed by ages of wild crowded racing on narrow ledges, along precipices, chasms, around sudden spurs and corners, only the leader seeing when, where and how to jump. If those behind jumped exactly as he did, they lived. If they stopped to exercise independent judgment, they were pushed off and perished; they and their judgment with them.

All these things, and many that are similar, occur to us when we think of sheep. They are also ewes and rams. Yes, truly; but what of it? All that has been said was said of sheep, genus ovis, that bland beast, compound of mutton, wool, and foolishness so widely known. If we think of the sheep-dog (and dog-ess), the shepherd (and shepherd-ess), of the ferocious sheep-eating bird of New Zealand, the Kea (and Kea-ess), all these herd, guard, or kill the sheep, both rams and ewes alike. In regard to mutton, to wool, to general character, we think only of their sheepishness, not at all of their ramishness or eweishness. That which is ovine or bovine, canine, feline or equine, is easily recognized as distinguishing that particular species of animal, and has no relation whatever to the sex thereof.

Returning to our muttons, let us consider the ram, and wherein his character differs from the sheep. We find he has a more quarrelsome disposition. He paws the earth and makes a noise. He has a tendency to butt. So has a goat—Mr. Goat. So has Mr. Buffalo, and Mr. Moose, and Mr. Antelope. This tendency to plunge head foremost at an adversary—and to find any other gentleman an adversary on sight—evidently does not pertain to sheep, to genus ovis; but to any male creature with horns.

As "function comes before organ," we may even give a reminiscent glance down the long path of evolution, and see how the mere act of butting—passionately and perpetually repeated—born of the belligerent spirit of the male—produced horns!

The ewe, on the other hand, exhibits love and care for her little ones, gives them milk and tries to guard them. But so does a goat—Mrs. Goat. So does Mrs. Buffalo and the rest. Evidently this mother instinct is no peculiarity of genus ovis, but of any female creature.

Even the bird, though not a mammal, shows the same mother-love and mother-care, while the father bird, though not a butter, fights with beak and wing and spur. His competition is more effective through display. The wish to please, the need to please, the overmastering necessity upon him that he secure the favor of the female, has made the male bird blossom like a butterfly. He blazes in gorgeous plumage, rears haughty crests and combs, shows drooping wattles and dangling blobs such as the turkey-cock affords; long splendid feathers for pure ornament appear upon him; what in her is a mere tail-effect becomes in him a mass of glittering drapery.

Partridge-cock, farmyard-cock, peacock, from sparrow to ostrich, observe his mien! To strut and languish; to exhibit every beauteous lure; to sacrifice ease, comfort, speed, everything—to beauty—for her sake—this is the nature of the he-bird of any species; the characteristic, not of the turkey, but of the cock! With drumming of loud wings, with crow and quack and bursts of glorious song, he woos his mate; displays his splendors before her; fights fiercely with his rivals. To butt—to strut—to make a noise—all for love's sake; these acts are common to the male.

We may now generalize and clearly state: That is masculine which belongs to the male—to any or all males, irrespective of species. That is feminine which belongs to the female, to any or all females, irrespective of species. That is ovine, bovine, feline, canine, equine or asinine which belongs to that species, irrespective of sex.

In our own species all this is changed. We have been so taken up with the phenomena of masculinity and femininity, that our common humanity has largely escaped notice. We know we are human, naturally, and are very proud of it; but we do not consider in what our humanness consists; nor how men and women may fall short of it, or overstep its bounds, in continual insistence upon their special differences. It is "manly" to do this; it is "womanly" to do that; but what a human being should do under the circumstances is not thought of.

The only time when we do recognize what we call "common humanity" is in extreme cases, matters of life and death; when either man or woman is expected to behave as if they were also human creatures. Since the range of feeling and action proper to humanity, as such, is far wider than that proper to either sex, it seems at first somewhat remarkable that we have given it so little recognition.

A little classification will help us here. We have certain qualities in common with inanimate matter, such as weight, opacity, resilience. It is clear that these are not human. We have other qualities in common with all forms of life; cellular construction, for instance, the reproduction of cells and the need of nutrition. These again are not human. We have others, many others, common to the higher mammals; which are not exclusively ours—are not distinctively "human." What then are true human characteristics? In what way is the human species distinguished from all other species?

Our human-ness is seen most clearly in three main lines: it is mechanical, psychical and social. Our power to make and use things is essentially human; we alone have extra-physical tools. We have added to our teeth the knife, sword, scissors, mowing machine; to our claws the spade, harrow, plough, drill, dredge. We are a protean creature, using the larger brain power through a wide variety of changing weapons. This is one of our main and vital distinctions. Ancient animal races are traced and known by mere bones and shells, ancient human races by their buildings, tools and utensils.

That degree of development which gives us the human mind is a clear distinction of race. The savage who can count a hundred is more human than the savage who can count ten.

More prominent than either of these is the social nature of humanity. We are by no means the only group-animal; that ancient type of industry the ant, and even the well-worn bee, are social creatures. But insects of their kind are found living alone. Human beings never. Our human-ness begins with some low form of social relation and increases as that relation develops.

Human life of any sort is dependent upon what Kropotkin calls "mutual aid," and human progress keeps step absolutely with that interchange of specialized services which makes society organic. The nomad, living on cattle as ants live on theirs, is less human than the farmer, raising food by intelligently applied labor; and the extension of trade and commerce, from mere village market-places to the world-exchanges of to-day, is extension of human-ness as well.

Humanity, thus considered, is not a thing made at once and unchangeable, but a stage of development; and is still, as Wells describes it, "in the making." Our human-ness is seen to lie not so much in what we are individually, as in our relations to one another; and even that individuality is but the result of our relations to one another. It is in what we do and how we do it, rather than in what we are. Some, philosophically inclined, exalt "being" over "doing." To them this question may be put: "Can you mention any form of life that merely 'is,' without doing anything?"

Taken separately and physically, we are animals, genus homo; taken socially and psychically, we are, in varying degree, human; and our real history lies in the development of this human-ness.

Our historic period is not very long. Real written history only goes back a few thousand years, beginning with the stone records of ancient Egypt. During this period we have had almost universally what is here called an Androcentric Culture. The history, such as it was, was made and written by men.

The mental, the mechanical, the social development, was almost wholly theirs. We have, so far, lived and suffered and died in a man-made world. So general, so unbroken, has been this condition, that to mention it arouses no more remark than the statement of a natural law. We have taken it for granted, since the dawn of civilization, that "mankind" meant men-kind, and the world was theirs.

Women we have sharply delimited. Women were a sex, "the sex," according to chivalrous toasts; they were set apart for special services peculiar to femininity. As one English scientist put it, in 1888, "Women are not only not the race—they are not even half the race, but a subspecies told off for reproduction only."

This mental attitude toward women is even more clearly expressed by Mr. H. B. Marriot-Watson in his article on "The American Woman" in the "Nineteenth Century" for June, 1904, where he says: "Her constitutional restlessness has caused her to abdicate those functions which alone excuse or explain her existence." This is a peculiarly happy and condensed expression of the relative position of women during our androcentric culture. The man was accepted as the race type without one dissentient voice; and the woman—a strange, diverse creature, quite disharmonious in the accepted scheme of things—was excused and explained only as a female.

She has needed volumes of such excuse and explanation; also, apparently, volumes of abuse and condemnation. In any library catalogue we may find books upon books about women: physiological, sentimental, didactic, religious—all manner of books about women, as such. Even to-day in the works of Marholm—poor young Weininger, Moebius, and others, we find the same perpetual discussion of women—as such.

This is a book about men—as such. It differentiates between the human nature and the sex nature. It will not go so far as to allege man's masculine traits to be all that excuse, or explain his existence: but it will point out what are masculine traits as distinct from human ones, and what has been the effect on our human life of the unbridled dominance of one sex.

We can see at once, glaringly, what would have been the result of giving all human affairs into female hands. Such an extraordinary and deplorable situation would have "feminized" the world. We should have all become "effeminate."

See how in our use of language the case is clearly shown. The adjectives and derivatives based on woman's distinctions are alien and derogatory when applied to human affairs; "effeminate"—too female, connotes contempt, but has no masculine analogue; whereas "emasculate"—not enough male, is a term of reproach, and has no feminine analogue. "Virile"—manly, we oppose to "puerile"—childish, and the very word "virtue" is derived from "vir"—a man.

Even in the naming of other animals we have taken the male as the race type, and put on a special termination to indicate "his female," as in lion, lioness; leopard, leopardess; while all our human scheme of things rests on the same tacit assumption; man being held the human type; woman a sort of accompaniment and subordinate assistant, merely essential to the making of people.

She has held always the place of a preposition in relation to man. She has been considered above him or below him, before him, behind him, beside him, a wholly relative existence—"Sydney's sister," "Pembroke's mother"—but never by any chance Sydney or Pembroke herself.

Acting on this assumption, all human standards have been based on male characteristics, and when we wish to praise the work of a woman, we say she has "a masculine mind."

It is no easy matter to deny or reverse a universal assumption. The human mind has had a good many jolts since it began to think, but after each upheaval it settles down as peacefully as the vine-growers on Vesuvius, accepting the last lava crust as permanent ground.

What we see immediately around us, what we are born into and grow up with, be it mental furniture or physical, we assume to be the order of nature.

If a given idea has been held in the human mind for many generations, as almost all our common ideas have, it takes sincere and continued effort to remove it; and if it is one of the oldest we have in stock, one of the big, common, unquestioned world ideas, vast is the labor of those who seek to change it.

Nevertheless, if the matter is one of importance, if the previous idea was a palpable error, of large and evil effect, and if the new one is true and widely important, the effort is worth making.

The task here undertaken is of this sort. It seeks to show that what we have all this time called "human nature" and deprecated, was in great part only male nature, and good enough in its place; that what we have called "masculine" and admired as such, was in large part human, and should be applied to both sexes: that what we have called "feminine" and condemned, was also largely human and applicable to both. Our androcentric culture is so shown to have been, and still to be, a masculine culture in excess, and therefore undesirable.

In the preliminary work of approaching these facts it will be well to explain how it can be that so wide and serious an error should have been made by practically all men. The reason is simply that they were men. They were males, avid saw women as females—and not otherwise.

So absolute is this conviction that the man who reads will say, "Of course! How else are we to look at women except as females? They are females, aren't they?" Yes, they are, as men are males unquestionably; but there is possible the frame of mind of the old marquise who was asked by an English friend how she could bear to have the footman serve her breakfast in bed—to have a man in her bed-chamber—and replied sincerely, "Call you that thing there a man?"

The world is full of men, but their principal occupation is human work of some sort; and women see in them the human distinction preponderantly. Occasionally some unhappy lady marries her coachman—long contemplation of broad shoulders having an effect, apparently; but in general women see the human creature most; the male creature only when they love.

To the man, the whole world was his world; his because he was male; and the whole world of woman was the home; because she was female. She had her prescribed sphere, strictly limited to her feminine occupations and interests; he had all the rest of life; and not only so, but, having it, insisted on calling it male.

This accounts for the general attitude of men toward the now rapid humanization of women. From her first faint struggles toward freedom and justice, to her present valiant efforts toward full economic and political equality, each step has been termed "unfeminine" and resented as an intrusion upon man's place and power. Here shows the need of our new classification, of the three distinct fields of life—masculine, feminine and human.

As a matter of fact, there is a "woman's sphere," sharply defined and quite different from his; there is also a "man's sphere," as sharply defined and even more limited; but there remains a common sphere—that of humanity, which belongs to both alike.

In the earlier part of what is known as "the woman's movement," it was sharply opposed on the ground that women would become "unsexed." Let us note in passing that they have become unsexed in one particular, most glaringly so, and that no one has noticed or objected to it.

As part of our androcentric culture we may point to the peculiar reversal of sex characteristics which make the human female carry the burden of ornament. She alone, of all human creatures, has adopted the essentially masculine attribute of special sex-decoration; she does not fight for her mate as yet, but she blooms forth as the peacock and bird of paradise, in poignant reversal of nature's laws, even wearing masculine feathers to further her feminine ends.

Woman's natural work as a female is that of the mother; man's natural work as a male is that of the father; their mutual relation to this end being a source of joy and well-being when rightly held: but human work covers all our life outside of these specialties. Every handicraft, every profession, every science, every art, all normal amusements and recreations, all government, education, religion; the whole living world of human achievement: all this is human.

That one sex should have monopolized all human activities, called them "man's work," and managed them as such, is what is meant by the phrase "Androcentric Culture."

II. THE MAN-MADE FAMILY.

The family is older than humanity, and therefore cannot be called a human institution. A post office, now, is wholly human; no other creature has a post office, but there are families in plenty among birds and beasts; all kinds permanent and transient; monogamous, polygamous and polyandrous.

We are now to consider the growth of the family in humanity; what is its rational development in humanness; in mechanical, mental and social lines; in the extension of love and service; and the effect upon it of this strange new arrangement—a masculine proprietor.

Like all natural institutions the family has a purpose; and is to be measured primarily as it serves that purpose; which is, the care and nurture of the young. To protect the helpless little ones, to feed and shelter them, to ensure them the benefits of an ever longer period of immaturity, and so to improve the race—this is the original purpose of the family.

When a natural institution becomes human it enters the plane of consciousness. We think about it; and, in our strange new power of voluntary action do things to it. We have done strange things to the family; or, more specifically, men have.

Balsac, at his bitterest, observed, "Women's virtue is man's best invention." Balsac was wrong. Virtue—the unswerving devotion to one mate—is common among birds and some of the higher mammals. If Balsac meant celibacy when he said virtue, why that is one of man's inventions—though hardly his best.

What man has done to the family, speaking broadly, is to change it from an institution for the best service of the child to one modified to his own service, the vehicle of his comfort, power and pride.

Among the heavy millions of the stirred East, a child—necessarily a male child—is desired for the credit and glory of the father, and his fathers; in place of seeing that all a parent is for is the best service of the child. Ancestor worship, that gross reversal of all natural law, is of wholly androcentric origin. It is strongest among old patriarchal races; lingers on in feudal Europe; is to be traced even in America today in a few sporadic efforts to magnify the deeds of our ancestors.

The best thing any of us can do for our ancestors is to be better than they were; and we ought to give our minds to it. When we use our past merely as a guide-book, and concentrate our noble emotions on the present and future, we shall improve more rapidly.

The peculiar changes brought about in family life by the predominance of the male are easily traced. In these studies we must keep clearly in mind the basic masculine characteristics: desire, combat, self-expression—all legitimate and right in proper use; only mischievous when excessive or out of place. Through them the male is led to strenuous competition for the favor of the female; in the overflowing ardours of song, as in nightingale and tomcat; in wasteful splendor of personal decoration, from the pheasant's breast to an embroidered waistcoat; and in direct struggle for the prize, from the stag's locked horns to the clashing spears of the tournament.

It is earnestly hoped that no reader will take offence at the necessarily frequent, reference to these essential features of maleness. In the many books about women it is, naturally, their femaleness that has been studied and enlarged upon. And though women, after thousands of years of such discussion, have become a little restive under the constant use of the word female: men, as rational beings, should not object to an analogous study—at least not for some time—a few centuries or so.

How, then, do we find these masculine tendencies, desire, combat and self-expression, affect the home and family when given too much power?

First comes the effect in the preliminary work of selection. One of the most uplifting forces of nature is that of sex selection. The males, numerous, varied, pouring a flood of energy into wide modifications, compete for the female, and she selects the victor, this securing to the race the new improvements.

In forming the proprietary family there is no such competition, no such selection. The man, by violence or by purchase, does the choosing—he selects the kind of woman that pleases him. Nature did not intend him to select; he is not good at it. Neither was the female intended to compete—she is not good at it.

If there is a race between males for a mate—the swiftest gets her first; but if one male is chasing a number of females he gets the slowest first. The one method improves our speed: the other does not. If males struggle and fight with one another for a mate, the strongest secures her; if the male struggles and fights with the female—(a peculiar and unnatural horror, known only among human beings) he most readily secures the weakest. The one method improves our strength—the other does not.

When women became the property of men; sold and bartered; "given away" by their paternal owner to their marital owner; they lost this prerogative of the female, this primal duty of selection. The males were no longer improved by their natural competition for the female; and the females were not improved; because the male did not select for points of racial superiority, but for such qualities as pleased him.

There is a locality in northern Africa, where young girls are deliberately fed with a certain oily seed, to make them fat,—that they may be the more readily married,—as the men like fat wives. Among certain more savage African tribes the chief's wives are prepared for him by being kept in small dark huts and fed on "mealies" and molasses; precisely as a Strasbourg goose is fattened for the gourmand. Now fatness is not a desirable race characteristic; it does not add to the woman's happiness or efficiency; or to the child's; it is merely an accessory pleasant to the master; his attitude being much as the amorous monad ecstatically puts it, in Sill's quaint poem, "Five Lives,"

"O the little female monad's lips!
O the little female monad's eyes!
O the little, little, female, female monad!"

This ultra littleness and ultra femaleness has been demanded and produced by our Androcentric Culture.

Following this, and part of it, comes the effect on motherhood. This function was the original and legitimate base of family life; and its ample sustaining power throughout the long early period of "the mother-right;" or as we call it, the matriarchate; the father being her assistant in the great work. The patriarchate, with its proprietary family, changed this altogether; the woman, as the property of the man was considered first and foremost as a means of pleasure to him; and while she was still valued as a mother, it was in a tributary capacity. Her children were now his; his property, as she was; the whole enginery of the family was turned from its true use to this new one, hitherto unknown, the service of the adult male.

To this day we are living under the influence of the proprietary family. The duty of the wife is held to involve man-service as well as child-service, and indeed far more; as the duty of the wife to the husband quite transcends the duty of the mother to the child.

See for instance the English wife staying with her husband in India and sending the children home to be brought up; because India is bad for children. See our common law that the man decides the place of residence; if the wife refuses to go with him to howsoever unfit a place for her and for the little ones, such refusal on her part constitutes "desertion" and is ground for divorce.

See again the idea that the wife must remain with the husband though a drunkard, or diseased; regardless of the sin against the child involved in such a relation. Public feeling on these matters is indeed changing; but as a whole the ideals of the man-made family still obtain.

The effect of this on the woman has been inevitably to weaken and overshadow her sense of the real purpose of the family; of the relentless responsibilities of her duty as a mother. She is first taught duty to her parents, with heavy religious sanction; and then duty to her husband, similarly buttressed; but her duty to her children has been left to instinct. She is not taught in girlhood as to her preeminent power and duty as a mother; her young ideals are all of devotion to the lover and husband: with only the vaguest sense of results.

The young girl is reared in what we call "innocence;" poetically described as "bloom;" and this condition is held one of her chief "charms." The requisite is wholly androcentric. This "innocence" does not enable her to choose a husband wisely; she does not even know the dangers that possibly confront her. We vaguely imagine that her father or brother, who do know, will protect her. Unfortunately the father and brother, under our current "double standard" of morality do not judge the applicants as she would if she knew the nature of their offenses.

Furthermore, if her heart is set on one of them, no amount of general advice and opposition serves to prevent her marrying him. "I love him!" she says, sublimely. "I do not care what he has done. I will forgive him. I will save him!"

This state of mind serves to forward the interests of the lover, but is of no advantage to the children. We have magnified the duties of the wife, and minified the duties of the mother; and this is inevitable in a family relation every law and custom of which is arranged from the masculine viewpoint.

From this same viewpoint, equally essential to the proprietary family, comes the requirement that the woman shall serve the man. Her service is not that of the associate and equal, as when she joins him in his business. It is not that of a beneficial combination, as when she practices another business and they share the profits; it is not even that of the specialist, as the service of a tailor or barber; it is personal service—the work of a servant.

In large generalization, the women of the world cook and wash, sweep and dust, sew and mend, for the men.

We are so accustomed to this relation; have held it for so long to be the "natural" relation, that it is difficult indeed to show that it is distinctly unnatural and injurious. The father expects to be served by the daughter, a service quite different from what he expects of the son. This shows at once that such service is no integral part of motherhood, or even of marriage; but is supposed to be the proper industrial position of women, as such.

Why is this so? Why, on the face of it, given a daughter and a son, should a form of service be expected of the one, which would be considered ignominious by the other?

The underlying reason is this. Industry, at its base, is a feminine function. The surplus energy of the mother does not manifest itself in noise, or combat, or display, but in productive industry. Because of her mother-power she became the first inventor and laborer; being in truth the mother of all industry as well as all people.

Man's entrance upon industry is late and reluctant; as will be shown later in treating his effect on economics. In this field of family life, his effect was as follows:

Establishing the proprietary family at an age when the industry was primitive and domestic; and thereafter confining the woman solely to the domestic area, he thereby confined her to primitive industry. The domestic industries, in the hands of women, constitute a survival of our remotest past. Such work was "woman's work" as was all the work then known; such work is still considered woman's work because they have been prevented from doing any other.

The term "domestic industry" does not define a certain kind of labor, but a certain grade of labor. Architecture was a domestic industry once—when every savage mother set up her own tepee. To be confined to domestic industry is no proper distinction of womanhood; it is an historic distinction, an economic distinction, it sets a date and limit to woman's industrial progress.

In this respect the man-made family has resulted in arresting the development of half the field. We have a world wherein men, industrially, live in the twentieth century; and women, industrially, live in the first—and back of it.

To the same source we trace the social and educational limitations set about women. The dominant male, holding his women as property, and fiercely jealous of them, considering them always as his, not belonging to themselves, their children, or the world; has hedged them in with restrictions of a thousand sorts; physical, as in the crippled Chinese lady or the imprisoned odalisque; moral, as in the oppressive doctrines of submission taught by all our androcentric religions; mental, as in the enforced ignorance from which women are now so swiftly emerging.

This abnormal restriction of women has necessarily injured motherhood. The man, free, growing in the world's growth, has mounted with the centuries, filling an ever wider range of world activities. The woman, bound, has not so grown; and the child is born to a progressive fatherhood and a stationary motherhood. Thus the man-made family reacts unfavorably upon the child. We rob our children of half their social heredity by keeping the mother in an inferior position; however legalized, hallowed, or ossified by time, the position of a domestic servant is inferior.

It is for this reason that child culture is at so low a level, and for the most part utterly unknown. Today, when the forces of education are steadily working nearer to the cradle, a new sense is wakening of the importance of the period of infancy, and its wiser treatment; yet those who know of such a movement are few, and of them some are content to earn easy praise—and pay—by belittling right progress to gratify the prejudices of the ignorant.

The whole position is simple and clear; and easily traceable to its root. Given a proprietary family, where the man holds the woman primarily for his satisfaction and service—then necessarily he shuts her up and keeps her for these purposes. Being so kept, she cannot develop humanly, as he has, through social contact, social service, true social life. (We may note in passing, her passionate fondness for the child-game called "society" she has been allowed to entertain herself withal; that poor simiacrum of real social life, in which people decorate themselves and madly crowd together, chattering, for what is called "entertainment.") Thus checked in social development, we have but a low grade motherhood to offer our children; and the children, reared in the primitive conditions thus artificially maintained, enter life with a false perspective, not only toward men and women, but toward life as a whole.

The child should receive in the family, full preparation for his relation to the world at large. His whole life must be spent in the world, serving it well or ill; and youth is the time to learn how. But the androcentric home cannot teach him. We live to-day in a democracy-the man-made family is a despotism. It may be a weak one; the despot may be dethroned and overmastered by his little harem of one; but in that case she becomes the despot—that is all. The male is esteemed "the head of the family;" it belongs to him; he maintains it; and the rest of the world is a wide hunting ground and battlefield wherein he competes with other males as of old.

The girl-child, peering out, sees this forbidden field as belonging wholly to men-kind; and her relation to it is to secure one for herself—not only that she may love, but that she may live. He will feed, clothe and adorn her—she will serve him; from the subjection of the daughter to that of the wife she steps; from one home to the other, and never enters the world at all—man's world.

The boy, on the other hand, considers the home as a place of women, an inferior place, and longs to grow up and leave it—for the real world. He is quite right. The error is that this great social instinct, calling for full social exercise, exchange, service, is considered masculine, whereas it is human, and belongs to boy and girl alike.

The child is affected first through the retarded development of his mother, then through the arrested condition of home industry; and further through the wrong ideals which have arisen from these conditions. A normal home, where there was human equality between mother and father, would have a better influence.

We must not overlook the effect of the proprietary family on the proprietor himself. He, too, has been held back somewhat by this reactionary force. In the process of becoming human we must learn to recognize justice, freedom, human rights; we must learn self-control and to think of others; have minds that grow and broaden rationally; we must learn the broad mutual interservice and unbounded joy of social intercourse and service. The petty despot of the man-made home is hindered in his humanness by too much manness.

For each man to have one whole woman to cook for and wait upon him is a poor education for democracy. The boy with a servile mother, the man with a servile wife, cannot reach the sense of equal rights we need to-day. Too constant consideration of the master's tastes makes the master selfish; and the assault upon his heart direct, or through that proverbial side-avenue, the stomach, which the dependent woman needs must make when she wants anything, is bad for the man, as well as for her.

We are slowly forming a nobler type of family; the union of two, based on love and recognized by law, maintained because of its happiness and use. We are even now approaching a tenderness and permanence of love, high pure enduring love; combined with the broad deep-rooted friendliness and comradeship of equals; which promises us more happiness in marriage than we have yet known. It will be good for all the parties concerned—man, woman and child: and promote our general social progress admirably.

If it needs "a head" it will elect a chairman pro tem. Friendship does not need "a head." Love does dot need "a head." Why should a family?

III. HEALTH AND BEAUTY.

NOTE—The word "Androcentric" we owe to Prof. Lester F. Ward. In his book, "Pure Sociology," Chap. 14, he describes the Androcentric Theory of life, hitherto universally accepted; and introduces his own "Gyneacocentric Theory." All who are interested in the deeper scientific aspects of this question are urged to read that chapter. Prof. Ward's theory is to my mind the most important that has been offered the world since the Theory of Evolution; and without exception the most important that has ever been put forward concerning women.

Among the many paradoxes which we find in human life is our low average standard of health and beauty, compared with our power and knowledge. All creatures suffer from conflict with the elements; from enemies without and within—the prowling devourers of the forest, and "the terror that walketh in darkness" and attacks the body from inside, in hidden millions.

Among wild animals generally, there is a certain standard of excellence; if you shoot a bear or a bird, it is a fair sample of the species; you do not say, "O what an ugly one!" or "This must have been an invalid!"

Where we have domesticated any animal, and interfered with its natural habits, illness has followed; the dog is said to have the most diseases second to man; the horse comes next; but the wild ones put us to shame by their superior health and the beauty that belongs to right development.

In our long ages of blind infancy we assume that sickness was a visitation frown the gods; some still believe this, holding it to be a special prerogative of divinity to afflict us in this way. We speak of "the ills that flesh is heir to" as if the inheritance was entailed and inalienable. Only of late years, after much study and long struggle with this old belief which made us submit to sickness as a blow from the hand of God, we are beginning to learn something of the many causes of our many diseases, and how to remove some of them.

It is still true, however, that almost every one of us is to some degree abnormal; the features asymmetrical, the vision defective, the digestion unreliable, the nervous system erratic—we are but a job lot even in what we call "good health"; and are subject to a burden of pain and premature death that would make life hideous if it were not so ridiculously unnecessary.

As to beauty—we do not think of expecting it save in the rarely exceptional case. Look at the faces—the figures—in any crowd you meet;

compare the average man or the average woman with the normal type of human beauty as given us in picture and statue; and consider if there is not some general cause for so general a condition of ugliness.

Moreover, leaving our defective bodies concealed by garments; what are those garments, as conducive to health and beauty? Is the practical ugliness of our men's attire, and the impractical absurdity of our women's, any contribution to human beauty? Look at our houses—are they beautiful? Even the houses of the rich?

We do not even know that we ought to live in a world of overflowing loveliness; and that our contribution to it should be the loveliest of all. We are so sodden in the dull ugliness of our interiors, so used to calling a tame weary low-toned color scheme "good taste," that only children dare frankly yearn for Beauty—and they are speedily educated out of it.

The reasons specially given for our low standards of health and beauty are ignorance, poverty, and the evil effects of special trades. The Man with the Hoe becomes brother to the ox because of over-much hoeing; the housepainter is lead-poisoned because of his painting; books have been written to show the injurious influence of nearly all our industries upon workers.

These causes are sound as far as they go; but do not cover the whole ground.

The farmer may be muscle-bound and stooping from his labor; but that does not account for his dyspepsia or his rheumatism.

Then we allege poverty as covering all. Poverty does cover a good deal. But when we find even a half-fed savage better developed than a well paid cashier; and a poor peasant woman a more vigorous mother than the idle wife of a rich man, poverty is not enough.

Then we say ignorance explains it. But there are most learned professors who are ugly and asthmathic; there are even doctors who can boast no beauty and but moderate health; there are some of the petted children of the wealthy, upon whom every care is lavished from birth, and who still are ill to look at and worse to marry.

All these special causes are admitted, given their due share in lowering our standards, but there is another far more universal in its application and its effects. Let us look back on our little ancestors the beasts, and see what keeps them so true to type.

The type itself set by that balance of conditions and forces we call "natural selection." As the environment changes they must be adapted to it, if they cannot so adapt themselves they die. Those who live are, by living, proven capable of maintaining themselves. Every creature which has remained on earth, while so many less effective kinds died out, remains as a conqueror. The speed of the deer—the constant use of speed—is what keeps it alive and makes it healthy and beautiful. The varied activities of the life of a leopard are what have developed the sinuous gracile strength we so admire. It is what the creature does for its living, its daily life-long exercise which makes it what it is.

But there is another great natural force which works steadily to keep all animals up to the race standard; that is sexual selection. Throughout nature the male is the variant, as we have already noted. His energy finds vent not only in that profuse output of decorative appendages Ward defines as "masculine efflorescence" but in variations not decorative, not useful or desirable at all.

The female, on the other hand, varies much less, remaining nearer the race type; and her function is to select among these varying males the specimens most valuable to the race. In the intense masculine competition the victor must necessarily be stronger than his fellows; he is first proven equal to his environment by having lived to grow up, then more than equal to his fellows by overcoming them. This higher grade of selection also develops not only the characteristics necessary to make a living; but secondary ones, often of a purely aesthetic nature, which make much of what we call beauty. Between the two, all who live must be up to a certain grade, and those who become parents must be above it; a masterly arrangement surely!

Here is where, during the period of our human history, we in our newborn consciousness and imperfect knowledge, have grievously interfered with the laws of nature. The ancient proprietary family, treating the woman as a slave, keeping her a prisoner and subject to the will of her master, cut her off at once from the exercise of those activities which alone develop and maintain the race type.

Take the one simple quality of speed. We are a creature built for speed, a free swift graceful animal; and among savages this is still seen—the capacity for running, mile after mile, hour after hour. Running is as natural a gait for genus homo as for genus cervus. Now suppose among deer, the doe was prohibited from running; the stag continuing free on the mountain; the doe living in caves and pens, unequal to any exercise. The effect on the species would be, inevitably, to reduce its speed.

In this way, by keeping women to one small range of duties, and in most cases housebound, we have interfered with natural selection and its resultant health and beauty. It can easily be seen what the effect on the race would have been if all men had been veiled and swathed, hidden in harems, kept to the tent or house, and confined to the activities of a house-servant. Our stalwart laborers, our proud soldiers, our athletes, would never have appeared under such circumstances. The confinement to the house alone, cutting women off from sunshine and air, is by itself an injury; and the range of occupation allowed them is not such as to develop a high standard of either health or beauty. Thus we have cut off half the race from the strengthening influence of natural selection, and so lowered our race-standards in large degree.

This alone, however, would not have hid such mischievous effects but for our further blunder in completely reversing nature's order of sexual selection. It is quite possible that even under confinement and restriction women could have kept up the race level, passably, through this great function of selection; but here is the great fundamental error of the Androcentric Culture. Assuming to be the possessor of women, their owner and master, able at will to give, buy and sell, or do with as he pleases, man became the selector.

It seems a simple change; and in those early days, wholly ignorant of natural laws, there was no suspicion that any mischief would result. In the light of modern knowledge, however, the case is clear. The woman was deprived of the beneficent action of natural selection, and the man was then, by his own act, freed from the stern but elevating effect of sexual selection. Nothing was required of the woman by natural selection save such capacity as should please her master; nothing was required of the man by sexual selection save power to take by force, or buy, a woman.

It does not take a very high standard of feminine intelligence, strength, skill, health, or beauty to be a houseservant, or even a housekeeper; witness the average.

It does not take a very high standard of masculine, intelligence, strength, skill, health or beauty to maintain a woman in that capacity—witness average.

Here at the very root of our physiological process, at the beginning of life, we have perverted the order of nature, and are suffering the consequences.

It has been held by some that man as the selector has developed beauty, more beauty than we had before; and we point to the charms of our women as compared with those of the squaw. The answer to this is that the squaw belongs to a decadent race; that she too is subject to the man, that the comparison to have weight should be made between our women and the women of the matriarchate—an obvious impossibility. We have not on earth women in a state of normal freedom and full development; but we have enough difference in their placing to learn that human strength and beauty grows with woman's freedom and activity.

The second answer is that much of what man calls beauty in woman is not human beauty at all, but gross overdevelopment of certain points which appeal to him as a male. The excessive fatness, previously referred to, is a case in point; that being considered beauty in a woman which is in reality an element of weakness, inefficiency and ill-health. The relatively small size of women, deliberately preferred, steadfastly chosen, and so built into the race, is a blow at real human progress in every particular. In our upward journey we should and do grow larger, leaving far behind us our dwarfish progenitors. Yet the male, in his unnatural position as selector, preferring for reasons both practical and sentimental, to have "his woman" smaller than himself, has deliberately striven to lower the standard of size in the race. We used to read in the novels of the last generation, "He was a magnificent specimen of manhood"—"Her golden head reached scarcely to his shoulder"—"She was a fairy creature—the tiniest of her sex." Thus we have mated, and yet expected that by some hocus pocus the boys would all "take after their father," and the girls, their mother. In his efforts to improve the breed of other animals, man has never tried to deliberately cross the large and small and expect to keep up the standard of size.

As a male he is appealed to by the ultra-feminine, and has given small thought to effects on the race. He was not designed to do the selecting. Under his fostering care we have bred a race of women who are physically weak enough to be handed about like invalids; or mentally weak enough to pretend they are—and to like it. We have made women who respond so perfectly to the force which made them, that they attach all their idea of beauty to those characteristics which attract men; sometimes humanly ugly without even knowing it.

For instance, our long restriction to house-limits, the heavy limitations of our clothing, and the heavier ones of traditional decorum, have made women disproportionately short-legged. This is a particularly undignified and injurious characteristic, bred in women and inherited by men, most seen among those races which keep their women most closely. Yet when one woman escapes the tendency and appears with a normal length of femur and tibia, a normal height of hip and shoulder, she is criticized and called awkward by her squatty sisters!

The most convenient proof of the inferiority of women in human beauty is shown by those composite statues prepared by Mr. Sargent for the World's Fair of '93. These were made from gymnasium measurements of thousands of young collegians of both sexes all over America. The statue of the girl has a pretty face, small hands and feet, rather nice arms, though weak; but the legs are too thick and short; the chest and shoulders poor; and the trunk is quite pitiful in its weakness. The figure of the man is much better proportioned.

Thus the effect on human beauty of masculine selection.

Beyond this positive deteriorative effect on women through man's arbitrary choice comes the negative effect of woman's lack of choice. Bought or stolen or given by her father, she was deprived of the innately feminine right and duty of choosing. "Who giveth this woman?" we still inquire in our archaic marriage service, and one man steps forward and gives her to another man.

Free, the female chose the victor, and the vanquished went unmated—

and without progeny. Dependent, having to be fed and cared for by some man, the victors take their pick perhaps, but the vanquished take what is left; and the poor women, "marrying for a home," take anything. As a consequence the inferior male is as free to transmit his inferiority as the superior to give better qualities, and does so—beyond computation. In modern days, women are freer, in some countries freer than in others; here in modern America freest of all; and the result is seen in our improving standards of health and beauty.

Still there remains the field of inter-masculine competition, does there not? Do not the males still struggle together? Is not that as of old, a source of race advantage?

To some degree it is. When life was simple and our activities consisted mainly in fighting and hard work; the male who could vanquish the others was bigger and stronger. But inter-masculine competition ceases to be of such advantage when we enter the field of social service. What is required in organized society is the specialization of the individual, the development of special talents, not always of immediate benefit to the man himself, but of ultimate benefit to society. The best social servant, progressive, meeting future needs, is almost always at a disadvantage besides the well-established lower types. We need, for social service, qualities quite different from the simple masculine characteristics—desire, combat, self-expression.

By keeping what we call "the outside world" so wholly male, we keep up masculine standards at the expense of human ones. This may be broadly seen in the slow and painful development of industry and science as compared to the easy dominance of warfare throughout all history until our own times.

The effect of all this ultra masculine competition upon health and beauty is but too plainly to be seen. Among men the male idea of what is good looking is accentuated beyond reason. Read about any "hero" you please; or study the products of the illustrator and note the broad shoulders, the rugged features, the strong, square, determined jaw. That jaw is in evidence if everything else fails. He may be cross-eyed, wide-eared, thick-necked, bandy-legged—what you please; but he must have a more or less prognathous jaw.

Meanwhile any anthropologist will show you that the line of human development is away from that feature of the bulldog and the alligator, and toward the measured dignity of the Greek type. The possessor of that kind of jaw may enable male to conquer male, but does not make him of any more service to society; of any better health or higher beauty.

Further, in the external decoration of our bodies, what is the influence here of masculine dominance.

We have before spoken of the peculiar position of our race in that the woman is the only female creature who carries the burden of sex ornament.

This amazing reversal of the order of nature results at its mildest in a perversion of the natural feminine instincts of love and service, and an appearance of the masculine instincts of self-expression and display. Alone among all female things do women decorate and preen themselves and exhibit their borrowed plumage (literally!) to attract the favor of the male. This ignominy is forced upon them by their position of economic dependence; and their general helplessness. As all broader life is made to depend, for them, on whom they marry, indeed as even the necessities of life so often depend on their marrying someone, they have been driven into this form of competition, so alien to the true female attitude.

The result is enough to make angels weep—and laugh. Perhaps no step in the evolution of beauty went farther than our human power of making a continuous fabric; soft and mobile, showing any color and texture desired. The beauty of the human body is supreme, and when we add to it the flow of color, the ripple of fluent motion, that comes of a soft, light garment over free limbs—it is a new field of loveliness and delight. Naturally this should have filled the whole world with a new pleasure. Our garments, first under right natural selection developing perfect use, under right sex selection developing beauty; and further, as our human aesthetic sense progresses, showing a noble symbolism, would have been an added strength and glory, a ceaseless joy.

What is the case?

Men, under a too strictly inter-masculine environment, have evolved the mainly useful but beautiless costume common to-day; and women—?

Women wear beautiful garments when they happen to be the fashion; and ugly garments when they are the fashion, and show no signs of knowing the difference. They show no added pride in the beautiful, no hint of mortification in the hideous, and are not even sensitive under criticism, or open to any persuasion or argument. Why should they be?

Their condition, physical and mental, is largely abnormal, their whole passionate absorption in dress and decoration is abnormal, and they have never looked, from a frankly human standpoint, at their position and its peculiarities, until the present age.

In the effect of our wrong relation on the world's health, we have spoken of the check to vigor and growth due to the housebound state of women and their burdensome clothes. There follow other influences, similar in origin, even more evil in result. To roughly and briefly classify we may distinguish the diseases due to bad air, to bad food, and that field of cruel mischief we are only now beginning to discuss—the diseases directly due to the erroneous relation between men and women.

We are the only race where the female depends on the male for a livelihood. We are the only race that practices prostitution. From the first harmless-looking but abnormal general relation follows the well recognized evil of the second, so long called "a social necessity," and from it, in deadly sequence, comes the "wages of sin;" death not only of the guilty, but of the innocent. It is no light part of our criticism of the Androcentric Culture that a society based on masculine desires alone, has willingly sacrificed such an army of women; and has repaid the sacrifice by the heaviest punishments.

That the unfortunate woman should sicken and die was held to be her just punishment; that man too should bear part penalty was found unavoidable, though much legislation and medical effort has been spent to shield him; but to the further consequences society is but now waking up.

IV. MEN AND ART.

Among the many counts in which women have been proven inferior to men in human development is the oft-heard charge that there are no great women artists. Where one or two are proudly exhibited in evidence, they are either pooh-poohed as not very great, or held to be the trifling exceptions which do but prove the rule.

Defenders of women generally make the mistake of over-estimating their performances, instead of accepting, and explaining, the visible facts. What are the facts as to the relation of men and women to art? And what, in especial, has been the effect upon art of a solely masculine expression?

When we look for the beginnings of art, we find ourselves in a period of crude decoration of the person and of personal belongings. Tattooing, for instance, is an early form of decorative art, still in practice among certain classes, even in advanced people. Most boys, if they are in contact with this early art, admire it, and wish to adorn themselves therewith; some do so—to later mortification. Early personal decoration consisted largely in direct mutilation of the body, and the hanging upon it, or fastening to it, of decorative objects. This we see among savages still, in its gross and primitive forms monopolized by men, then shared by women, and, in our time, left almost wholly to them. In personal decoration today, women are still near the savage. The "artists" developed in this field of art are the tonsorial, the sartorial, and all those specialized adorners of the body commonly known as "beauty doctors."

Here, as in other cases, the greatest artists are men. The greatest milliners, the greatest dressmakers and tailors, the greatest hairdressers, and the masters and designers in all our decorative toilettes and accessories, are men. Women, in this as in so many other lines, consume rather than produce. They carry the major part of personal decoration today; but the decorator is the man. In the decoration of objects, woman, as the originator of primitive industry, originated also the primitive arts; and in the pottery, basketry, leatherwork, needlework, weaving, with all beadwork, dyeing and embroideries of ancient peoples we see the work of the woman decorator. Much of this is strong and beautiful, but its time is long past. The art which is part of industry, natural, simple, spontaneous, making beauty in every object of use, adding pleasure to labor and to life, is not Art with a large A, the Art which requires Artists, among whom are so few women of note.

Art as a profession, and the Artist as a professional, came later; and by that time women had left the freedom and power of the matriarchate and become slaves in varying degree. The women who were idle pets in harems, or the women who worked hard as servants, were alike cut off from the joy of making things. Where constructive work remained to them, art remained, in its early decorative form. Men, in the proprietary family, restricting the natural industry of women to personal service, cut off their art with their industry, and by so much impoverished the world.

There is no more conspicuously pathetic proof of the aborted development of women than this commonplace—their lack of a civilized art sense. Not only in the childish and savage display upon their bodies, but in the pitiful products they hang upon the walls of the home, is seen the arrest in normal growth.

After ages of culture, in which men have developed Architecture, Sculpture, Painting, Music and the Drama, we find women in their primitive environment making flowers of wax, and hair, and worsted; doing mottoes of perforated cardboard, making crazy quilts and mats and "tidies"—as if they lived in a long past age, or belonged to a lower race.

This, as part of the general injury to women dating from the beginning of our androcentric culture, reacts heavily upon the world at large. Men, specializing, giving their lives to the continuous pursuit of one line of service, have lifted our standard in aesthetic culture, as they have in other matters; but by refusing the same growth to women, they have not only weakened and reduced the output, but ruined the market as it were, hopelessly and permanently kept down the level of taste.

Among the many sides of this great question, some so terrible, some so pathetic, some so utterly absurd, this particular phase of life is especially easy to study and understand, and has its own elements of amusement. Men, holding women at the level of domestic service, going on themselves to lonely heights of achievement, have found their efforts hampered and their attainments rendered barren and unsatisfactory by the amazing indifference of the world at large. As the world at large consists half of women, and wholly of their children, it would seem patent to the meanest understanding that the women must be allowed to rise in order to lift the world. But such has not been the method—heretofore.

We have spoken so far in this chapter of the effect of men on art through their interference with the art of women. There are other sides to the question. Let us consider once more the essential characteristics of maleness, and see how they have affected art, keeping always in mind the triune distinction between masculine, feminine and human. Perhaps we shall best see this difference by considering what the development of art might have been on purely human terms.

The human creature, as such, naturally delights in construction, and adds decoration to construction as naturally. The cook, making little regular patterns around the edge of the pie, does so from a purely human instinct, the innate eye-pleasure in regularity, symmetry, repetition, and alternation. Had this natural social instinct grown unchecked in us, it would have manifested itself in a certain proportion of specialists—artists of all sorts—

and an accompanying development of appreciation on the part of the rest of us. Such is the case in primitive art; the maker of beauty is upheld and rewarded by a popular appreciation of her work—or his.

Had this condition remained, we should find a general level of artistic expression and appreciation far higher than we see now. Take the one field of textile art, for instance: that wide and fluent medium of expression, the making of varied fabrics, the fashioning of garments and the decoration of them—all this is human work and human pleasure. It should have led us to a condition where every human being was a pleasure to the eye, appropriately and beautifully clothed.

Our real condition in this field is too patent to need emphasis; the stiff, black ugliness of our men's attire; the irritating variegated folly of our women's; the way in which we spoil the beauty and shame the dignity of childhood by modes of dress.

In normal human growth, our houses would be a pleasure to the eye; our furniture and utensils, all our social products, would blossom into beauty as naturally as they still do in those low stages of social evolution where our major errors have not yet borne full fruit.

Applied art in all its forms is a human function, common to every one to some degree, either in production or appreciation, or both. "Pure art," as an ideal, is also human; and the single-hearted devotion of the true artist to this ideal is one of the highest forms of the social sacrifice. Of all the thousand ways by which humanity is specialized for inter-service, none is more exquisite than this; the evolution of the social Eye, or Ear, or Voice, the development of those whose work is wholly for others, and to whom the appreciation of others is as the bread of life. This we should have in a properly developed community; the pleasure of applied art in the making and using of everything we have; and then the high joy of the Great Artist, and the noble work thereof, spread far and wide.

What do we find?

Applied art at a very low level; small joy either for the maker or the user. Pure art, a fine-spun specialty, a process carried on by an elect few who openly despise the unappreciative many. Art has become an occult profession requiring a long special education even to enjoy, and evolving a jargon of criticism which becomes more esoteric yearly.

Let us now see what part in this undesirable outcome is due to our Androcentric Culture.

As soon as the male of our species assumed the exclusive right to perform all social functions, he necessarily brought to that performance the advantages—and disadvantages—of maleness, of those dominant characteristics, desire, combat, self-expression.

Desire has overweighted art in many visible forms; it is prominent in painting and music, almost monopolizes fiction, and has pitifully degraded dancing.

Combat is not so easily expressed in art, where even competition is on a high plane; but the last element is the main evil, self-expression. This impulse is inherently and ineradicably masculine. It rests on that most basic of distinctions between the sexes, the centripetal and centrifugal forces of the universe. In the very nature of the sperm-cell and the germ-cell we find this difference: the one attracts, gathers, draws in; the other repels, scatters, pushes out. That projective impulse is seen in the male nature everywhere; the constant urge toward expression, to all boasting and display. This spirit, like all things masculine, is perfectly right and admirable in its place.

It is the duty of the male, as a male, to vary; bursting forth in a thousand changing modifications—the female, selecting, may so incorporate beneficial changes in the race. It is his duty to thus express himself—an essentially masculine duty; but masculinity is one thing, and art is another. Neither the masculine nor the feminine has any place in art—Art is Human.

It is not in any faintest degree allied to the personal processes of reproduction; but is a social process, a most distinctive social process, quite above the plane of sex. The true artist transcends his sex, or her sex. If this is not the case, the art suffers.

Dancing is an early, and a beautiful art; direct expression of emotion through the body; beginning in subhuman type, among male birds, as the bower-bird of New Guinea, and the dancing crane, who swing and caper before their mates. Among early peoples we find it a common form of social expression in tribal dances of all sorts, religious, military, and other. Later it becomes a more explicit form of celebration, as among the Greeks; in whose exquisite personal culture dancing and music held high place.

But under the progressive effects of purely masculine dominance we find the broader human elements of dancing left out, and the sex-element more and more emphasized. As practiced by men alone dancing has become a mere display of physical agility, a form of exhibition common to all males. As practiced by men and women together we have our social dances, so lacking in all the varied beauty of posture and expression, so steadily becoming a pleasant form of dalliance.

As practiced by women alone we have one of the clearest proofs of the degrading effect of masculine dominance:—the dancing girl. In the frank sensualism of the Orient, this personage is admired and enjoyed on her merits. We, more sophisticated in this matter, joke shamefacedly about "the bald-headed row," and occasionally burst forth in shrill scandal over some dinner party where ladies clad in a veil and a bracelet dance on the table. Nowhere else in the whole range of life on earth, is this degradation found—the female capering and prancing before the male. It is absolutely and essentially his function, not hers. That we, as a race, present this pitiful spectacle, a natural art wrested to unnatural ends, a noble art degraded to ignoble ends, has one clear cause.

Architecture, in its own nature, is least affected by that same cause. The human needs secured by it, are so human, so unescapably human, that we find less trace of excessive masculinity than in other arts. It meets our social demands, it expresses in lasting form our social feeling, up to the highest; and it has been injured not so much by an excess of masculinity as by a lack of femininity.

The most universal architectural expression is in the home; the home is essentially a place for the woman and the child; yet the needs of woman and child are not expressed in our domestic architecture. The home is built on lines of ancient precedent, mainly as an industrial form; the kitchen is its working centre rather than the nursery.

Each man wishes his home to preserve and seclude his woman, his little harem of one; and in it she is to labor for his comfort or to manifest his ability to maintain her in idleness. The house is the physical expression of the limitations of women; and as such it fills the world with a small drab ugliness. A dwelling house is rarely a beautiful object. In order to be such, it should truly express simple and natural relations; or grow in larger beauty as our lives develop.

The deadlock for architectural progress, the low level of our general taste, the everlasting predominance of the commonplace in buildings, is the natural result of the proprietary family and its expression in this form.

In sculpture we have a noble art forcing itself into some service through many limitations. Its check, as far as it comes under this line of study, has been indicated in our last chapter; the degradation of the human body, the vicious standards of sex-consciousness enforced under the name of modesty, the covered ugliness, which we do not recognize, all this is a deadly injury to free high work in sculpture.

With a nobly equal womanhood, stalwart and athletic; with the high standards of beauty and of decorum which we can never have without free womanhood; we should show a different product in this great art.

An interesting note in passing is this: when we seek to express socially our noblest, ideas, Truth; Justice; Liberty; we use the woman's body as the highest human type. But in doing this, the artist, true to humanity and not biassed by sex, gives us a strong, grand figure, beautiful indeed, but never decorated. Fancy Liberty in ruffles and frills, with rings in her ears—or nose.

Music is injured by a one-sided handling, partly in the excess of the one dominant masculine passion, partly by the general presence of egoism; that tendency to self-expression instead of social expression, which so disfigures our art; and this is true also of poetry.

Miles and miles of poetry consist of the ceaseless outcry of the male for the female, which is by no means so overwhelming as a feature of human life as he imagines it; and other miles express his other feelings, with that ingenuous lack of reticence which is at its base essentially masculine. Having a pain, the poet must needs pour it forth, that his woe be shared and sympathized with.

As more and more women writers flock into the field there is room for fine historic study of the difference in sex feeling, and the gradual emergence of the human note.

Literature, and in especial the art of fiction, is so large a field for this study that it will have a chapter to itself; this one but touching on these various forms; and indicating lines of observation.

That best known form of art which to my mind needs no qualifying description—painting—is also a wide field; and cannot be done full justice to within these limits. The effect upon it of too much masculinity is not so much in choice of subject as in method and spirit. The artist sees beauty of form and color where the ordinary observer does not; and paints the old and ugly with as much enthusiasm as the young and beautiful—sometimes. If there is in some an over-emphasis of feminine attractions it is counterbalanced in others by a far broader line of work.

But the main evils of a too masculine art lie in the emphasis laid on self-expression. The artist, passionately conscious of how he feels, strives to make other people aware of these sensations. This is now so generally accepted by critics, so seriously advanced by painters, that what is called "the art world" accepts it as established.

If a man paints the sea, it is not to make you see and feel as a sight of that same ocean would, but to make you see and feel how he, personally, was affected by it; a matter surely of the narrowest importance. The ultra-masculine artist, extremely sensitive, necessarily, and full of the natural urge to expression of the sex, uses the medium of art as ingenuously as the partridge-cock uses his wings in drumming on the log; or the bull moose stamps and bellows; not narrowly as a mate call, but as a form of expression of his personal sensations.

The higher the artist the more human he is, the broader his vision, the more he sees for humanity, and expresses for humanity, and the less personal, the less ultra-masculine, is his expression.

V. MASCULINE LITERATURE.

When we are offered a "woman's" paper, page, or column, we find it filled with matter supposed to appeal to women as a sex or class; the writer mainly dwelling upon the Kaiser's four K's—Kuchen, Kinder, Kirche, Kleider. They iterate and reiterate endlessly the discussion of cookery, old and new; of the care of children; of the overwhelming subject of clothing; and of moral instruction. All this is recognized as "feminine" literature, and it must have some appeal else the women would not read it. What parallel have we in "masculine" literature?

"None!" is the proud reply. "Men are people! Women, being 'the sex,' have their limited feminine interests, their feminine point of view, which must be provided for. Men, however, are not restricted—to them belongs the world's literature!"

Yes, it has belonged to them—ever since there was any. They have written it and they have read it. It is only lately that women, generally speaking, have been taught to read; still more lately that they have been allowed to write. It is but a little while since Harriet Martineau concealed her writing beneath her sewing when visitors came in—writing was "masculine"—sewing "feminine."

We have not, it Is true, confined men to a narrowly construed "masculine sphere," and composed a special literature suited to it. Their effect on literature has been far wider than that, monopolizing this form of art with special favor. It was suited above all others to the dominant impulse of self-expression; and being, as we have seen essentially and continually "the sex;" they have impressed that sex upon this art overwhelmingly; they have given the world a masculized literature.

It is hard for us to realize this. We can readily see, that if women had always written the books, no men either writing or reading them, that would have surely "feminized" our literature; but we have not in our minds the concept, much less the word, for an overmasculized influence.

Men having been accepted as humanity, women but a side-issue; (most literally if we accept the Hebrew legend!), whatever men did or said was human—and not to be criticized. In no department of life is it easier to contravert this old belief; to show how the male sex as such differs from the human type; and how this maleness has monopolized and disfigured a great social function.

Human life is a very large affair; and literature is its chief art. We live, humanly, only through our power of communication. Speech gives us this power laterally, as it were, in immediate personal contact. For permanent use speech becomes oral tradition—a poor dependence. Literature gives not only an infinite multiplication to the lateral spread of communion but adds the vertical reach. Through it we know the past, govern the present, and influence the future. In its servicable common forms it is the indispensable daily servant of our lives; in its nobler flights as a great art no means of human inter-change goes so far.

In these brief limits we can touch but lightly on some phases of so great a subject; and will rest the case mainly on the effect of an exclusively masculine handling of the two fields of history and fiction. In poetry and the drama the same influence is easily traced, but in the first two it is so baldly prominent as to defy objection.

History is, or should be, the story of our racial life. What have men made it? The story of warfare and conquest. Begin at the very beginning with the carven stones of Egypt, the clay records of Chaldea, what do we find of history?

"I Pharaoh, King of Kings! Lord of Lords! (etc. etc.), went down into the miserable land of Kush, and slew of the inhabitants thereof an hundred and forty and two thousands!" That, or something like it, is the kind of record early history gives us.

The story of Conquering Kings, who and how many they killed and enslaved; the grovelling adulation of the abased; the unlimited jubilation of the victor; from the primitive state of most ancient kings, and the Roman triumphs where queens walked in chains, down to our omni present soldier's monuments: the story of war and conquest—war and conquest—over and over; with such boasting and triumph, such cock-crow and flapping of wings as show most unmistakably the natural source.

All this will strike the reader at first as biased and unfair. "That was the way people lived in those days!" says the reader.

No—it was not the way women lived.

"O, women!" says the reader, "Of course not! Women are different."

Yea, women are different; and men are different! Both of them, as sexes, differ from the human norm, which is social life and all social development. Society was slowly growing in all those black blind years. The arts, the sciences, the trades and crafts and professions, religion, philosophy, government, law, commerce, agriculture—all the human processes were going on as well as they were able, between wars.

The male naturally fights, and naturally crows, triumphs over his rival and takes the prize—therefore was he made male. Maleness means war.

Not only so; but being male, he cares only for male interests. Men, being the sole arbiters of what should be done and said and written, have given us not only a social growth scarred and thwarted from the beginning by continual destruction; but a history which is one unbroken record of courage and red cruelty, of triumph and black shame.

As to what went on that was of real consequence, the great slow steps of the working world, the discoveries and inventions, the real progress of humanity—that was not worth recording, from a masculine point of view. Within this last century, "the woman's century," the century of the great awakening, the rising demand for freedom, political, economic, and domestic, we are beginning to write real history, human history, and not merely masculine history. But that great branch of literature—Hebrew, Greek, Roman, and all down later times, shows beyond all question, the influence of our androcentric culture.

Literature is the most powerful and necessary of the arts, and fiction is its broadest form. If art "holds the mirror up to nature" this art's mirror is the largest of all, the most used. Since our very life depends on some communication; and our progress is in proportion to our fullness and freedom of communication; since real communication requires mutual understanding; so in the growth of the social consciousness, we note from the beginning a passionate interest in other people's lives.

The art which gives humanity consciousness is the most vital art. Our greatest dramatists are lauded for their breadth of knowledge of "human nature," their range of emotion and understanding; our greatest poets are those who most deeply and widely experience and reveal the feelings of the human heart; and the power of fiction is that it can reach and express this great field of human life with no limits but those of the author.

When fiction began it was the legitimate child of oral tradition; a product of natural brain activity; the legend constructed instead of remembered. (This stage is with us yet as seen in the constant changes in repetition of popular jokes and stories.)

Fiction to-day has a much wider range; yet it is still restricted, heavily and most mischievously restricted.

What is the preferred subject matter of fiction?

There are two main branches found everywhere, from the Romaunt of the Rose to the Purplish Magazine;—the Story of Adventure, and the Love Story.

The Story-of-Adventure branch is not so thick as the other by any means, but it is a sturdy bough for all that. Stevenson and Kipling have proved its immense popularity, with the whole brood of detective stories and the tales of successful rascality we call "picaresque" Our most popular weekly shows the broad appeal of this class of fiction.

All these tales of adventure, of struggle and difficulty; of hunting and fishing and fighting; of robbing and murdering, catching and punishing, are distinctly and essentially masculine. They do not touch on human processes, social processes, but on the special field of predatory excitement so long the sole province of men.

It is to be noted here that even in the overwhelming rise of industrial interests to-day, these, when used as the basis for a story, are forced into line with one, or both, of these two main branches of fiction;—conflict or love. Unless the story has one of these "interests" in it, there is no story—so holds the editor; the dictum being, put plainly, "life has no interests except conflict and love!"

It is surely something more than a coincidence that these are the two essential features of masculinity—Desire and Combat—Love and War.

As a matter of fact the major interests of life are in line with its major processes; and these—in our stage of human development—are more varied than our fiction would have us believe. Half the world consists of women, we should remember, who are types of human life as well as men, and their major processes are not those of conflict and adventure, their love means more than mating. Even on so poor a line of distinction as the "woman's column" offers, if women are to be kept to their four Ks, there should be a "men's column" also; and all the "sporting news" and fish stories be put in that; they are not world interests; they are male interests.

Now for the main branch—the Love Story. Ninety per cent. of fiction is In this line; this is preeminently the major interest of life—given in fiction. What is the love-story, as rendered by this art?

It is the story of the pre-marital struggle. It is the Adventures of Him in Pursuit of Her—and it stops when he gets her! Story after story, age after age, over and over and over, this ceaseless repetition of the Preliminaries.

Here is Human Life. In its large sense, its real sense, it is a matter of inter-relation between individuals and groups, covering all emotions, all processes, all experiences. Out of this vast field of human life fiction arbitrarily selects one emotion, one process, one experience, as its necessary base.

"Ah! but we are persons most of all!" protests the reader. "This is personal experience—it has the universal appeal!"

Take human life personally then. Here is a Human Being, a life, covering some seventy years; involving the changing growth of many faculties; the ever new marvels of youth, the long working time of middle life, the slow ripening of age. Here is the human soul, in the human body, Living. Out of this field of personal life, with all of its emotions, processes, and experiences, fiction arbitrarily selects one emotion, one process, one experience, mainly of one sex.

The "love" of our stories is man's love of woman. If any dare dispute this, and say it treats equally of woman's love for man, I answer, "Then why do the stories stop at marriage?"

There is a current jest, revealing much, to this effect:

The young wife complains that the husband does not wait upon and woo her as he did before marriage; to which he replies, "Why should I run after the street-car when I've caught it?"

Woman's love for man, as currently treated in fiction is largely a reflex; it is the way he wants her to feel, expects her to feel; not a fair representation of how she does feel. If "love" is to be selected as the most important thing in life to write about, then the mother's love should be the principal subject: This is the main stream. This is the general underlying, world-lifting force. The "life-force," now so glibly chattered about, finds its fullest expression in motherhood; not in the emotions of an assistant in the preliminary stages.

What has literature, what has fiction, to offer concerning mother-love, or even concerning father-love, as compared to this vast volume of excitement about lover-love? Why is the search-light continually focussed upon a two or three years space of life "mid the blank miles round about?" Why indeed, except for the clear reason, that on a starkly masculine basis this is his one period of overwhelming interest and excitement.

If the beehive produced literature, the bee's fiction would be rich and broad; full of the complex tasks of comb-building and filling; the care and feeding of the young, the guardian-service of the queen; and far beyond that it would spread to the blue glory of the summer sky, the fresh winds, the endless beauty and sweetness of a thousand thousand flowers. It would treat of the vast fecundity of motherhood, the educative and selective processes of the group-mothers; and the passion of loyalty, of social service, which holds the hive together.

But if the drones wrote fiction, it would have no subject matter save the feasting of many; and the nuptial flight, of one.

To the male, as such, this mating instinct is frankly the major interest of life; even the belligerent instincts are second to it. To the female, as such, it is for all its intensity, but a passing interest. In nature's economy, his is but a temporary devotion, hers the slow processes of life's fulfillment.

In Humanity we have long since, not outgrown, but overgrown, this stage of feeling. In Human Parentage even the mother's share begins to pale beside that ever-growing Social love and care, which guards and guides the children of to-day.

The art of literature in this main form of fiction is far too great a thing to be wholly governed by one dominant note. As life widened and intensified, the artist, if great enough, has transcended sex; and in the mightier works of the real masters, we find fiction treating of life, life in general, in all its complex relationships, and refusing to be held longer to the rigid canons of an androcentric past.

This was the power of Balzac—he took in more than this one field. This was the universal appeal of Dickens; he wrote of people, all kinds of people, doing all kinds of things. As you recall with pleasure some preferred novel of this general favorite, you find yourself looking narrowly for the "love story" in it. It is there—for it is part of life; but it does not dominate the whole scene—any more than it does in life.

The thought of the world is made and handed out to us in the main. The makers of books are the makers of thoughts and feelings for people in general. Fiction is the most popular form in which this world-food is taken. If it were true, it would teach us life easily, swiftly, truly; teach not by preaching but by truly re-presenting; and we should grow up becoming acquainted with a far wider range of life in books than could even be ours in person. Then meeting life in reality we should be wise—and not be disappointed.

As it is, our great sea of fiction is steeped and dyed and flavored all one way. A young man faces life—the seventy year stretch, remember, and is given book upon book wherein one set of feelings is continually vocalized and overestimated. He reads forever of love, good love and bad love, natural and unnatural, legitimate and illegitimate; with the unavoidable inference that there is nothing else going on.

If he is a healthy young man he breaks loose from the whole thing, despises "love stories" and takes up life as he finds it. But what impression he does receive from fiction is a false one, and he suffers without knowing it from lack of the truer broader views of life it failed to give him.

A young woman faces life—the seventy year stretch remember; and is given the same books—with restrictions. Remember the remark of Rochefoucauld, "There are thirty good stories in the world and twenty-nine cannot be told to women." There is a certain broad field of literature so grossly androcentric that for very shame men have tried to keep it to themselves. But in a milder form, the spades all named teaspoons, or at the worst appearing as trowels—the young woman is given the same fiction. Love and love and love—from "first sight" to marriage. There it stops—just the fluttering ribbon of announcement, "and lived happily ever after."

Is that kind of fiction any sort of picture of a woman's life? Fiction, under our androcentric culture, has not given any true picture of woman's life, very little of human life, and a disproportioned section of man's life.

As we daily grow more human, both of us, this noble art is changing for the better so fast that a short lifetime can mark the growth. New fields are opening and new laborers are working in them. But it is no swift and easy matter to disabuse the race mind from attitudes and habits inculcated for a thousand years. What we have been fed upon so long we are well used to, what we are used to we like, what we like we think is good and proper.

The widening demand for broader, truer fiction is disputed by the slow racial mind: and opposed by the marketers of literature on grounds of visible self-interest, as well as lethargic conservatism.

It is difficult for men, heretofore the sole producers and consumers of literature; and for women, new to the field, and following masculine canons because all the canons were masculine; to stretch their minds to a recognition of the change which is even now upon us.

This one narrow field has been for so long overworked, our minds are so filled with heroes and heroes continually repeating the one-act play, that when a book like David Harum is offered the publisher refuses it repeatedly, and finally insists on a "heart interest" being injected by force.

Did anyone read David Harum for that heart interest? Does anyone remember that heart interest? Has humanity no interests but those of the heart?

Robert Ellesmere was a popular book—but not because of its heart interest.

Uncle Tom's Cabin appealed to the entire world, more widely than any work of fiction that was ever written; but if anybody fell in love and married in it they have been forgotten. There was plenty of love in that book, love of family, love of friends, love of master for servant and servant for master; love of mother for child; love of married people for each other; love of humanity and love of God.

It was extremely popular. Some say it was not literature. That opinion will live, like the name of Empedocles.

The art of fiction is being re-born in these days. Life is discovered to be longer, wider, deeper, richer, than these monotonous players of one June would have us believe.

The humanizing of woman of itself opens five distinctly fresh fields of fiction: First the position of the young woman who is called upon to give up her "career"—her humanness—for marriage, and who objects to it; second, the middle-aged woman who at last discovers that her discontent is social starvation—that it is not more love that she wants, but more business in life: Third the interrelation of women with women—a thing we could never write about before because we never had it before: except in harems and convents: Fourth the inter-action between mothers and children; this not the eternal "mother and child," wherein the child is always a baby, but the long drama of personal relationship; the love and hope, the patience and power, the lasting joy and triumph, the slow eating disappointment which must never be owned to a living soul—here are grounds for novels that a million mothers and many million children would eagerly read: Fifth the new attitude of the full-grown woman who faces the demands of love with the high standards of conscious motherhood.

There are other fields, broad and brilliantly promising, but this chapter is meant merely to show that our one-sided culture has, in this art, most disproportionately overestimated the dominant instincts of the male—Love and War—an offense against art and truth, and an injury to life.

VI. GAMES AND SPORTS

One of the sharpest distinctions both between the essential characters and the artificial positions of men and women, is in the matter of games and sports. By far the greater proportion of them are essentially masculine, and as such alien to women; while from those which are humanly interesting, women have been largely debarred by their arbitrary restrictions.

The play instinct is common to girls and boys alike; and endures in some measure throughout life. As other young animals express their abounding energies in capricious activities similar to those followed in the business of living, so small children gambol, physically, like lambs and kids; and as the young of higher kinds of animals imitate in their play the more complex activities of their elders, so do children imitate whatever activities they see about them. In this field of playing there is no sex.

Similarly in adult life healthy and happy persons, men and women, naturally express surplus energy in various forms of sport. We have here one of the most distinctively human manifestations. The great accumulation of social energy, and the necessary limitations of one kind of work, leave a human being tired of one form of action, yet still uneasy for lack of full expression; and this social need has been met by our great safety valve of games and sports.

In a society of either sex, or in a society without sex, there would still be both pleasure and use in games; they are vitally essential to human life. In a society of two sexes, wherein one has dictated all the terms of life, and the other has been confined to an extremely limited fraction of human living, we may look to see this great field of enjoyment as disproportionately divided.

It is not only that we have reduced the play impulse in women by restricting them to one set of occupations, and overtaxing their energies with mother-work and housework combined; and not only that by our androcentric conventions we further restrict their amusements; but we begin in infancy, and forcibly differentiate their methods of play long before any natural distinction would appear.

Take that universal joy the doll, or puppet, as an instance. A small imitation of a large known object carries delight to the heart of a child of either sex. The worsted cat, the wooden horse, the little wagon, the tin soldier, the wax doll, the toy village, the "Noah's Ark," the omnipresent "Teddy Bear," any and every small model of a real thing is a delight to the young human being. Of all things the puppet is the most intimate, the little image of another human being to play with. The fancy of the child, making endless combinations with these visible types, plays as freely as a kitten in the leaves; or gravely carries out some observed forms of life, as the kitten imitates its mother's hunting.

So far all is natural and human.

Now see our attitude toward child's play—under a masculine culture. Regarding women only as a sex, and that sex as manifest from infancy, we make and buy for our little girls toys suitable to this view. Being females—which means mothers, we must needs provide them with babies before they cease to be babies themselves; and we expect their play to consist in an imitation of maternal cares. The doll, the puppet, which interests all children, we have rendered as an eternal baby; and we foist them upon our girl children by ceaseless millions.

The doll, as such, is dear to the little boy as well as the girl, but not as a baby. He likes his jumping-jack, his worsted Sambo, often a genuine rag-doll; but he is discouraged and ridiculed in this. We do not expect the little boy to manifest a father's love and care for an imitation child—but we do expect the little girl to show maternal feelings for her imitation baby. It has not yet occurred to us that this is monstrous.

Little children should not be expected to show, in painful precocity, feelings which ought never to be experienced till they come at the proper age. Our kittens play at cat-sports, little Tom and Tabby together; but little Tabby does not play she is a mother!

Beyond the continuous dolls and their continuous dressing, we provide for our little girls tea sets and kitchen sets, doll's houses, little work-boxes—the imitation tools of their narrow trades. For the boy there is a larger choice. We make for them not only the essentially masculine toys of combat—all the enginery of mimic war; but also the models of human things, like boats, railroads, wagons. For them, too, are the comprehensive toys of the centuries, the kite, the top, the ball. As the boy gets old enough to play the games that require skill, he enters the world-lists, and the little sister, left inside, with her everlasting dolls, learns that she is "only a girl," and "mustn't play with boys—boys are so rough!" She has her doll and her tea set. She "plays house." If very active she may jump rope, in solitary enthusiasm, or in combination of from two to four. Her brother is playing games. From this time on he plays the games of the world. The "sporting page" should be called "the Man's Page" as that array of recipes, fashions and cheap advice is called "the Woman's Page."

One of the immediate educational advantages of the boy's position is that he learns "team work." This is not a masculine characteristic, it is a human one; a social power. Women are equally capable of it by nature; but not by education. Tending one's imitation baby is not team-work; nor is playing house. The little girl is kept forever within the limitations of her mother's "sphere" of action; while the boy learns life, and fancies that his new growth is due to his superior sex.

Now there are certain essential distinctions in the sexes, which would manifest themselves to some degree even in normally reared children; as for instance the little male would be more given to fighting and destroying; the little female more to caring for and constructing things.

"Boys are so destructive!" we say with modest pride—as if it was in some way a credit to them. But early youth is not the time to display sex distinction; and they should be discouraged rather than approved.

The games of the world, now the games of men, easily fall into two broad classes—games of skill and games of chance.

The interest and pleasure in the latter is purely human, and as such is shared by the two sexes even now. Women, in the innocent beginnings or the vicious extremes of this line of amusement, make as wild gamblers as men. At the races, at the roulette wheel, at the bridge table, this is clearly seen.

In games of skill we have a different showing. Most of these are developed by and for men; but when they are allowed, women take part in them with interest and success. In card games, in chess, checkers, and the like, in croquet and tennis, they play, and play well if well-trained. Where they fall short in so many games, and are so wholly excluded in others, is not for lack of human capacity, but for lack of masculinity. Most games are male. In their element of desire to win, to get the prize, they are male; and in their universal attitude of competition they are male, the basic spirit of desire and of combat working out through subtle modern forms.

There is something inherently masculine also in the universal dominance of the projectile in their games. The ball is the one unescapable instrument of sport. From the snapped marble of infancy to the flying missile of the bat, this form endures. To send something forth with violence; to throw it, bat it, kick it, shoot it; this impulse seems to date back to one of the twin forces of the universe—the centrifugal and centripetal energies between which swing the planets.

The basic feminine impulse is to gather, to put together, to construct; the basic masculine impulse to scatter, to disseminate, to destroy. It seems to give pleasure to a man to bang something and drive it from him; the harder he hits it and the farther it goes the better pleased he is.

Games of this sort will never appeal to women. They are not wrong; not necessarily evil in their place; our mistake is in considering them as human, whereas they are only masculine.

Play, in the childish sense is an expression of previous habit; and to be studied in that light. Play in the educational sense should be encouraged or discouraged to develop desired characteristics. This we know, and practice; only we do it under androcentric canons; confining the girl to the narrow range we consider proper for women, and assisting the boy to cover life with the expression of masculinity, when we should be helping both to a more human development.

Our settled conviction that men are people—the people, and that masculine qualities are the main desideratam in life, is what keeps up this false estimate of the value of our present games. Advocates of football, for instance, proudly claim that it fits a man for life. Life—from the wholly male point of view—is a battle, with a prize. To want something beyond measure, and to fight to get—that is the simple proposition. This view of life finds its most naive expression in predatory warfare; and still tends to make predatory warfare of the later and more human processes of industry. Because they see life in this way they imagine that skill and practice in the art of fighting, especially in collective fighting, is so valuable in our modern life. This is an archaism which would be laughable if it were not so dangerous in its effects.

The valuable processes to-day are those of invention, discovery, all grades of industry, and, most especially needed, the capacity for honest service and administration of our immense advantages. These are not learned on the football field. This spirit of desire and combat may be seen further in all parts of this great subject. It has developed into a cult of sportsmanship; so universally accepted among men as of superlative merit as to quite blind them to other standards of judgment.

In the Cook-Peary controversy of 1909, this canon was made manifest. Here, one man had spent a lifetime in trying to accomplish something; and at the eleventh hour succeeded. Then, coming out in the rich triumph long deferred, he finds another man, of character well known to him, impudently and falsely claiming that he had done it first. Mr. Peary expressed himself, quite restrainedly and correctly, in regard to the effrontery and falsity of this claim—and all the country rose up and denounced him as "unsportsmanlike!"

Sport and the canons of sport are so dominant in the masculine mind that what they considered a deviation from these standards was of far more importance than the question of fact involved; to say nothing of the moral obliquity of one lying to the whole world, for money; and that at the cost of another's hard-won triumph.

If women had condemned the conduct of one or the other as "not good house-wifery," this would have been considered a most puerile comment. But to be "unsportsmanlike" is the unpardonable sin.

Owing to our warped standards we glaringly misjudge the attitude of the two sexes in regard to their amusements. Of late years more women than ever before have taken to playing cards; and some, unfortunately, play for money. A steady stream of comment and blame follows upon this. The amount of card playing among men—and the amount of money lost and won, does not produce an equivalent comment.

Quite aside from this one field of dissipation, look at the share of life, of time, of strength, of money, given by men to their wide range of recreation. The primitive satisfaction of hunting and fishing they maintain at enormous expense. This is the indulgence of a most rudimentary impulse; pre-social and largely pre-human, of no service save as it affects bodily health, and of a most deterring influence on real human development. Where hunting and fishing is of real human service, done as a means of livelihood, it is looked down upon like any other industry; it is no longer "sport."

The human being kills to eat, or to sell and eat from the returns; he kills for the creature's hide or tusks, for use of some sort; or to protect his crops from vermin, his flocks from depredation; but the sportsman kills for the gratification of a primeval instinct, and under rules of an arbitrary cult. "Game" creatures are his prey; bird, beast or fish that is hard to catch, that requires some skill to slay; that will give him not mere meat and bones, but "the pleasure of the chase."

The pleasure of the chase is a very real one. It is exemplified, in its broad sense in children's play. The running and catching games, the hiding and finding games, are always attractive to our infancy, as they are to that of cubs and kittens. But the long continuance of this indulgence among mature civilized beings is due to their masculinity. That group of associated sex instincts, which in the woman prompts to the patient service and fierce defence of the little child, in the man has its deepest root in seeking, pursuing and catching. To hunt is more than a means of obtaining food, in his long ancestry; it is to follow at any cost, to seek through all difficulties, to struggle for and secure the central prize of his being—a mate.

His "protective instincts" are far later and more superficial. To support and care for his wife, his children, is a recent habit, in plain sight historically; but "the pleasure of the chase" is older than that. We should remember that associate habits and impulses last for ages upon ages in living forms; as in the tree climbing instincts of our earliest years, of Simian origin; and the love of water, which dates back through unmeasured time. Where for millions of years the strongest pleasure a given organism is fitted for, is obtained by a certain group of activities, those activities will continue to give pleasure long after their earlier use is gone.

This is why men enjoy "the ardor of pursuit" far more than women. It is an essentially masculine ardor. To come easily by what he wants does not satisfy him. He wants to want it. He wants to hunt it, seek it, chase it, catch it. He wants it to be "game." He is by virtue of his sex a sportsman.

There is no reason why these special instincts should not be gratified so long as it does no harm to the more important social processes; but it is distinctly desirable that we should understand their nature. The reason why we have the present overwhelming mass of "sporting events," from the ball game to the prize fight, is because our civilization is so overwhelmingly masculine. We shall criticize them more justly when we see that all this mass of indulgence is in the first place a form of sex-expression, and in the second place a survival of instincts older than the oldest savagery.

Besides our games and sports we have a large field of "amusements" also worth examining. We not only enjoy doing things, but we enjoy seeing them done by others. In these highly specialized days most of our amusement consists in paying two dollars to sit three hours and see other people do things.

This in its largest sense is wholly human. We, as social creatures, can enjoy a thousand forms of expression quite beyond the personal. The birds must each sing his own song; the crickets chirp in millionfold performance; but human being feels the deep thrill of joy in their special singers, actors, dancers, as well as in their own personal attempts. That we should find pleasure in watching one another is humanly natural, but what it is we watch, the kind of pleasure and the kind of performance, opens a wide field of choice.

We know, for instance, something of the crude excesses of aboriginal Australian dances; we know more of the gross license of old Rome; we know the breadth of the jokes in medieval times, and the childish brutality of the bull-ring and the cockpit. We know, in a word, that amusements vary; that they form a ready gauge of character and culture; that they have a strong educational influence for good or bad. What we have not hitherto observed is the predominant masculine influence on our amusements. If we recall once more the statement with regard to entertaining anecdotes, "There are thirty good stories in the world, and twenty-nine of them cannot be told to women," we get a glaring sidelight on the masculine specialization in jokes.

"Women have no sense of humor" has been frequently said, when "Women have not a masculine sense of humor" would be truer. If women had thirty "good stories" twenty-nine of which could not be told to men, it is possible that men, if they heard some of the twenty-nine, would not find them funny. The overweight of one sex has told in our amusements as everywhere else.

Because men are further developed in humanity than women are as yet, they have built and organized great places of amusement; because they carried into their humanity their unchecked masculinity, they have made these amusements to correspond. Dramatic expression, is in its true sense, not only a human distinction, but one of our noblest arts. It is allied with the highest emotions; is religious, educational, patriotic, covering the whole range of human feeling. Through it we should be able continually to express, in audible, visible forms, alive and moving, whatever phase of life we most enjoyed or wished to see. There was a time when the drama led life; lifted, taught, inspired, enlightened. Now its main function is to amuse.

Under the demand for amusement, it has cheapened and coarsened, and now the thousand vaudevilles and picture shows give us the broken fragments of a degraded art of which our one main demand is that it shall make us laugh.

There are many causes at work here; and while this study seeks to show in various fields one cause, it does not claim that cause is the only one. Our economic conditions have enormous weight upon our amusements, as on all other human phenomena; but even under economic pressure the reactions of men and women are often dissimilar. Tired men and women both need amusement, the relaxation and restful change of irresponsible gayety. The great majority of women, who work longer hours than any other class, need it desperately and never get it. Amusement, entertainment, recreation, should be open to us all, enjoyed by all. This is a human need, and not a distinction of either sex. Like most human things it is not only largely monopolized by men, but masculized throughout. Many forms of amusement are for men only; more for men mostly; all are for men if they choose to go.

The entrance of women upon the stage, and their increased attendance at theatres has somewhat modified the nature of the performance; even the "refined vaudeville" now begins to show the influence of women. It would be no great advantage to have this department of human life feminized; the improvement desired is to have it less masculized; to reduce the excessive influence of one, and to bring out those broad human interests and pleasures which men and women can equally participate in and enjoy.

VII. ETHICS AND RELIGION.

The laws of physics were at work before we were on earth, and continued to work on us long before we had intelligence enough to perceive, much less understand, them. Our proven knowledge of these processes constitutes "the science of physics"; but the laws were there before the science.

Physics is the science of material relation, how things and natural forces work with and on one another. Ethics is the science of social relation, how persons and social forces work with and on one another.

Ethics is to the human world what physics is to the material world; ignorance of ethics leaves us in the same helpless position in regard to one another that ignorance of physics left us in regard to earth, air, fire and water.

To be sure, people lived and died and gradually improved, while yet ignorant of the physical sciences; they developed a rough "rule of thumb" method, as animals do, and used great forces without understanding them. But their lives were safer and their improvement more rapid as they learned more, and began to make servants of the forces which had been their masters.

We have progressed, lamely enough, with terrible loss and suffering, from stark savagery to our present degree of civilization; we shall go on more safely and swiftly when we learn more of the science of ethics.

Let us note first that while the underlying laws of ethics remain steady and reliable, human notions of them have varied widely and still do so. In different races, ages, classes, sexes, different views of ethics obtain; the conduct of the people is modified by their views, and their prosperity is modified by their conduct.

Primitive man became very soon aware that conduct was of importance. As consciousness increased, with the power to modify action from within, instead of helplessly reacting to stimuli from without, there arose the crude first codes of ethics, the "Thou shalt" and "Thou shalt not" of the blundering savage. It was mostly "Thou shalt not." Inhibition, the checking of an impulse proven disadvantageous, was an earlier and easier form of action than the later human power to consciously decide on and follow a course of action with no stimulus but one's own will.

Primitive ethics consists mostly of Tabus—the things that are forbidden; and all our dim notions of ethics to this day, as well as most of our religions, deal mainly with forbidding.

This is almost the whole of our nursery government, to an extent shown by the well-worn tale of the child who said her name was "Mary." "Mary what?" they asked her. And she answered, "Mary Don't." It is also the main body of our legal systems—a complex mass of prohibitions and preventions. And even in manners and conventions, the things one should not do far outnumber the things one should. A general policy of negation colors our conceptions of ethics and religion.

When the positive side began to be developed, it was at first in purely arbitrary and artificial form. The followers of a given religion were required to go through certain motions, as prostrating themselves, kneeling, and the like; they were required to bring tribute to the gods and their priests, sacrifices, tithes, oblations; they were set little special performances to go through at given times; the range of things forbidden was broad; the range of things commanded was narrow. The Christian religion, practically interpreted, requires a fuller "change of heart" and change of life than any preceding it; which may account at once for its wide appeal to enlightened peoples, and to its scarcity of application.

Again, in surveying the field, it is seen that as our grasp of ethical values widened, as we called more and more acts and tendencies "right" and "wrong," we have shown astonishing fluctuations and vagaries in our judgment. Not only in our religions, which have necessarily upheld each its own set of prescribed actions as most "right," and its own special prohibitions as most "wrong"; but in our beliefs about ethics and our real conduct, we have varied absurdly.

Take, for instance, the ethical concept among "gentlemen" a century or so since, which put the paying of one's gambling debts as a well-nigh sacred duty, and the paying of a tradesman who had fed and clothed one as a quite negligible matter. If the process of gambling was of social service, and the furnishing of food and clothes was not, this might be good ethics; but as the contrary is true, we have to account for this peculiar view on other grounds.

Again, where in Japan a girl, to maintain her parents, is justified in leading a life of shame, we have a peculiar ethical standard difficult for Western minds to appreciate. Yet in such an instance as is described in "Auld Robin Gray," we see precisely the same code; the girl, to benefit her parents, marries a rich old man she does not love—which is to lead a life of shame. The ethical view which justifies this, puts the benefit of parents above the benefit of children, robs the daughter of happiness and motherhood, injures posterity to assist ancestors.

This is one of the products of that very early religion, ancestor worship; and here we lay a finger on a distinctly masculine influence.

We know little of ethical values during the matriarchate; whatever they were, they must have depended for sanction on a cult of promiscuous but efficient maternity. Our recorded history begins in the patriarchal period, and it is its ethics alone which we know.

The mother instinct, throughout nature, is one of unmixed devotion, of love and service, care and defence, with no self-interest. The animal father, in such cases as he is of service to the young, assists the mother in her work in similar fashion. But the human father in the family with the male head soon made that family an instrument of desire, and combat, and self-expression, following the essentially masculine impulses. The children were his, and if males, valuable to serve and glorify him. In his dominance over servile women and helpless children, free rein was given to the growth of pride and the exercise of irresponsible tyranny. To these feelings, developed without check for thousands of years, and to the mental habits resultant, it is easy to trace much of the bias of our early ethical concepts.

Perhaps it is worth while to repeat here that the effort of this book is by no means to attribute a wholly evil influence to men, and a wholly good one to women; it is not even claimed that a purely feminine culture would have advanced the world more successfully. It does claim that the influence of the two together is better than that of either one alone; and in especial to point out what special kind of injury is due to the exclusive influence of one sex heretofore.

We have to-day reached a degree of human development where both men and women are capable of seeing over and across the distinctions of sex, and mutually working for the advancement of the world. Our progress is, however, seriously impeded by what we may call the masculine tradition, the unconscious dominance of a race habit based on this long androcentric period; and it is well worth while, in the interests of both sexes, to show the mischievous effects of the predominance of one.

We have in our ethics not only a "double standard" in one special line, but in nearly all. Man, as a sex, has quite naturally deified his own qualities rather than those of his opposite. In his codes of manners, of morals, of laws, in his early concepts of God, his ancient religions, we see masculinity written large on every side. Confining women wholly to their feminine functions, he has required of them only what he called feminine virtues, and the one virtue he has demanded, to the complete overshadowing of all others, is measured by wholly masculine requirements.

In the interests of health and happiness, monogamous marriage proves its superiority in our race as it has in others. It is essential to the best growth of humanity that we practice the virtue of chastity; it is a human virtue, not a feminine one. But in masculine hands this virtue was enforced upon women under penalties of hideous cruelty, and quite ignored by men. Masculine ethics, colored by masculine instincts, always dominated by sex, has at once recognized the value of chastity in the woman, which is right; punished its absence unfairly, which is wrong; and then reversed the whole matter when applied to men, which is ridiculous.

Ethical laws are laws—not idle notions. Chastity is a virtue because it promotes human welfare—not because men happen to prize it in women and ignore it themselves. The underlying reason for the whole thing is the benefit of the child; and to that end a pure and noble fatherhood is requisite, as well as such a motherhood. Under the limitations of a too masculine ethics, we have developed on this one line social conditions which would be absurdly funny if they were not so horrible.

Religion, be it noticed, does not bear out this attitude. The immense human need of religion, the noble human character of the great religious teachers, has always set its standards, when first established, ahead of human conduct.

Some there are, men of learning and authority, who hold that the deadening immobility of our religions, their resistance to progress and relentless preservation of primitive ideals, is due to the conservatism of women. Men, they say, are progressive by nature; women are conservative. Women are more religious than men, and so preserve old religious forms unchanged after men have outgrown them.

If we saw women in absolute freedom, with a separate religion devised by women, practiced by women, and remaining unchanged through the centuries; while men, on the other hand, bounded bravely forward, making new ones as fast as they were needed, this belief might be maintained. But what do we see? All the old religions made by men, and forced on the women whether they liked it or not. Often women not even considered as part of the scheme—denied souls—given a much lower place in the system—going from the service of their father's gods to the service of their husbands—having none of their own. We see religions which make practically no place for women, as with the Moslem, as rigidly bigoted and unchanging as any other.

We see also this: that the wider and deeper the religion, the more human, the more it calls for practical applications in Christianity—the more it appeals to women. Further, in the diverging sects of the Christian religion, we find that its progressiveness is to be measured, not by the numbers of its women adherents, but by their relative freedom. The women of America, who belong to a thousand sects, who follow new ones with avidity, who even make them, and who also leave them all as men do, are women, as well as those of Spain, who remain contented Romanists, but in America the status of women is higher.

The fact is this: a servile womanhood is in a state of arrested development, and as such does form a ground for the retention of ancient ideas. But this is due to the condition of servility, not to womanhood. That women at present are the bulwark of the older forms of our religions is due to the action of two classes of men: the men of the world, who keep women in their restricted position, and the men of the church, who take every advantage of the limitations of women. When we have for the first time in history a really civilized womanhood, we can then judge better of its effect on religion.

Meanwhile, we can see quite clearly the effect of manhood. Keeping in mind those basic masculine impulses—desire and combat—we see them reflected from high heaven in their religious concepts. Reward! Something to want tremendously and struggle to achieve! This is a concept perfectly masculine and most imperfectly religious. A religion is partly explanation—a theory of life; it is partly emotion—an attitude of mind, it is partly action—a system of morals. Man's special effect on this large field of human development is clear. He pictured his early gods as like to himself, and they behaved in accordance with his ideals. In the dimmest, oldest religions, nearest the matriarchate, we find great goddesses—types of Motherhood, Mother-love, Mother-care and Service. But under masculine dominance, Isis and Ashteroth dwindle away to an alluring Aphrodite—not Womanhood for the child and the World—but the incarnation of female attractiveness for man.

As the idea of heaven developed in the man's mind it became the Happy

Hunting Ground of the savage, the beery and gory Valhalla of the Norseman, the voluptuous, many-houri-ed Paradise of the Mohammedan. These are men's heavens all. Women have never been so fond of hunting, beer or blood; and their houris would be of the other kind. It may be said that the early Christian idea of heaven is by no means planned for men. That is trite, and is perhaps the reason why it has never had so compelling an attraction for them.

Very early in his vague efforts towards religious expression, man voiced his second strongest instinct—that of combat. His universe is always dual, always a scene of combat. Born with that impulse, exercising it continually, he naturally assumed it to be the major process in life. It is not. Growth is the major process. Combat is a useful subsidiary process, chiefly valuable for its initial use, to transmit the physical superiority of the victor. Psychic and social advantages are not thus secured or transmitted.

In no one particular is the androcentric character of our common thought more clearly shown than in the general deification of what are now described as "conflict stimuli." That which is true of the male creature as such is assumed to be true of life in general; quite naturally, but by no means correctly. To this universal masculine error we may trace in the field of religion and ethics the great devil theory, which has for so long obscured our minds. A God without an Adversary was inconceivable to the masculine mind. From this basic misconception we find all our ideas of ethics distorted; that which should have been treated as a group of truths to be learned and habits to be cultivated was treated in terms of combat, and moral growth made an everlasting battle. This combat theory we may follow later into our common notions of discipline, government, law and punishment; here is it enough to see its painful effects in this primary field of ethics and religion?

The third essential male trait of self-expression we may follow from its innocent natural form in strutting cock or stamping stag up to the characteristics we label vanity and pride. The degradation of women in forcing them to adopt masculine methods of personal decoration as a means of livelihood, has carried with the concomitant of personal vanity: but to this day and at their worst we do not find in women the naive exultant glow of pride which swells the bosom of the men who march in procession with brass bands, in full regalia of any sort, so that it be gorgeous, exhibiting their glories to all.

It is this purely masculine spirit which has given to our early concepts of Deity the unadmirable qualities of boundless pride and a thirst for constant praise and prostrate admiration, characteristics certainly unbefitting any noble idea of God. Desire, combat and self-expression all have had their unavoidable influence on masculine religions. What deified Maternity a purely feminine culture might have put forth we do not know, having had none such. Women are generally credited with as much moral sense as men, and as much religious instinct; but so far it has had small power to modify our prevailing creeds.

As a matter of fact, no special sex attributes should have any weight in our ideas of right and wrong. Ethics and religion are distinctly human concerns; they belong to us as social factors, not as physical ones. As we learn to recognize our humanness, and to leave our sex characteristics where they belong, we shall at last learn something about ethics as a simple and practical science, and see that religions grow as the mind grows to formulate them.

If anyone seeks for a clear, simple, easily grasped proof of our ethics, it is to be found in a popular proverb. Struggling upward from beast and savage into humanness, man has seen, reverenced, and striven to attain various human virtues.

He was willing to check many primitive impulses, to change many barbarous habits, to manifest newer, nobler powers. Much he would concede to Humanness, but not his sex—that was beyond the range of Ethics or Religion. By the state of what he calls "morals," and the laws he makes to regulate them, by his attitude in courtship and in marriage, and by the gross anomaly of militarism, in all its senseless waste of life and wealth and joy, we may perceive this little masculine exception:

"All's fair in love and war."

VIII. EDUCATION.

The origin of education is maternal. The mother animal is seen to teach her young what she knows of life, its gains and losses; and, whether consciously done or not, this is education. In our human life, education, even in its present state, is the most important process. Without it we could not maintain ourselves, much less dominate and improve conditions as we do; and when education is what it should be, our power will increase far beyond present hopes.

In lower animals, speaking generally, the powers of the race must be lodged in each individual. No gain of personal experience is of avail to the others. No advantages remain, save those physically transmitted. The narrow limits of personal gain and personal inheritance rigidly hem in sub-human progress. With us, what one learns may be taught to the others. Our life is social, collective. Our gain is for all, and profits us in proportion as we extend it to all. As the human soul develops in us, we become able to grasp more fully our common needs and advantages; and with this growth has come the extension of education to the people as a whole. Social functions are developed under natural laws, like physical ones, and may be studied similarly.

In the evolution of this basic social function, what has been the effect of wholly masculine influence?

The original process, instruction of individual child by individual mother, has been largely neglected in our man-made world. That was considered as a subsidiary sex-function of the woman, and as such, left to her "instinct." This is the main reason why we show such great progress in education for older children, and especially for youths, and so little comparatively in that given to little ones.

We have had on the one side the natural current of maternal education, with its first assistant, the nursemaid, and its second, the "dame-school"; and on the other the influence of the dominant class, organized in university, college, and public school, slowly filtering downward.

Educational forces are many. The child is born into certain conditions, physical and psychic, and "educated" thereby. He grows up into social, political and economic conditions, and is further modified by them. All these conditions, so far, have been of androcentric character; but what we call education as a special social process is what the child is deliberately taught and subjected to; and it is here we may see the same dominant influence so clearly.

This conscious education was, for long, given to boys alone, the girls being left to maternal influence, each to learn what her mother knew, and no more. This very clear instance of the masculine theory is glaring enough by itself to rest a case on. It shows how absolute was the assumption that the world was composed of men, and men alone were to be fitted for it. Women were no part of the world, and needed no training for its uses. As females they were born and not made; as human beings they were only servants, trained as such by their servant mothers.

This system of education we are outgrowing more swiftly with each year. The growing humanness of women, and its recognition, is forcing an equal education for boy and girl. When this demand was first made, by women of unusual calibre, and by men sufficiently human to overlook sex-prejudice, how was it met? What was the attitude of woman's "natural protector" when she began to ask some share in human life?

Under the universal assumption that men alone were humanity, that the world was masculine and for men only, the efforts of the women were met as a deliberate attempt to "unsex" themselves and become men. To be a woman was to be ignorant, uneducated; to be wise, educated, was to be a man. Women were not men, visibly; therefore they could not be educated, and ought not to want to be.

Under this androcentric prejudice, the equal extension of education to women was opposed at every step, and is still opposed by many. Seeing in women only sex, and not humanness, they would confine her exclusively to feminine interests. This is the masculine view, par excellence. In spite of it, the human development of women, which so splendidly characterizes our age, has gone on; and now both woman's colleges and those for both sexes offer "the higher education" to our girls, as well as the lower grades in school and kindergarten.

In the special professional training, the same opposition was experienced, even more rancorous and cruel. One would think that on the entrance of a few straggling and necessarily inferior feminine beginners into a trade or profession, those in possession would extend to them the right hand of fellowship, as comrades, extra assistance as beginners, and special courtesy as women.

The contrary occurred. Women were barred out, discriminated against, taken advantage of, as competitors; and as women they have had to meet special danger and offence instead of special courtesy. An unforgettable instance of this lies in the attitude of the medical colleges toward women students. The men, strong enough, one would think, in numbers, in knowledge, in established precedent, to be generous, opposed the newcomers first with absolute refusal; then, when the patient, persistent applicants did get inside, both students and teachers met them not only with unkindness and unfairness, but with a weapon ingeniously well chosen, and most discreditable—namely, obscenity. Grave professors, in lecture and clinic, as well as grinning students, used offensive language, and played offensive tricks, to drive the women out—a most androcentric performance.

Remember that the essential masculine attitude is one of opposition, of combat; his desire is obtained by first overcoming a competitor; and then see how this dominant masculinity stands out where it has no possible use or benefit—in the field of education. All along the line, man, long master of a subject sex, fought every step of woman toward mental equality. Nevertheless, since modern man has become human enough to be just, he has at last let her have a share in the advantages of education; and she has proven her full power to appreciate and use these advantages.

Then to-day rises a new cry against "women in education." Here is Mr. Barrett Wendell, of Harvard, solemnly claiming that teaching women weakens the intellect of the teacher, and every now and then bursts out a frantic sputter of alarm over the "feminization" of our schools. It is true that the majority of teachers are now women. It is true that they do have an influence on growing children. It would even seem to be true that that is largely what women are for.

But the male assumes his influence to be normal, human, and the female influence as wholly a matter of sex; therefore, where women teach boys, the boys become "effeminate"—a grievous fall. When men teach girls, do the girls become ———? Here again we lack the analogue. Never has it occurred to the androcentric mind to conceive of such a thing as being too masculine. There is no such word! It is odd to notice that which ever way the woman is placed, she is supposed to exert this degrading influence; if the teacher, she effeminizes her pupils; if the pupil, she effeminizes her teachers.

Now let us shake ourselves free, if only for a moment, from the androcentric habit of mind.

As a matter of sex, the female is the more important. Her share of the processes which sex distinction serves is by far the greater. To be feminine—if one were nothing else, is a far more extensive and dignified office than to be masculine—and nothing else.

But as a matter of humanity the male of our species is at present far ahead of the female. By this superior humanness, his knowledge, his skill, his experience, his organization and specialization, he makes and manages the world. All this is human, not male. All this is as open to the woman as the man by nature, but has been denied her during our androcentric culture.

But even if, in a purely human process, such as education, she does bring her special feminine characteristics to bear, what are they, and what are the results?

We can see the masculine influence everywhere still dominant and superior. There is the first spur, Desire, the base of the reward system, the incentive of self-interest, the attitude which says, "Why should I make an effort unless it will give me pleasure?" with its concomitant laziness, unwillingness to work without payment. There is the second spur, Combat, the competitive system, which sets one against another, and finds pleasure not in learning, not exercising the mind, but in getting ahead of one's fellows. Under these two wholly masculine influences we have made the educational process a joy to the few who successfully attain, and a weary effort, with failure and contumely attached, to all the others. This may be a good method in sex-competition, but is wholly out of place and mischievous in education. Its prevalence shows the injurious masculization of this noble social process.

What might we look for in a distinctly feminine influence? What are these much-dreaded feminine characteristics?

The maternal ones, of course. The sex instincts of the male are of a preliminary nature, leading merely to the union preceding parenthood. The sex instincts of the female cover a far larger field, spending themselves most fully in the lasting love, the ceaseless service, the ingenuity and courage of efficient motherhood. To feminize education would be to make it more motherly. The mother does not rear her children by a system of prizes to be longed for and pursued; nor does she set them to compete with one another, giving to the conquering child what he needs, and to the vanquished, blame and deprivation. That would be "unfeminine."

Motherhood does all it knows to give to each child what is most needed, to teach all to their fullest capacity, to affectionately and efficiently develop the whole of them.

But this is not what is meant by those who fear so much the influence of women. Accustomed to a wholly male standard of living, to masculine ideals, virtues, methods and conditions, they say—and say with some justice—that feminine methods and ideals would be destructive to what they call "manliness." For instance, education to-day is closely interwoven with games and sports, all of an excessively masculine nature. "The education of a boy is carried on largely on the playground!" say the objectors to women teachers. Women cannot join them there; therefore, they cannot educate them.

What games are these in which women cannot join? There are forms of fighting, of course, violent and fierce, modern modifications of the instinct of sex-combat. It is quite true that women are not adapted, or inclined, to baseball or football or any violent game. They are perfectly competent to take part in all normal athletic development, the human range of agility and skill is open to them, as everyone knows who has been to the circus; but they are not built for physical combat; nor do they find ceaseless pleasure in throwing, hitting or kicking things.

But is it true that these strenuous games have the educational value attributed to them? It seems like blasphemy to question it. The whole range of male teachers, male pupils, male critics and spectators, are loud in their admiration for the "manliness" developed by the craft, courage, co-ordinative power and general "sportsmanship" developed by the game of football, for instance; that a few young men are killed and many maimed, is nothing in comparison to these advantages.

Let us review the threefold distinction on which this whole study rests, between masculine, feminine and human. Grant that woman, being feminine, cannot emulate man in being masculine—and does not want to. Grant that the masculine qualities have their use and value, as well as feminine ones. There still remain the human qualities shared by both, owned by neither, most important of all. Education is a human process, and should develop human qualities—not sex qualities. Surely our boys are sufficiently masculine, without needing a special education to make them more so.

The error lies here. A strictly masculine world, proud of its own sex and despising the other, seeing nothing in the world but sex, either male or female, has "viewed with alarm" the steady and rapid growth of humanness. Here, for instance, is a boy visibly tending to be an artist, a musician, a scientific discoverer. Here is another boy not particularly clever in any line, nor ambitious for any special work, though he means in a general way to "succeed"; he is, however, a big, husky fellow, a good fighter, mischievous as a monkey, and strong in the virtues covered by the word "sportsmanship." This boy we call "a fine manly fellow."

We are quite right. He is. He is distinctly and excessively male, at the expense of his humanness. He may make a more prepotent sire than the other, though even that is not certain; he may, and probably will, appeal more strongly to the excessively feminine girl, who has even less humanness than he; but he is not therefore a better citizen.

The advance of civilization calls for human qualities, in both men and women. Our educational system is thwarted and hindered, not as Prof. Wendell and his life would have us believe, by "feminization," but by an overweening masculization.

Their position is a simple one. "We are men. Men are human beings. Women are only women. This is a man's world. To get on in it you must do it man-fashion—i.e., fight, and overcome the others. Being civilized, in part, we must arrange a sort of 'civilized warfare,' and learn to play the game, the old crude, fierce male game of combat, and we must educate our boys thereto." No wonder education was denied to women. No wonder their influence is dreaded by an ultra-masculine culture.

It will change the system in time. It will gradually establish an equal place in life for the feminine characteristics, so long belittled and derided, and give pre-eminent dignity to the human power.

Physical culture, for both boys and girls, will be part of such a modified system. All things that both can do together will be accepted as human; but what either boys or girls have to retire apart to practice will be frankly called masculine and feminine, and not encouraged in children.

The most important qualities are the human ones, and will be so named and honored. Courage is a human quality, not a sex-quality. What is commonly called courage in male animals is mere belligerence, the fighting instinct. To meet an adversary of his own sort is a universal masculine trait; two father cats may fight fiercely each other, but both will run from a dog as quickly as a mother cat. She has courage enough, however, in defence of her kittens.

What this world most needs to-day in both men and women, is the power to recognize our public conditions; to see the relative importance of measures; to learn the processes of constructive citizenship. We need an education which shall give its facts in the order of their importance; morals and manners based on these facts; and train our personal powers with careful selection, so that each may best serve the community.

At present, in the larger processes of extra-scholastic education, the advantage is still with the boy. From infancy we make the gross mistake of accentuating sex in our children, by dress and all its limitations, by special teaching of what is "ladylike" and "manly." The boy is allowed a freedom of experience far beyond the girl. He learns more of his town and city, more of machinery, more of life, passing on from father to son the truths as well as traditions of sex superiority.

All this is changing before our eyes, with the advancing humanness of women. Not yet, however, has their advance affected, to any large extent, the base of all education; the experience of a child's first years. Here is where the limitations of women have checked race progress most thoroughly. Here hereditary influence was constantly offset by the advance of the male. Social selection did develop higher types of men, though sex-selection reversed still insisted on primitive types of women. But the educative influence of these primitive women, acting most exclusively on the most susceptible years of life, has been a serious deterrent to race progress.

Here is the dominant male, largely humanized, yet still measuring life from male standards. He sees women only as a sex. (Note here the criticism of Europeans on American women. "Your women are so sexless!" they say, meaning merely that our women have human qualities as well as feminine.) And children he considers as part and parcel of the same domain, both inferior classes, "women and children."

I recall in Rimmer's beautiful red chalk studies, certain profiles of man, woman and child, and careful explanation that the proportion of the woman's face and head were far more akin to the child than to the man. What Mr. Rimmer should have shown, and could have, by profuse illustration, was that the faces of boy and girl differ but slightly, and the faces of old men and women differ as little, sometimes not at all; while the face of the woman approximates the human more closely than that of the man; while the child, representing race more than sex, is naturally more akin to her than to him. The male reserves more primitive qualities, the hairiness, the more pugnacious jaw; the female is nearer to the higher human types.

An ultra-male selection has chosen women for their femininity first, and next for qualities of submissiveness and patient service bred by long ages of servility.

This servile womanhood, or the idler and more excessively feminine type, has never appreciated the real power and place of the mother, and has never been able to grasp or to carry out any worthy system of education for little children. Any experienced teacher, man or woman, will own how rare it is to find a mother capable of a dispassionate appreciation of educative values. Books in infant education and child culture generally are read by teachers more than mothers, so our public libraries prove. The mother-instinct, quite suitable and sufficient in animals, is by no means equal to the requirements of civilized life. Animal motherhood furnishes a fresh wave of devotion for each new birth; primitive human motherhood extends that passionate tenderness over the growing family for a longer period; but neither can carry education beyond its rudiments.

So accustomed are we to our world-old method of entrusting the first years of the child to the action of untaught, unbridled mother-instinct, that suggestions as to a better education for babies are received with the frank derision of massed ignorance.

That powerful and brilliant writer, Mrs. Josephine Daskam Bacon, among others has lent her able pen to ridicule and obstruct the gradual awakening of human intelligence in mothers, the recognition that babies are no exception to the rest of us in being better off for competent care and service. It seems delightfully absurd to these reactionaries that ages of human progress should be of any benefit to babies, save, indeed, as their more human fathers, specialized and organized, are able to provide them with better homes and a better world to grow up in. The idea that mothers, more human, should specialize and organize as well, and extend to their babies these supreme advantages, is made a laughing stock.

It is easy and profitable to laugh with the majority; but in the judgment of history, those who do so, hold unenviable positions. The time is coming when the human mother will recognize the educative possibilities of early childhood, learn that the ability to rightly teach little children is rare and precious, and be proud and glad to avail themselves of it.

We shall then see a development of the most valuable human qualities in our children's minds such as would now seem wildly Utopian. We shall learn from wide and long experience to anticipate and provide for the steps of the unfolding mind, and train it, through carefully prearranged experiences, to a power of judgment, of self-control, of social perception, now utterly unthought of.

Such an education would begin at birth; yes, far before it, in the standards of a conscious human motherhood. It would require a quite different status of wifehood, womanhood, girlhood. It would be wholly impossible if we were never to outgrow our androcentric culture.

IX. "SOCIETY" AND "FASHION"

Among our many naive misbeliefs is the current fallacy that "society" is made by women; and that women are responsible for that peculiar social manifestation called "fashion."

Men and women alike accept this notion; the serious essayist and philosopher, as well as the novelist and paragrapher, reflect it in their pages. The force of inertia acts in the domain of psychics as well as physics; any idea pushed into the popular mind with considerable force will keep on going until some opposing force—or the slow resistance of friction—stops it at last.

"Society" consists mostly of women. Women carry on most of its processes, therefore women are its makers and masters, they are responsible for it, that is the general belief.

We might as well hold women responsible for harems—or prisoners for jails. To be helplessly confined to a given place or condition does not prove that one has chosen it; much less made it.

No; in an androcentric culture "society," like every other social relation, is dominated by the male and arranged for his convenience. There are, of course, modifications due to the presence of the other sex; where there are more women than men there are inevitable results of their influence; but the character and conditions of the whole performance are dictated by men.

Social intercourse is the prime condition of human life. To meet, to mingle, to know one another, to exchange, not only definite ideas, facts, and feelings, but to experience that vague general stimulus and enlarged power that comes of contact—all this is essential to our happiness as well as to our progress.

This grand desideratum has always been monopolized by men as far as possible. What intercourse was allowed to women has been rigidly hemmed its by man-made conventions. Women accept these conventions, repeat them, enforce them upon their daughters; but they originate with men.

The feet of the little Chinese girl are bound by her mother and her nurse—but it is not for woman's pleasure that this crippling torture was invented. The Oriental veil is worn by women, but it is not for any need of theirs that veils were decreed them.

When we look at society in its earlier form we find that the public house has always been with us. It is as old almost as the private house; the need for association is as human as the need for privacy. But the public house was—and is—for men only. The woman was kept as far as possible at home. Her female nature was supposed to delimit her life satisfactorily, and her human stature was completely ignored.

Under the pressure of that human nature she has always rebelled at the social restrictions which surrounded her; and from the women of older lands gathered at the well, or in the market place, to our own women on the church steps or in the sewing circle, they have ceaselessly struggled for the social intercourse which was as much a law of their being as of man's.

When we come to the modern special field that we call "society," we find it to consist of a carefully arranged set of processes and places wherein women may meet one another and meet men. These vary, of course, with race, country, class, and period; from the clean licence of our western customs to the strict chaperonage of older lands; but free as it is in

America, even here there are bounds.

Men associate without any limit but that of inclination and financial capacity. Even class distinction only works one way—the low-class man may not mingle with high-class women; but the high-class man may—and does—mingle with low-class women. It is his society—may not a man do what he will with his own?

Caste distinctions, as have been ably shown by Prof. Lester F. Ward, are relics of race distinction; the subordinate caste was once a subordinate race; and while mating, upward, was always forbidden to the subject race; mating, downward, was always practiced by the master race.

The elaborate shading of "the color line" in slavery days, from pure black up through mulatto, quadroon, octoroon, quinteroon, griffada, mustafee, mustee, and sang d'or—to white again; was not through white mothers—but white fathers; never too exclusive in their tastes. Even in slavery, the worst horrors were strictly androcentric.

"Society" is strictly guarded—that is its women are. As always, the main tabu is on the woman. Consider carefully the relation between "society" and the growing girl. She must, of course, marry; and her education, manners, character, must of course be pleasing to the prospective wooer. That which is desirable in young girls means, naturally, that which is desirable to men. Of all cultivated accomplishments the first is "innocence." Beauty may or may not be forthcoming; but "innocence" is "the chief charm of girlhood."

Why? What good does it do her? Her whole life's success is made to depend on her marrying; her health and happiness depends on her marrying the right man. The more "innocent" she is, the less she knows, the easier it is for the wrong man to get her.

As is so feelingly described in "The Sorrows of Amelia," in "The Ladies' Literary Cabinet," a magazine taken by my grandmother; "The only foible which the delicate Amelia possessed was an unsuspecting breast to lavish esteem. Unversed in the secret villanies of a base degenerate world, she ever imagined all mankind to be as spotless as herself. Alas for Amelia! This fatal credulity was the source of all her misfortunes." It was. It is yet.

Just face the facts with new eyes—look at it as if you had never seen "society" before; and observe the position of its "Queen."

Here is Woman. Let us grant that Motherhood is her chief purpose. (As a female it is. As a human being she has others!) Marriage is our way of safeguarding motherhood; of ensuring "support" and "protection" to the wife and children.

"Society" is very largely used as a means to bring together young people, to promote marriage. If "society" is made and governed by women we should naturally look to see its restrictions and encouragements such as would put a premium on successful maternity and protect women—and their children—from the evils of ill-regulated fatherhood.

Do we find this? By no means.

"Society" allows the man all liberty—all privilege—all license. There are certain offences which would exclude him; such as not paying gambling debts, or being poor; but offences against womanhood—against motherhood—do not exclude him.

How about the reverse?

If "society" is made by women, for women, surely a misstep by a helplessly "innocent" girl, will not injure her standing!

But it does. She is no longer "innocent." She knows now. She has lost her market value and is thrown out of the shop. Why not? It is his shop—not hers. What women may and may not be, what they must and must not do, all is measured from the masculine standard.

A really feminine "society" based on the needs and pleasures of women, both as females and as human beings, would in the first place accord them freedom and knowledge; the knowledge which is power. It would not show us "the queen of the ballroom" in the position of a wall-flower unless favored by masculine invitation; unable to eat unless he brings her something; unable to cross the floor without his arm. Of all blind stultified "royal sluggards" she is the archetype. No, a feminine society would grant at least equality to women in this, their so-called special field.

Its attitude toward men, however, would be rigidly critical.

Fancy a real Mrs. Grundy (up to date it has been a Mr., his whiskers hid in capstrings) saying, "No, no, young man. You won't do. You've been drinking. The habit's growing on you. You'll make a bad husband."

Or still more severely, "Out with you, sir! You've forfeited your right to marry! Go into retirement for seven years, and when you come back bring a doctor's certificate with you."

That sounds ridiculous, doesn't it—for "Society" to say? It is ridiculous, in a man's "society."

The required dress and decoration of "society"; the everlasting eating and drinking of "society," the preferred amusements of "society," the absolute requirements and absolute exclusions of "society," are of men, by men, for men,—to paraphrase a threadbare quotation. And then, upon all that vast edifice of masculine influence, they turn upon women as Adam did; and blame them for severity with their fallen sisters! "Women are so hard upon women!"

They have to be. What man would "allow" his wife, his daughters, to visit and associate with "the fallen"? His esteem would be forfeited, they would lose their "social position," the girl's chance of marrying would be gone.

Men are not so stern. They may visit the unfortunate women, to bring them help, sympathy, re-establishment—or for other reasons; and it does not forfeit their social position. Why should it? They make the regulation.

Women are to-day, far more conspicuously than men, the exponents and victims of that mysterious power we call "Fashion." As shown in mere helpless imitation of one another's idea, customs, methods, there is not much difference; in patient acquiescence with prescribed models of architecture, furniture, literature, or anything else; there is not much difference; but in personal decoration there is a most conspicuous difference. Women do to-day submit to more grotesque ugliness and absurdity than men; and there are plenty of good reasons for it. Confining our brief study of fashion to fashion in dress, let us observe why it is that women wear these fine clothes at all; and why they change them as they do.

First, and very clearly, the human female carries the weight of sex decoration, solely because of her economic dependence on the male. She alone in nature adds to the burdens of maternity, which she was meant for, this unnatural burden of ornament, which she was not meant for. Every other female in the world is sufficiently attractive to the male without trimmings. He carries the trimmings, sparing no expense of spreading antlers or trailing plumes; no monstrosity of crest and wattles, to win her favor.

She is only temporarily interested in him. The rest of the time she is getting her own living, and caring for her own young. But our women get their bread from their husbands, and every other social need. The woman depends on the man for her position in life, as well as the necessities of existence. For herself and for her children she must win and hold him who is the source of all supplies. Therefore she is forced to add to her own natural attractions this "dance of the seven veils," of the seventeen gowns, of the seventy-seven hats of gay delirium.

There are many who think in one syllable, who say, "women don't dress to please men—they dress to please themselves—and to outshine other women." To these I would suggest a visit to some summer shore resort during the week and extending over Saturday night. The women have all the week to please themselves and outshine one another; but their array on Saturday seems to indicate the approach of some new force or attraction.

If all this does not satisfy I would then call their attention to the well-known fact that the young damsel previous to marriage spends far more time and ingenuity in decoration than she does afterward. This has long been observed and deprecated by those who write Advice to Wives, on the ground that this difference is displeasing to the husband—that she loses her influence over him; which is true. But since his own "society," knowing his weakness, has tied him to her by law; why should she keep up what is after all an unnatural exertion?

That excellent magazine "Good Housekeeping" has been running for some months a rhymed and illustrated story of "Miss Melissa Clarissa McRae," an extremely dainty and well-dressed stenographer, who captured and married a fastidious young man, her employer, by the force of her artificial attractions—and then lost his love after marriage by a sudden unaccountable slovenliness—the same old story.

If this in not enough, let me instance further the attitude toward "Fashion" of that class of women who live most openly and directly upon the favor of men. These know their business. To continually attract the vagrant fancy of the male, nature's born "variant," they must not only pile on artificial charms, but change them constantly. They do. From the leaders of this profession comes a steady stream of changing fashions; the more extreme and bizarre, the more successful—and because they are successful they are imitated.

If men did not like changes in fashion be assured these professional men-pleasers would not change them, but since Nature's Variant tires of any face in favor of a new one, the lady who would hold her sway and cannot change her face (except in color) must needs change her hat and gown.

But the Arbiter, the Ruling Cause, he who not only by choice demands, but as a business manufactures and supplies this amazing stream of fashions; again like Adam blames the woman—for accepting what he both demands and supplies.

A further proof, if more were needed, is shown in this; that in exact proportion as women grow independent, educated, wise and free, do they become less submissive to men-made fashions. Was this improvement hailed with sympathy and admiration—crowned with masculine favor?

The attitude of men toward those women who have so far presumed to "unsex themselves" is known to all. They like women to be foolish, changeable, always newly attractive; and while women must "attract" for a living—why they do, that's all.

It is a pity. It is humiliating to any far-seeing woman to have to recognize this glaring proof of the dependent, degraded position of her sex; and it ought to be humiliating to men to see the results of their mastery. These crazily decorated little creatures do not represent womanhood.

When the artist uses the woman as the type of every highest ideal; as Justice, Liberty, Charity, Truth—he does not represent her trimmed. In any part of the world where women are even in part economically independent there we find less of the absurdities of fashion. Women who work cannot be utterly absurd.

But the idle woman, the Queen of Society, who must please men within their prescribed bounds; and those of the half-world, who must please them at any cost—these are the vehicles of fashion.

X. LAW AND GOVERNMENT.

It is easy to assume that men are naturally the lawmakers and law-enforcers, under the plain historic fact that they have been such since the beginning of the patriarchate.

Back of law lies custom and tradition. Back of government lies the correlative activity of any organized group. What group-insects and group-animals evolve unconsciously and fulfill by their social instincts, we evolve consciously and fulfill by arbitrary systems called laws and governments. In this, as in all other fields of our action, we must discriminate between the humanness of the function in process of development, and the influence of the male or female upon it. Quite apart from what they may like or dislike as sexes, from their differing tastes and faculties, lies the much larger field of human progress, in which they equally participate.

On this plane the evolution of law and government proceeds somewhat as follows:—The early woman-centered group organized on maternal lines of common love and service. The early combinations of men were first a grouped predacity—organized hunting; then a grouped belligerency,—organized warfare.

By special development some minds are able to perceive the need of certain lines of conduct over others, and to make this clear to their fellows; whereby, gradually, our higher social nature establishes rules and precedents to which we personally agree to submit. The process of social development is one of progressive co-ordination.

From independent individual action for individual ends, up to interdependent social action for social ends we slowly move; the "devil" in the play being the old Ego, which has to be harmonized with the new social spirit. This social process, like all others, having been in masculine hands, we may find in it the same marks of one-sided Specialization so visible in our previous studies.

The coersive attitude is essentially male. In the ceaseless age-old struggle of sex combat he developed the desire to overcome, which is always stimulated by resistance; and in this later historic period of his supremacy, he further developed the habit of dominance and mastery. We may instance the contrast between the conduct of a man when "in love" and while courting; in which period he falls into the natural position of his sex towards the other—namely, that of a wooer; and his behavior when, with marriage, they enter the, artificial relation of the master male and servile female. His "instinct of dominance" does not assert itself during the earlier period, which was a million times longer than the latter; it only appears in the more modern and arbitrary relation.

Among other animals monogamous union is not accompanied by any such discordant and unnatural features. However recent as this habit is when considered biologically, it is as old as civilization when we consider it historically: quite old enough to be a serious force. Under its pressure we see the legal systems and forms of government slowly evolving, the general human growth always heavily perverted by the special masculine influence. First we find the mere force of custom governing us, the mores of the ancient people. Then comes the gradual appearance of authority, from the purely natural leadership of the best hunter or fighter up through the unnatural mastery of the patriarch, owning and governing his wives, children, slaves and cattle, and making such rules and regulations as pleased him.

Our laws as we support them now are slow, wasteful, cumbrous systems, which require a special caste to interpret and another to enforce; wherein the average citizen knows nothing of the law, and cares only to evade it when he can, obey it when he must. In the household, that stunted, crippled rudiment of the matriarchate, where alone we can find what is left of the natural influence of woman, the laws and government, so far as she is responsible for them, are fairly simple, and bear visible relation to the common good, which relation is clearly and persistently taught.

In the larger household of city and state the educational part of the law is grievously neglected. It makes no allowance for ignorance. If a man breaks a law of which he never heard he is not excused therefore; the penalty rolls on just the same. Fancy a mother making solemn rules and regulations for her family, telling the children nothing about them, and then punishing them when they disobeyed the unknown laws!

The use of force is natural to the male; while as a human being he must needs legislate somewhat in the interests of the community, as a male being he sees no necessity for other enforcement than by penalty. To violently oppose, to fight, to trample to the earth, to triumph in loud bellowings of savage joy,—these are the primitive male instincts; and the perfectly natural social instinct which leads to peaceful persuasion, to education, to an easy harmony of action, are contemptuously ranked as "feminine," or as "philanthropic,"—which is almost as bad. "Men need stronger measures" they say proudly. Yes, but four-fifths of the world are women and children!

As a matter of fact the woman, the mother, is the first co-ordinator, legislator, administrator and executive. From the guarding and guidance of her cubs and kittens up to the longer, larger management of human youth, she is the first to consider group interests and co-relate them.

As a father the male grows to share in these original feminine functions, and with us, fatherhood having become socialized while motherhood has not, he does the best he can, alone, to do the world's mother-work in his father way.

In study of any long established human custom it is very difficult to see it clearly and dispassionately. Our minds are heavily loaded with precedent, with race-custom, with the iron weight called authority. These heavy forces reach their most perfect expression in the absolutely masculine field of warfare. The absolute authority; the brainless, voiceless obedience; the relentless penalty. Here we have male coercion at its height; law and government wholly arbitrary. The result is as might be expected, a fine machine of destruction. But destruction is not a human process—merely a male process of eliminating the unfit.

The female process is to select the fit; her elimination is negative and painless.

Greater than either is the human process, to develop fitness.

Men are at present far more human than women. Alone upon their self-seized thrones they have carried as best they might the burdens of the state; and the history of law and government shows them as changing slowly but irresistably in the direction of social improvement.

The ancient kings were the joyous apotheosis of masculinity. Power and Pride were theirs; Limitless Display; Boundless Self-indulgence; Irresistable Authority. Slaves and courtiers bowed before them, subjects obeyed them, captive women filled their harems. But the day of the masculine monarchy is passing, and the day of the human democracy is coming in. In a Democracy Law and Government both change. Laws are no longer imposed on the people by one above them, but are evolved from the people themselves. How absurd that the people should not be educated in the laws they make; that the trailing remnants of blind submission should still becloud their minds and make them bow down patiently under the absurd pressure of outgrown tradition!

Democratic government is no longer an exercise of arbitrary authority from one above, but is an organization for public service of the people themselves—or will be when it is really attained.

In this change government ceases to be compulsion, and becomes agreement; law ceases to be authority and becomes co-ordination. When we learn the rules of whist or chess we do not obey them because we fear to be punished if we don't, but because we want to play the game. The rules of human conduct are for our own happiness and service—any child can see that. Every child will see it when laws are simplified, based on sociology, and taught in schools. A child of ten should be considered grossly uneducated who could not rewrite the main features of the laws of his country, state, and city; and those laws should be so simple in their principles that a child of ten could understand them.

Teacher: "What is a tax?"

Child: "A tax is the money we agree to pay to keep up our common advantages."

Teacher: "Why do we all pay taxes?"

Child: "Because the country belongs to all of us, and we must all pay our share to keep it up."

Teacher: "In what proportion do we pay taxes?"

Child: "In proportion to how much money we have." (Sotto voce: "Of course!")

Teacher: "What is it to evade taxes?"

Child: "It is treason." (Sotto voce: "And a dirty mean trick.")

In masculine administration of the laws we may follow the instinctive love of battle down through the custom of "trial by combat"—only recently outgrown, to our present method, where each contending party hires a champion to represent him, and these fight it out in a wordy war, with tricks and devices of complex ingenuity, enjoying this kind of struggle as they enjoy all other kinds.

It is the old masculine spirit of government as authority which is so slow in adapting itself to the democratic idea of government as service. That it should be a representative government they grasp, but representative of what? of the common will, they say; the will of the majority;—never thinking that it is the common good, the common welfare, that government should represent.

It is the inextricable masculinity in our idea of government which so revolts at the idea of women as voters. "To govern:" that means to boss, to control, to have authority; and that only, to most minds. They cannot bear to think of the woman as having control over even their own affairs; to control is masculine, they assume. Seeing only self-interest as a natural impulse, and the ruling powers of the state as a sort of umpire, an authority to preserve the rules of the game while men fight it out forever; they see in a democracy merely a wider range of self interest, and a wider, freer field to fight in.

The law dictates the rules, the government enforces them, but the main business of life, hitherto, has been esteemed as one long fierce struggle; each man seeking for himself. To deliberately legislate for the service of all the people, to use the government as the main engine of that service, is a new process, wholly human, and difficult of development under an androcentric culture.

Furthermore they put forth those naively androcentric protests,—women cannot fight, and in case their laws were resisted by men they could not enforce them,—therefore they should not vote!

What they do not so plainly say, but very strongly think, is that women should not share the loot which to their minds is so large a part of politics.

Here we may trace clearly the social heredity of male government.

Fix clearly in your mind the first head-ship of man—the leader of the pack as it were—the Chief Hunter. Then the second head-ship, the Chief Fighter. Then the third head-ship, the Chief of the Family. Then the long line of Chiefs and Captains, Warlords and Landlords, Rulers and Kings.

The Hunter hunted for prey, and got it. The Fighter enriched himself with the spoils of the vanquished. The Patriarch lived on the labor of women and slaves. All down the ages, from frank piracy and robbery to the measured toll of tribute, ransom and indemnity, we see the same natural instinct of the hunter and fighter. In his hands the government is a thing to sap and wreck, to live on. It is his essential impulse to want something very much; to struggle and fight for it; to take all he can get.

Set against this the giving love that comes with motherhood; the endless service that comes of motherhood; the peaceful administration in the interest of the family that comes of motherhood. We prate much of the family as the unit of the state. If it is—why not run the state on that basis? Government by women, so far as it is influenced by their sex, would be influenced by motherhood; and that would mean care, nurture, provision, education. We have to go far down the scale for any instance of organized motherhood, but we do find it in the hymenoptera; in the overflowing industry, prosperity, peace and loving service of the ant-hill and bee-hive. These are the most highly socialized types of life, next to ours, and they are feminine types.

We as human beings have a far higher form of association, with further issues than mere wealth and propagation of the species. In this human process we should never forget that men are far more advanced than women, at present. Because of their humanness has come all the noble growth of civilization, in spite of their maleness.

As human beings both male and female stand alike useful and honorable, and should in our government be alike used and honored; but as creatures of sex, the female is fitter than the male for administration of constructive social interests. The change in governmental processes which marks our times is a change in principle. Two great movements convulse the world to-day, the woman's movement and the labor movement. Each regards the other as of less moment than itself. Both are parts of the same world-process.

We are entering upon a period of social consciousness. Whereas so far almost all of us have seen life only as individuals, and have regarded the growing strength and riches of the social body as merely so much the more to fatten on; now we are beginning to take an intelligent interest in our social nature, to understand it a little, and to begin to feel the vast increase of happiness and power that comes of real Human Life.

In this change of systems a government which consisted only of prohibition and commands; of tax collecting and making war; is rapidly giving way to a system which intelligently manages our common interests, which is a growing and improving method of universal service. Here the socialist is perfectly right in his vision of the economic welfare to be assured by the socialization of industry, though that is but part of the new development; and the individualist who opposes socialism, crying loudly for the advantage of "free competition" is but voicing the spirit of the predacious male.

So with the opposers to the suffrage of women. They represent, whether men or women, the male viewpoint. They see the woman only as a female, utterly absorbed in feminine functions, belittled and ignored as her long tutelage has made her; and they see the man as he sees himself, the sole master of human affairs for as long as we have historic record.

This, fortunately, is not long. We can now see back of the period of his supremacy, and are beginning to see beyond it. We are well under way already in a higher stage of social development, conscious, well-organized, wisely managed, in which the laws shall be simple and founded on constructive principles instead of being a set of ring-regulations within which people may fight as they will; and in which the government shall be recognized in its full use; not only the sternly dominant father, and the wisely servicable mother, but the real union of all people to sanely and economically manage their affairs.

XI. CRIME AND PUNISHMENT.

The human concept of Sin has had its uses no doubt; and our special invention of a thing called Punishment has also served a purpose.

Social evolution has worked in many ways wastefully, and with unnecessary pain, but it compares very favorably with natural evolution.

As we grow wiser; as our social consciousness develops, we are beginning to improve on nature in more ways than one; a part of the same great process, but of a more highly sublimated sort.

Nature shows a world of varied and changing environment. Into this comes Life—flushing and spreading in every direction. A pretty hard time Life has of it. In the first place it is dog eat dog in every direction; the joy of the hunter and the most unjoyous fear of the hunted.

But quite outside of this essential danger, the environment waits, grim and unappeasable, and continuously destroys the innocent myriads who fail to meet the one requirement of life—Adaptation. So we must not be too severe in self-condemnation when we see how foolish, cruel, crazily wasteful, is our attitude toward crime and punishment.

We become socially conscious largely through pain, and as we begin to see how much of the pain is wholly of our own causing we are overcome with shame. But the right way for society to face its past is the same as for the individual; to see where it was wrong and stop it—but to waste no time and no emotion over past misdeeds.

What is our present state as to crime? It is pretty bad. Some say it is worse than it used to be; others that it is better. At any rate it is bad enough, and a disgrace to our civilization. We have murderers by the thousand and thieves by the million, of all kinds and sizes; we have what we tenderly call "immorality," from the "errors of youth" to the sodden grossness of old age; married, single, and mixed. We have all the old kinds of wickedness and a lot of new ones, until one marvels at the purity and power of human nature, that it should carry so much disease and still grow on to higher things.

Also we have punishment still with us; private and public; applied like a rabbit's foot, with as little regard to its efficacy. Does a child offend? Punish it! Does a woman offend? Punish her! Does a man offend? Punish him! Does a group offend? Punish them!

"What for?" some one suddenly asks.

"To make them stop doing it!"

"But they have done it!"

"To make them not do it again, then."

"But they do do it again—and worse."

"To prevent other people's doing it, then."

"But it does not prevent them—the crime keeps on. What good is your punishment?"

What indeed!

What is the application of punishment to crime? Its base, its prehistoric base, is simple retaliation; and this is by no means wholly male, let us freely admit. The instinct of resistance, of opposition, of retaliation, lies deeper than life itself. Its underlying law is the law of physics—action and reaction are equal. Life's expression of this law is perfectly natural, but not always profitable. Hit your hand on a stone wall, and the stone wall hits your hand. Very good; you learn that stone walls are hard, and govern yourself accordingly.

Conscious young humanity observed and philosophized, congratulating itself on its discernment. "A man hits me—I hit the man a little harder—then he won't do it again." Unfortunately he did do it again—a little harder still. The effort to hit harder carried on the action and reaction till society, hitting hardest of all, set up a system of legal punishment, of unlimited severity. It imprisoned, it mutilated, it tortured, it killed; it destroyed whole families, and razed contumelious cities to the ground.

Therefore all crime ceased, of course? No? But crime was mitigated, surely! Perhaps. This we have proven at last; that crime does not decrease in proportion to the severest punishment. Little by little we have ceased to raze the cities, to wipe out the families, to cut off the ears, to torture; and our imprisonment is changing from slow death and insanity to a form of attempted improvement.

But punishment as a principle remains in good standing, and is still the main reliance where it does the most harm—in the rearing of children. "Spare the rod and spoil the child" remains in belief, unmodified by the millions of children spoiled by the unspared rod.

The breeders of racehorses have learned better, but not the breeders of children. Our trouble is simply the lack of intelligence. We face the babyish error and the hideous crime in exactly the same attitude.

"This person has done something offensive."

Yes?—and one waits eagerly for the first question of the rational mind—but does not hear it. One only hears "Punish him!"

What is the first question of the rational mind?

"Why?"

Human beings are not first causes. They do not evolve conduct out of nothing. The child does this, the man does that, because of something; because of many things. If we do not like the way people behave, and wish them to behave better, we should, if we are rational beings, study the conditions that produce the conduct.

The connection between our archaic system of punishment and our androcentric culture is two-fold. The impulse of resistance, while, as we have seen, of the deepest natural origin, is expressed more strongly in the male than in the female. The tendency to hit back and hit harder has been fostered in him by sex-combat till it has become of great intensity. The habit of authority too, as old as our history; and the cumulative weight of all the religions and systems of law and government, have furthermore built up and intensified the spirit of retaliation and vengeance.

They have even deified this concept, in ancient religions, crediting to God the evil passions of men. As the small boy recited; "Vengeance. A mean desire to get even with your enemies: 'Vengeance is mine saith the Lord'—'I will repay.'"

The Christian religion teaches better things; better than its expositors and upholders have ever understood—much less practised.

The teaching of "Love your enemies, do good unto them that hate you, and serve them that despitefully use you and persecute you," has too often resulted, when practised at all, in a sentimental negation; a pathetically useless attitude of non-resistance. You might as well base a religion on a feather pillow!

The advice given was active; direct; concrete. "Love!" Love is not non-resistance. "Do good!" Doing good is not non-resistance. "Serve!" Service is not non-resistance.

Again we have an overwhelming proof of the far-reaching effects of our androcentric culture. Consider it once more. Here is one by nature combative and desirous, and not by nature intended to monopolize the management of his species. He assumes to be not only the leader, but the whole thing—to be humanity itself, and to see in woman as Grant Allen so clearly put it "Not only not the race; she is not even half the race, but a subspecies, told off for purposes of reproduction merely."

Under this monstrous assumption, his sex-attributes wholly identified with his human attributes, and overshadowing them, he has imprinted on every human institution the tastes and tendencies of the male. As a male he fought, as a male human being he fought more, and deified fighting; and in a culture based on desire and combat, loud with strident self-expression, there could be but slow acceptance of the more human methods urged by Christianity. "It is a religion for slaves and women!" said the warrior of old. (Slaves and women were largely the same thing.) "It is a religion for slaves and women" says the advocate of the Superman.

Well? Who did the work of all the ancient world? Who raised the food and garnered it and cooked it and served it? Who built the houses, the temples, the aqueducts, the city wall? Who made the furniture, the tools, the weapons, the utensils, the ornaments—made them strong and beautiful and useful? Who kept the human race going, somehow, in spite of the constant hideous waste of war, and slowly built up the real industrial civilization behind that gory show?—Why just the slaves and the women.

A religion which had attractions for the real human type is not therefore to be utterly despised by the male.

In modern history we may watch with increasing ease the slow, sure progress of our growing humanness beneath the weakening shell of an all-male dominance. And in this field of what begins in the nurse as "discipline," and ends on the scaffold as "punishment," we can clearly see that blessed change.

What is the natural, the human attribute? What does this "Love," and "Do good," and "Serve" mean? In the blundering old church, still androcentric, there was a great to-do to carry out this doctrine, in elaborate symbolism. A set of beggars and cripples, gathered for the occasion, was exhibited, and kings and cardinals went solemnly through the motions of serving them. As the English schoolboy phrased it, "Thomas Becket washed the feet of leopards."

Service and love and doing good must always remain side issues in a male world. Service and love and doing good are the spirit of motherhood, and the essence of human life.

Human life is service, and is not combat. There you have the nature of the change now upon us.

What has the male mind made of Christianity?

Desire—to save one's own soul. Combat—with the Devil. Self-expression—the whole gorgeous outpouring of pageant and display, from the jewels of the high priest's breastplate to the choir of mutilated men to praise a male Deity no woman may so serve.

What kind of mind can imagine a kind of god who would like a eunuch better than a woman?

For woman they made at last a place—the usual place—of renunciation, sacrifice and service, the Sisters of Mercy and their kind; and in that loving service the woman soul has been content, not yearning for cardinal's cape or bishop's mitre.

All this is changing—changing fast. Everywhere the churches are broadening out into more service, and the service broadening out beyond a little group of widows and fatherless, of sick and in prison, to embrace its true field—all human life. In this new attitude, how shall we face the problems of crime?

Thus: "It is painfully apparent that a certain percentage of our people do not function properly. They perform antisocial acts. Why? What is the matter with them?"

Then the heart and mind of society is applied to the question, and certain results are soon reached; others slowly worked toward.

First result. Some persons are so morally diseased that they must have hospital treatment. The world's last prison will be simply a hospital for moral incurables. They must by no means reproduce their kind,—that can be attended to at once. Some are morally diseased, but may be cured, and the best powers of society will be used to cure them. Some are only morally diseased because of the conditions in which they are born and reared, and here society can save millions at once.

An intelligent society will no more neglect its children than an intelligent mother will neglect her children; and will see as clearly that ill-fed, ill-dressed, ill-taught and vilely associated little ones must grow up gravely injured.

As a matter of fact we make our crop of criminals, just as we make our idiots, blind, crippled, and generally defective. Everyone is a baby first, and a baby is not a criminal, unless we make it so. It never would be,—in right conditions. Sometimes a pervert is born, as sometimes a two-headed calf is born, but they are not common.

The older, simpler forms of crime we may prevent with case and despatch, but how of the new ones?—big, terrible, far-reaching, wide-spread crimes, for which we have as yet no names; and before which our old system of anti-personal punishment falls helpless? What of the crimes of poisoning a community with bad food; of defiling the water; of blackening the air; of stealing whole forests? What of the crimes of working little children; of building and renting tenements that produce crime and physical disease as well? What of the crime of living on the wages of fallen women—of hiring men to ruin innocent young girls; of holding them enslaved and selling them for profit? (These things are only "misdemeanors" in a man-made world!)

And what about a crime like this; to use the public press to lie to the public for private ends? No name yet for this crime; much less a penalty.

And this: To bring worse than leprosy to an innocent clean wife who loves and trusts you?

Or this: To knowingly plant poison in an unborn child?

No names, for these; no "penalties"; no conceivable penalty that could touch them.

The whole punishment system falls to the ground before the huge mass of evil that confronts us. If we saw a procession of air ships flying over a city and dropping bombs, should we rush madly off after each one crying, "Catch him! Punish him!" or should we try to stop the procession?

The time is coming when the very word "crime" will be disused, except in poems and orations; and "punishment," the word and deed, be obliterated. We are beginning to learn a little of the nature of humanity its goodness, its beauty, its lovingness; and to see that even its stupidity is only due to our foolish old methods of education.

It is not new power, new light, new hope that we need, but to understand what ails us.

We know enough now, we care enough now, we are strong enough now, to make the whole world a thousand fold better in a generation; but we are shackled, chained, blinded, by old false notions. The ideas of the past, the sentiments of the past, the attitude and prejudices of the past, are in our way; and among them none more universally mischievous than this great body of ideas and sentiments, prejudices and habits, which make up the offensive network of the androcentric culture.

XII. POLITICS AND WARFARE.

I go to my old dictionary, and find; "Politics, I. The science of government; that part of ethics which has to do with the regulation and government of a nation or state, the preservation of its safety, peace and prosperity; the defence of its existence and rights against foreign control or conquest; the augmentation of its strength and resources, and the protection of its citizens in their rights; with the preservation and improvement of their morals. 2. The management of political parties; the advancement of candidates to office; in a bad sense, artful or dishonest management to secure the success of political measures or party schemes, political trickery."

From present day experience we might add, 3. Politics, practical; The art of organizing and handling men in large numbers, manipulating votes, and, in especial, appropriating public wealth.

We can easily see that the "science of government" may be divided into "pure" and "applied" like other sciences, but that it is "a part of ethics" will be news to many minds.

Yet why not? Ethics is the science of conduct, and politics is merely one field of conduct; a very common one. Its connection with Warfare in this chapter is perfectly legitimate in view of the history of politics on the one hand, and the imperative modern issues which are to-day opposed to this established combination.

There are many to-day who hold that politics need not be at all connected with warfare, and others who hold that politics is warfare front start to finish.

In order to dissociate the two ideas completely let us give a paraphrase of the above definition, applying it to domestic management;—that part of ethics which has to do with the regulation and government of a family; the preservation of its safety, peace and prosperity; the defense of its existence and rights against any strangers' interference or control; the augmentation of its strength and resources, and the protection of its members in their rights; with the preservation and improvement of their morals.

All this is simple enough, and in no way masculine; neither is it feminine, save in this; that the tendency to care for, defend and manage a group, is in its origin maternal.

In every human sense, however, politics has left its maternal base far in the background; and as a field of study and of action is as well adapted to men as to women. There is no reason whatever why men should not develop great ability in this department of ethics, and gradually learn how to preserve the safety, peace and prosperity of their nation; together with those other services as to resources, protection of citizens, and improvement of morals.

Men, as human beings, are capable of the noblest devotion and efficiency in these matters, and have often shown them; but their devotion and efficiency have been marred in this, as in so many other fields, by the constant obtrusion of an ultra-masculine tendency.

In warfare, per se, we find maleness in its absurdest extremes. Here is to be studied the whole gamut of basic masculinity, from the initial instinct of combat, through every form of glorious ostentation, with the loudest possible accompaniment of noise.

Primitive warfare had for its climax the possession of the primitive prize, the female. Without dogmatising on so remote a period, it may be suggested as a fair hypothesis that this was the very origin of our organized raids. We certainly find war before there was property in land, or any other property to tempt aggressors. Women, however, there were always, and when a specially androcentric tribe had reduced its supply of women by cruel treatment, or they were not born in sufficient numbers, owing to hard conditions, men must needs go farther afield after other women. Then, since the men of the other tribes naturally objected to losing their main labor supply and comfort, there was war.

Thus based on the sex impulse, it gave full range to the combative instinct, and further to that thirst for vocal exultation so exquisitely male. The proud bellowings of the conquering stag, as he trampled on his prostrate rival, found higher expression in the "triumphs" of old days, when the conquering warrior returned to his home, with victims chained to his chariot wheels, and braying trumpets.

When property became an appreciable factor in life, warfare took on a new significance. What was at first mere destruction, in the effort to defend or obtain some hunting ground or pasture; and, always, to secure the female; now coalesced with the acquisitive instinct, and the long black ages of predatory warfare closed in upon the world.

Where the earliest form exterminated, the later enslaved, and took tribute; and for century upon century the "gentleman adventurer," i.e., the primitive male, greatly preferred to acquire wealth by the simple old process of taking it, to any form of productive industry.

We have been much misled as to warfare by our androcentric literature. With a history which recorded nothing else; a literature which praised and an art which exalted it; a religion which called its central power "the God of Battles"—never the God of Workshops, mind you!—with a whole complex social structure man-prejudiced from center to circumference, and giving highest praise and honor to the Soldier; it is still hard for its to see what warfare really is in human life.

Someday we shall have new histories written, histories of world progress, showing the slow uprising, the development, the interservice of the nations; showing the faint beautiful dawn of the larger spirit of world-consciousness, and all its benefitting growth.

We shall see people softening, learning, rising; see life lengthen with the possession of herds, and widen in rich prosperity with agriculture. Then industry, blossoming, fruiting, spreading wide; art, giving light and joy; the intellect developing with companionship and human intercourse; the whole spreading tree of social progress, the trunk of which is specialized industry, and the branches of which comprise every least and greatest line of human activity and enjoyment. This growing tree, springing up wherever conditions of peace and prosperity gave it a chance, we shall see continually hewed down to the very root by war.

To the later historian will appear throughout the ages, like some Hideous Fate, some Curse, some predetermined check, to drag down all our hope and joy and set life forever at its first steps over again, this Red Plague of War.

The instinct of combat, between males, worked advantageously so long as it did not injure the female or the young. It is a perfectly natural instinct, and therefore perfectly right, in its place; but its place is in a pre-patriarchal era. So long as the animal mother was free and competent to care for herself and her young; then it was an advantage to have "the best man win;" that is the best stag or lion; and to have the vanquished die, or live in sulky celibacy, was no disadvantage to any one but himself.

Humanity is on a stage above this plan. The best man in the social structure is not always the huskiest. When a fresh horde of ultra-male savages swarmed down upon a prosperous young civilization, killed off the more civilized males and appropriated the more civilized females; they did, no doubt, bring in a fresh physical impetus to the race; but they destroyed the civilization.

The reproduction of perfectly good savages is not the main business of humanity. Its business is to grow, socially; to develop, to improve; and warfare, at its best, retards human progress; at its worst, obliterates it.

Combat is not a social process at all; it is a physical process, a subsidiary sex process, purely masculine, intended to improve the species by the elimination of the unfit. Amusingly enough, or absurdly enough; when applied to society, it eliminates the fit, and leaves the unfit to perpetuate the race!

We require, to do our organized fighting, a picked lot of vigorous young males, the fittest we can find. The too old or too young; the sick, crippled, defective; are all left behind, to marry and be fathers; while the pick of the country, physically, is sent off to oppose the pick of another country, and kill—kill—kill!

Observe the result on the population! In the first place the balance is broken—there are not enough men to go around, at home; many women are left unmated. In primitive warfare, where women were promptly enslaved, or, at the best, polygamously married, this did not greatly matter to the population; but as civilization advances and monogamy obtains, whatever eugenic benefits may once have sprung from warfare are completely lost, and all its injuries remain.

In what we innocently call "civilized warfare" (we might as well speak of "civilized cannibalism!"), this steady elimination of the fit leaves an everlowering standard of parentage at home. It makes a widening margin of what we call "surplus women," meaning more than enough to be monogamously married; and these women, not being economically independent, drag steadily upon the remaining men, postponing marriage, and increasing its burdens.

The birth rate is lowered in quantity by the lack of husbands, and lowered in quality both by the destruction of superior stock, and by the wide dissemination of those diseases which invariably accompany the wife-lessness of the segregated males who are told off to perform our military functions.

The external horrors and wastes of warfare we are all familiar with; A. It arrests industry and all progress. B. It destroys the fruits of industry and progress. C. It weakens, hurts and kills the combatants. D. It lowers the standard of the non-combatants. Even the conquering nation is heavily injured; the conquered sometimes exterminated, or at least absorbed by the victor.

This masculine selective process, when applied to nations, does not produce the same result as when applied to single opposing animals. When little Greece was overcome it did not prove that the victors were superior, nor promote human interests in any way; it injured them.

The "stern arbitrament of war" may prove which of two peoples is the better fighter, but ft does not prove it therefor the fittest to survive.

Beyond all these more or less obvious evils, comes a further result, not enough recognized; the psychic effects of military standard of thought and feeling.

Remember that an androcentric culture has always exempted its own essential activities from the restraints of ethics,—"All's fair in love and war!" Deceit, trickery, lying, every kind of skulking underhand effort to get information; ceaseless endeavor to outwit and overcome "the enemy"; besides as cruelty and destruction; are characteristic of the military process; as well as the much praised virtues of courage, endurance and loyalty, personal and public.

Also classed as a virtue, and unquestionably such from the military point of view, is that prime factor in making and keeping an army, obedience.

See how the effect of this artificial maintenance of early mental attitudes acts on our later development. True human progress requires elements quite other than these. If successful warfare made one nation unquestioned master of the earth its social progress would not be promoted by that event. The rude hordes of Genghis Khan swarmed over Asia and into Europe, but remained rude hordes; conquest is not civilization, nor any part of it.

When the northern tribes-men overwhelmed the Roman culture they paralysed progress for a thousand years or so; set back the clock by that much. So long as all Europe was at war, so long the arts and sciences sat still, or struggled in hid corners to keep their light alive.

When warfare itself ceases, the physical, social and psychic results do not cease. Our whole culture is still hag-ridden by military ideals.

Peace congresses have begun to meet, peace societies write and talk, but the monuments to soldiers and sailors (naval sailors of course), still go up, and the tin soldier remains a popular toy. We do not see boxes of tin carpenters by any chance; tin farmers, weavers, shoemakers; we do not write our "boys books" about the real benefactors and servers of society; the adventurer and destroyer remains the idol of an Androcentric Culture.

In politics the military ideal, the military processes, are so predominant as to almost monopolise "that part of ethics." The science of government, the plain wholesome business of managing a community for its own good; doing its work, advancing its prosperity, improving its morals—this is frankly understood and accepted as A Fight from start to finish. Marshall your forces and try to get in, this is the political campaign. When you are in, fight to stay in, and to keep the other fellow out. Fight for your own hand, like an animal; fight for your master like any hired bravo; fight always for some desired "victory"—and "to the victors belong the spoils."

This is not by any means the true nature of politics. It is not even a fair picture of politics to-day; in which man, the human being, is doing noble work for humanity; but it is the effect of man, the male, on politics.

Life, to the "male mind" (we have heard enough of the "female mind" to use the analogue!) is a fight, and his ancient military institutions and processes keep up the delusion.

As a matter of fact life is growth. Growth comes naturally, by multiplication of cells, and requires three factors to promote it; nourishment, use, rest. Combat is a minor incident of life; belonging to low levels, and not of a developing influence socially.

The science of politics, in a civilized community, should have by this time a fine accumulation of simplified knowledge for diffusion in public schools; a store of practical experience in how to promote social advancement most rapidly, a progressive economy and ease of administration, a simplicity in theory and visible benefit in practice, such as should make every child an eager and serviceable citizen.

What do we find, here in America, in the field of "politics?"

We find first a party system which is the technical arrangement to carry on a fight. It is perfectly conceivable that a flourishing democratic government be carried on without any parties at all; public functionaries being elected on their merits, and each proposed measure judged on its merits; though this sounds impossible to the androcentric mind.

"There has never been a democracy without factions and parties!" is protested.

There has never been a democracy, so far—only an androcracy.

A group composed of males alone, naturally divides, opposes, fights; even a male church, under the most rigid rule, has its secret undercurrents of antagonism.

"It is the human heart!" is again protested. No, not essentially the human heart, but the male heart. This is so well recognized by men in general, that, to their minds, in this mingled field of politics and warfare, women have no place.

In "civilized warfare" they are, it is true, allowed to trail along and practice their feminine function of nursing; but this is no part of war proper, it is rather the beginning of the end of war. Some time it will strike our "funny spot," these strenuous efforts to hurt and destroy, and these accompanying efforts to heal and save.

But in our politics there is not even provision for a nursing corps; women are absolutely excluded.

"They cannot play the game!" cries the practical politician. There is loud talk of the defilement, the "dirty pool" and its resultant darkening of fair reputations, the total unfitness of lovely woman to take part in "the rough and tumble of politics."

In other words men have made a human institution into an ultra-masculine performance; and, quite rightly, feel that women could not take part in politics as men do. That it is not necessary to fulfill this human custom in so masculine a way does not occur to them. Few men can overlook the limitations of their sex and see the truth; that this business of taking care of our common affairs is not only equally open to women and men, but that women are distinctly needed in it.

Anyone will admit that a government wholly in the hands of women would be helped by the assistance of men; that a gynaecocracy must, of its own nature, be one sided. Yet it is hard to win reluctant admission of the opposite fact; that an androcracy must of its own nature be one sided also, and would be greatly improved by the participation of the other sex.

The inextricable confusion of politics and warfare is part of the stumbling block in the minds of men. As they see it, a nation is primarily a fighting organization; and its principal business is offensive and defensive warfare; therefore the ultimatum with which they oppose the demand for political equality—"women cannot fight, therefore they cannot vote."

Fighting, when all is said, is to them the real business of life; not to be able to fight is to be quite out of the running; and ability to solve our growing mass of public problems; questions of health, of education, of morals, of economics; weighs naught against the ability to kill.

This naive assumption of supreme value in a process never of the first importance; and increasingly injurious as society progresses, would be laughable if it were not for its evil effects. It acts and reacts upon us to our hurt. Positively, we see the ill effects already touched on; the evils not only of active war; but of the spirit and methods of war; idealized, inculcated and practiced in other social processes. It tends to make each man-managed nation an actual or potential fighting organization, and to give us, instead of civilized peace, that "balance of power" which is like the counted time in the prize ring—only a rest between combats.

It leaves the weaker nations to be "conquered" and "annexed" just as they used to be; with tariffs instead of tribute. It forces upon each the burden of armament; upon many the dreaded conscription; and continually lowers the world's resources in money and in life.

Similarly in politics, it adds to the legitimate expenses of governing the illegitimate expenses of fighting; and must needs have a "spoils system" by which to pay its mercenaries.

In carrying out the public policies the wheels of state are continually clogged by the "opposition;" always an opposition on one side or the other; and this slow wiggling uneven progress, through shorn victories and haggling concessions, is held to be the proper and only political method.

"Women do not understand politics," we are told; "Women do not care for politics;" "Women are unfitted for politics."

It is frankly inconceivable, from the androcentric view-point, that nations can live in peace together, and be friendly and serviceable as persons are. It is inconceivable also, that in the management of a nation, honesty, efficiency, wisdom, experience and love could work out good results without any element of combat.

The "ultimate resort" is still to arms. "The will of the majority" is only respected on account of the guns of the majority. We have but a partial civilization, heavily modified to sex—the male sex.

WOMAN AND THE STATE

[A Discussion of Political Equality of Men and Women. To be read in connection with chapter 12 of Our Androcentric Culture.]

Here are two vital factors in human life; one a prime essential to our existence; the other a prime essential to our progress.

Both of them we idealize in certain lines, and exploit in others. Both of them are misinterpreted, balked of their full usefulness, and humanity thus injured.

The human race does not get the benefit of the full powers of women, nor of the full powers of the state.

In all civilized races to-day there is a wide and growing sense of discontent among women; a criticism of their assigned limitations, and a demand for larger freedom and opportunity. Under different conditions the demand varies; it is here for higher education, there for justice before the law; here for economic independence, and there for political equality.

This last is at present the most prominent Issue of "the woman question" in England and America, as the activity of the "militant suffragists" has forced it upon the attention of the world.

Thoughtful people in general are now studying this point more seriously than ever before, genuinely anxious to adopt the right side, and there is an alarmed uprising of sincere objection to the political equality of women.

Wasting no time on ignorance, prejudice, or the resistance of special interests, let us fairly face the honest opposition, and do it justice.

The conservative position is this:

"Men and women have different spheres in life. To men belong the creation and management of the state, and the financial maintenance of the home and family:

"To women belong the physical burden of maternity, and the industrial management of the home and family; these duties require all their time and strength:

"The prosperity of the state may be sufficiently conserved by men alone; the prosperity of the family requires the personal presence and services of the mother in the home: if women assume the cares of the state, the home and family will suffer:"

Some go even farther than this, and claim an essential limitation in "the female mind" which prevents it from grasping large political interests; holding, therefore, that if women took part in state affairs it would be to the detriment of the community:

Others advance a theory that "society," in the special sense, is the true sphere of larger service for women, and that those of them not exclusively confined to "home duties" may find full occupation in "social duties," including the time honored fields of "religion" and "charity":

Others again place their main reliance on the statement that, as to the suffrage, "women do not want it."

Let us consider these points in inverse order, beginning with the last one.

We will admit that at present the majority of women are not consciously desirous of any extension of their political rights and privileges, but deny that this indifference is any evidence against the desirability of such extension.

It has long been accepted that the position of women is an index of civilization. Progressive people are proud of the freedom and honor given their women, and our nation honestly believes itself the leader in this line. "American women are the freest in the world!" we say; and boast of it.

Since the agitation for women's rights began, many concessions have been made to further improve their condition. Men, seeing the justice of certain demands, have granted in many states such privileges as admission to schools, colleges, universities, and special instruction for professions; followed by admission to the bar, the pulpit, and the practice of medicine. Married women, in many states, have now a right to their own earnings; and in a few, mothers have an equal right in the guardianship of their children.

We are proud and glad that our women are free to go unveiled, to travel alone, to choose their own husbands; we are proud and glad of every extension of justice already granted by men to women.

Now:—Have any of these concessions been granted because a majority of women asked for them? Was it advanced in opposition to any of them that "women did not want it?" Have as many women ever asked for these things as are now asking for the ballot? If it was desirable to grant these other rights and privileges without the demand of a majority, why is the demand of a majority required before this one is granted?

The child widows of India did not unitedly demand the abolition of the "suttee."

The tortured girl children of China did not rise in overwhelming majority to demand free feet; yet surely no one would refuse to lift these burdens because only a minority of progressive women insisted on justice.

It is a sociological impossibility that a majority of an unorganized class should unite in concerted demand for a right, a duty, which they have never known.

The point to be decided is whether political equality is to the advantage of women and of the state—not whether either, as a body, is asking for it.

Now for the "society" theory. There is a venerable fiction to the effect that women make—and manage, "society." No careful student of comparative history can hold this belief for a moment. Whatever the conditions of the age or place; industrial, financial, religious, political, educational; these conditions are in the hands of men; and these conditions dictate the "society" of that age or place.

"Society" in a constitutional monarchy is one thing; in a primitive despotism another; among millionaires a third; but women do not make the despotism, the monarchy, or the millions. They take social conditions as provided by men, precisely as they take all other conditions at their hands. They do not even modify an existing society to their own interests, being powerless to do so. The "double standard of morals," ruling everywhere in "society," proves this; as does the comparative helplessness of women to enjoy even social entertainments, without the constant attendance and invitation of men.

Even in its great function of exhibition leading to marriage, it is the girls who are trained and exhibited, under closest surveillance; while the men stroll in and out, to chose at will, under no surveillance whatever.

That women, otherwise powerful, may use "society" to further their ends, is as true as that men do; and in England, where women, through their titled and landed position, have always had more political power than here, "society" is a very useful vehicle for the activities of both sexes.

But, in the main, the opportunities of "society" to women, are merely opportunities to use their "feminine influence" in extra domestic lines—a very questionable advantage to the home and family, to motherhood, to women, or to the state.

In religion women have always filled and more than filled the place allowed them. Needless to say it was a low one. The power of the church, its whole management and emoluments, were always in the hands of men, save when the Lady Abbess held her partial sway; but the work of the church has always been helped by women—the men have preached and the women practised!

Charity, as a vocation, is directly in line with the mother instinct, and has always appealed to women. Since we have learned how injurious to true social development this mistaken kindness is, it might almost be classified as a morbid by-product of suppressed femininity!

In passing we may note that charity as a virtue is ranked highest among those nations and religions where women are held lowest. With the Moslems it is a universal law—and in the Moslem Paradise there are no women—save the Houries!

The playground of a man-fenced "society"; the work-ground of a man-taught church; and this "osmosis" of social nutrition, this leakage and seepage of values which should circulate normally, called charity; these are not a sufficient field for the activities of women.

As for those limitations of the "feminine mind" which render her unfit to consider the victuallage of a nation, or the justice of a tax on sugar; it hardly seems as if the charge need be taken seriously. Yet so able a woman as Mrs. Humphry Ward has recently advanced it in all earnestness.

In her view women are capable of handling municipal, but not state affairs. Since even this was once denied them; and since, in England, they have had municipal suffrage for some time; it would seem as if their abilities grew with use, as most abilities do; which is in truth the real answer.

Most women spend their whole lives, and have spent their whole lives for uncounted generations, in the persistent and exclusive contemplation of their own family affairs. They are near-sighted, or near-minded, rather; the trouble is not with the nature of their minds, but with the use of them.

If men as a class had been exclusively confined to the occupation of house-service since history began, they would be similarly unlikely to manifest an acute political intelligence.

We may agree with Tennyson that "Woman is not undeveloped man, but diverse;" that is women are not undeveloped men; but the feminine half of humanity is undeveloped human. They have exercised their feminine functions, but not their human-functions; at least not to their full extent.

Here appears a distinction which needs to be widely appreciated.

We are not merely male and female—all animals are that—our chief distinction is that of race, our humanness.

Male characteristics we share with all males, bird and beast; female characteristics we share with all females, similarly; but human characteristics belong to genus homo alone; and are possessed by both sexes. A female horse is just as much a horse as a male of her species; a female human being is just as human as the male of her species—or ought to be!

In the special functions and relations of sex there is no contest, no possible rivalry or confusion; but in the general functions of humanity there is great misunderstanding.

Our trouble is that we have not recognized these human functions as such; but supposed them to be exclusively masculine; and, acting under that idea, strove to prevent women from an unnatural imitation of men.

Hence this minor theory of the limitations of the "female mind."

The mind is pre-eminently human. That degree of brain development which distinguishes our species, is a human, not a sex characteristic.

There may be, has been, and still is, a vast difference in our treatment of the minds of the two sexes. We have given them a different education, different exercises, different conditions in all ways. But all these differences are external, and their effect disappears with them.

The "female mind" has proven its identical capacity with the "male mind," in so far as it has been given identical conditions. It will take a long time, however, before conditions are so identical, for successive generations, as to give the "female mind" a fair chance.

In the meantime, considering its traditional, educational and associative drawbacks, the "female mind" has made a remarkably good showing.

The field of politics is an unfortunate one in which to urge this alleged limitation; because politics is one of the few fields in which some women have been reared and exercised under equal conditions with men.

We have had queens as long as we have had kings, perhaps longer; and history does not show the male mind, in kings, to have manifested a numerically proportionate superiority over the female mind, in queens. There have been more kings than queens, but have there been more good and great ones, in proportion?

Even one practical and efficient queen is proof enough that being a woman does not preclude political capacity. Since England has had such an able queen for so long, and that within Mrs. Humphry Ward's personal memory, her position seems fatuous in the extreme.

It has been advanced that great queens owed their power to the association and advice of the noble and high-minded men who surrounded them; and, further, that the poor showing made by many kings, was due to the association and vice of the base and low-minded women who surrounded them.

This is a particularly pusillanimous claim in the first place; is not provable in the second place; and, if it were true, opens up a very pretty field of study in the third place. It would seem to prove, if it proves anything, that men are not fit to be trusted with political power on account of an alarming affinity for the worst of women; and, conversely, that women, as commanding the assistance of the best of men, are visibly the right rulers! Also it opens a pleasant sidelight on that oft-recommended tool—"feminine influence."

We now come to our opening objection; that society and state, home, and family, are best served by the present division of interests: and its corollary, that if women enlarge that field of interest it would reduce their usefulness in their present sphere.

The corollary is easily removed. We are now on the broad ground of established facts; of history, recent, but still achieved.

Women have had equal political rights with men in several places, for considerable periods of time. In Wyoming, to come near home, they have enjoyed this status for more than a generation. Neither here nor in any other state or country where women vote, is there the faintest proof of injury to the home or family relation. In Wyoming, indeed, divorce has decreased, while gaining so fast in other places.

Political knowledge, political interest, does not take up more time and strength than any other form of mental activity; nor does it preclude a keen efficiency in other lines; and as for the actual time required to perform the average duties of citizenship—it is a contemptible bit of trickery in argument, if not mere ignorance and confusion of idea, to urge the occasional attendance on political meetings, or the annual or bi-annual dropping of a ballot, as any interference with the management of a house.

It is proven, by years on years of established experience, that women can enjoy full political equality and use their power, without in the least ceasing to be contented and efficient wives and mothers, cooks and housekeepers.

What really horrifies the popular mind at the thought of women in politics, is the picture of woman as a "practical politician;" giving her time to it as a business, and making money by it, in questionable, or unquestionable, ways; and, further, as a politician in office, as sheriff, alderman, senator, judge.

The popular mind becomes suffused with horror at the first idea, and scarcely less so at the second. It pictures blushing girlhood on the Bench; tender motherhood in the Senate; the housewife turned "ward-heeler;" and becomes quite sick in contemplation of these abominations.

No educated mind, practical mind, no mind able and willing to use its faculties, need be misled for a moment by these sophistries.

There is absolutely no evidence that women as a class will rush into "practical politics." Where they have voted longest they do not manifest this dread result. Neither is there any proof that they will all desire to hold office; or that any considerable portion of them will; or that, if they did, they would get it.

We seem unconsciously to assume that when women begin to vote, men will stop; or that the women will outnumber the men; also that, outnumbering them, they will be completely united in their vote; and, still further, that so outnumbering and uniting, they will solidly vote for a ticket composed wholly of women candidates.

Does anyone seriously imagine this to be likely?

This may be stated with assurance; if ever we do see a clever, designing, flirtatious, man-twisting woman; or a pretty, charming, irresistable young girl, elected to office—it will not be by the votes of women!

Where women are elected to office, by the votes of both men and women, they are of suitable age and abilities, and do their work well. They have already greatly improved some of the conditions of local politics, and the legislation they advocate is of a beneficial character.

What is the true relation of women to the state?

It is precisely identical with that of men. Their forms of service may vary, but their duty, their interest, their responsibility, is the same.

Here are the people on earth, half of them women, all of them her children. It is her earth as much as his; the people are their people, the state their state; compounded of them all, in due relation.

As the father and mother, together; shelter, guard, teach and provide for their children in the home; so should all fathers and mothers, together; shelter, guard, teach and provide for their common children, the community.

The state is no mystery; no taboo place of masculine secrecy; it is simply us.

Democracy is but a half-grown child as yet, one of twins? Its boy-half is a struggling thing, with "the diseases of babyhood"; its girl-half has hardly begun to take notice.

As human creatures we have precisely the same duty and privilege, interest, and power in the state; sharing its protection, its advantages, and its services. As women we have a different relation.

Here indeed we will admit, and glory in, our "diversity." The "eternal womanly" is a far more useful thing in the state than the "eternal manly."

To be woman means to be mother. To be mother means to give love, defense, nourishment, care, instruction. Too long, far too long has motherhood neglected its real social duties, its duties to humanity at large. Even in her position of retarded industrial development, as the housekeeper and houseworker of the world, woman has a contribution of special value to the state.

As the loving mother, the patient teacher, the tender nurse, the wise provider and care-taker, she can serve the state, and the state needs her service.

XIII. INDUSTRY AND ECONOMICS.

The forest of Truth, on the subject of industry and economics, is difficult to see on account of the trees.

We have so many Facts on this subject; so many Opinions; so many Traditions and Habits; and the pressure of Immediate Conclusions is so intense upon us all; that it is not easy to form a clear space in one's mind and consider the field fairly.

Possibly the present treatment of the subject will appeal most to the minds of those who know least about it; such as the Average Woman. To her, Industry is a daylong and lifelong duty, as well as a natural impulse; and economics means going without things. To such untrained but also unprejudiced minds it should be easy to show the main facts on these lines.

Let us dispose of Economics first, as having a solemn scientific appearance.

Physical Economics treats of the internal affairs of the body; the whole machinery and how it works; all organs, members, functions; each last and littlest capillary and leucocyte, are parts of that "economy."

Nature's "economy" is not in the least "economical." The waste of life, the waste of material, the waste of time and effort, are prodigious, yet she achieves her end as we see.

Domestic Economics covers the whole care and government of the household; the maintenance of peace, health, order, and morality; the care and nourishment of children as far as done at home; the entire management of the home, as well as the spending and saving of money; are included in it. Saving is the least and poorest part of it; especially as in mere abstinence from needed things; most especially when this abstinence is mainly "Mother's." How best to spend; time, strength, love, care, labor, knowledge, and money—this should be the main study in Domestic Economics.

Social, or, as they are used to call it, Political Economics, covers a larger, but not essentially different field. A family consists of people, and the Mother is their natural manager. Society consists of people—the same people—only more of them. All the people, who are members of Society, are also members of families—except some incubated orphans maybe. Social Economics covers the whole care and management of the people, the maintenance of peace and health and order and morality; the care of children, as far as done out of the home; as well as the spending and saving of the public money—all these are included in it.

This great business of Social Economics is at present little understood and most poorly managed, for this reason; we approach it from an individual point of view; seeking not so much to do our share in the common service, as to get our personal profit from the common wealth. Where the whole family labors together to harvest fruit and store it for the winter, we have legitimate Domestic Economics: but where one member takes and hides a lot for himself, to the exclusion of the others, we have no Domestic Economics at all—merely individual selfishness.

In Social Economics we have a large, but simple problem. Here is the earth, our farm. Here are the people, who own the earth. How can the most advantage to the most people be obtained from the earth with the least labor? That is the problem of Social Economics.

Looking at the world as if you held it in your hands to study and discuss, what do we find at present?

We find people living too thickly for health and comfort in some places, and too thinly for others; we find most people working too hard and too long at honest labor; some people working with damaging intensity at dishonest labor; and a few wretched paupers among the rich and poor, degenerate idlers who do not work at all, the scum and the dregs of Society.

All this is bad economics. We do not get the comfort out of life we easily could; and work far too hard for what we do get. Moreover, there is no peace, no settled security. No man is sure of his living, no matter how hard he works, a thousand things may occur to deprive him of his job, or his income. In our time there is great excitement along this line of study; and more than one proposition is advanced whereby we may improve, most notably instanced in the world-covering advance of Socialism.

In our present study the principal fact to be exhibited is the influence of a male culture upon Social Economics and Industry.

Industry, as a department of Social Economics, is little understood. Heretofore we have viewed this field from several wholly erroneous positions. From the Hebrew (and wholly androcentric) religious teaching, we have regarded labor as a curse.

Nothing could be more absurdly false. Labor is not merely a means of supporting human life—it is human life. Imagine a race of beings living without labor! They must be the rudest savages.

Human work consists in specialized industry and the exchange of its products; and without it is no civilization. As industry develops, civilization develops; peace expands; wealth increases; science and art help on the splendid total. Productive industry, and its concomitant of distributive industry cover the major field of human life.

If our industry was normal, what should we see?

A world full of healthy, happy people; each busily engaged in what he or she most enjoys doing. Normal Specialization, like all our voluntary processes, is accompanied by keen pleasure; and any check or interruption to it gives pain and injury. Whosoever works at what he loves is well and happy. Whoso works at what he does not love is ill and miserable. It is very bad economics to force unwilling industry. That is the weakness of slave labor; and of wage labor also where there is not full industrial education and freedom of choice.

Under normal conditions we should see well developed, well trained specialists happily engaged in the work they most enjoyed; for reasonable hours (any work, or play either, becomes injurious if done too long); and as a consequence the whole output of the world would be vastly improved, not only in quantity but in quality.

Plain are the melancholy facts of what we do see. Following that pitiful conception of labor as a curse, comes the very old and androcentric habit of despising it as belonging to women, and then to slaves.

As a matter of fact industry is in its origin feminine; that is, maternal. It is the overflowing fountain of mother-love and mother-power which first prompts the human race to labor; and for long ages men performed no productive industry at all; being merely hunters and fighters.

It is this lack of natural instinct for labor in the male of our species, together with the ideas and opinions based on that lack, and voiced by him in his many writings, religious and other, which have given to the world its false estimate of this great function, human work. That which is our very life, our greatest joy, our road to all advancement, we have scorned and oppressed; so that "working people," the "working classes," "having to work," etc., are to this day spoken of with contempt. Perhaps drones speak so among themselves of the "working bees!"

Normally, widening out from the mother's careful and generous service in the family, to careful, generous service in the world, we should find labor freely given, with love and pride.

Abnormally, crushed under the burden of androcentric scorn and prejudice, we have labor grudgingly produced under pressure of necessity; labor of slaves under fear of the whip, or of wage-slaves, one step higher, under fear of want. Long ages wherein hunting and fighting were the only manly occupations, have left their heavy impress. The predacious instinct and the combative instinct weigh down and disfigure our economic development. What Veblen calls "the instinct of workmanship" grows on, slowly and irresistably; but the malign features of our industrial life are distinctively androcentric: the desire to get, of the hunter; interfering with the desire to give, of the mother; the desire to overcome an antagonist—originally masculine, interfering with the desire to serve and benefit—originally feminine.

Let the reader keep in mind that as human beings, men are able to over-live their masculine natures and do noble service to the world; also that as human beings they are today far more highly developed than women, and doing far more for the world. The point here brought out is that as males their unchecked supremacy has resulted in the abnormal predominance of masculine impulses in our human processes; and that this predominance has been largely injurious.

As it happens, the distinctly feminine or maternal impulses are far more nearly in line with human progress than are those of the male; which makes her exclusion from human functions the more mischievous.

Our current teachings in the infant science of Political Economy are naively masculine. They assume as unquestionable that "the economic man" will never do anything unless he has to; will only do it to escape pain or attain pleasure; and will, inevitably, take all he can get, and do all he can to outwit, overcome, and if necessary destroy his antagonist.

Always the antagonist; to the male mind an antagonist is essential to progress, to all achievement. He has planted that root-thought in all the human world; from that old hideous idea of Satan, "The Adversary," down to the competitor in business, or the boy at the head of the class, to be superseded by another.

Therefore, even in science, "the struggle for existence" is the dominant law—to the male mind, with the "survival of the fittest" and "the elimination of the unfit."

Therefore in industry and economics we find always and everywhere the antagonist; the necessity for somebody or something to be overcome—else why make an effort? If you have not the incentive of reward, or the incentive of combat, why work? "Competition is the life of trade."

Thus the Economic Man.

But how about the Economic Woman?

To the androcentric mind she does not exist. Women are females, and that's all; their working abilities are limited to personal service.

That it would be possible to develop industry to far greater heights, and to find in social economics a simple and beneficial process for the promotion of human life and prosperity, under any other impulse than these two, Desire and Combat, is hard indeed to recognize—for the "male mind."

So absolutely interwoven are our existing concepts of maleness and humanness, so sure are we that men are people and women only females, that the claim of equal weight and dignity in human affairs of the feminine instincts and methods is scouted as absurd. We find existing industry almost wholly in male hands; find it done as men do it; assume that that is the way it must be done.

When women suggest that it could be done differently, their proposal is waved aside—they are "only women"—their ideas are "womanish."

Agreed. So are men "only men," their ideas are "mannish"; and of the two the women are more vitally human than the men.

The female is the race-type—the man the variant.

The female, as a race-type, having the female processes besides; best performs the race processes. The male, however, has with great difficulty developed them, always heavily handicapped by his maleness; being in origin essentially a creature of sex, and so dominated almost exclusively by sex impulses.

The human instinct of mutual service is checked by the masculine instinct of combat; the human tendency to specialize in labor, to rejoicingly pour force in lines of specialized expression, is checked by the predacious instinct, which will exert itself for reward; and disfigured by the masculine instinct of self-expression, which is an entirely different thing from the great human outpouring of world force.

Great men, the world's teachers and leaders, are great in humanness; mere maleness does not make for greatness unless it be in warfare—a disadvantageous glory! Great women also must be great in humanness; but their female instincts are not so subversive of human progress as are the instincts of the male. To be a teacher and leader, to love and serve, to guard and guide and help, are well in line with motherhood.

"Are they not also in line with fatherhood?" will be asked; and, "Are not the father's paternal instincts masculine?"

No, they are not; they differ in no way from the maternal, in so far as they are beneficial. Parental functions of the higher sort, of the human sort, are identical. The father can give his children many advantages which the mother can not; but that is due to his superiority as a human being. He possesses far more knowledge and power in the world, the human world; he himself is more developed in human powers and processes; and is therefore able to do much for his children which the mother can not; but this is in no way due to his masculinity. It is in this development of human powers in man, through fatherhood, that we may read the explanation of our short period of androcentric culture.

So thorough and complete a reversal of previous relation, such continuance of what appears in every way an unnatural position, must have had some justification in racial advantages, or it could not have endured. This is its justification; the establishment of humanness in the male; he being led into it, along natural lines, by the exercise of previously existing desires.

In a male culture the attracting forces must inevitably have been, we have seen, Desire and Combat. These masculine forces, acting upon human processes, while necessary to the uplifting of the man, have been anything but uplifting to civilization. A sex which thinks, feels and acts in terms of combat is difficult to harmonize in the smooth bonds of human relationship; that they have succeeded so well is a beautiful testimony to the superior power of race tendency over sex tendency. Uniting and organizing, crudely and temporarily, for the common hunt; and then, with progressive elaboration, for the common fight; they are now using the same tactics—and the same desires, unfortunately—in common work.

Union, organization, complex interservice, are the essential processes of a growing society; in them, in the ever-increasing discharge of power along widening lines of action, is the joy and health of social life. But so far men combine in order to better combat; the mutual service held incidental to the common end of conquest and plunder.

In spite of this the overmastering power of humanness is now developing among modern men immense organizations of a wholly beneficial character, with no purpose but mutual advantage. This is true human growth, and as such will inevitably take the place of the sex-prejudiced earlier processes.

The human character of the Christian religion is now being more and more insisted on; the practical love and service of each and all; in place of the old insistence on Desire—for a Crown and Harp in Heaven, and Combat—with that everlasting adversary.

In economics this great change is rapidly going on before our eyes. It is a change in idea, in basic concept, in our theory of what the whole thing is about. We are beginning to see the world, not as "a fair field and no favor"—not a place for one man to get ahead of others, for a price; but as an establishment belonging to us, the proceeds of which are to be applied, as a matter of course, to human advantage.

In the old idea, the wholly masculine idea, based on the processes of sex-combat, the advantage of the world lay in having "the best man win." Some, in the first steps of enthusiasm for Eugenics, think so still; imagining that the primal process of promoting evolution through the paternity of the conquering male is the best process.

To have one superior lion kill six or sixty inferior lions, and leave a progeny of more superior lions behind him, is all right—for lions; the superiority in fighting being all the superiority they need.

But the man able to outwit his follows, to destroy them in physical, or ruin in financial, combat, is not therefore a superior human creature. Even physical superiority, as a fighter, does not prove the kind of vigor best calculated to resist disease, or to adapt itself to changing conditions.

That our masculine culture in its effect on Economics and Industry is injurious, is clearly shown by the whole open page of history. From the simple beneficent activities of a matriarchal period we follow the same lamentable steps; nation after nation. Women are enslaved and captives are enslaved; a military despotism is developed; labor is despised and discouraged. Then when the irresistible social forces do bring us onward, in science, art, commerce, and all that we call civilization, we find the same check acting always upon that progress; and the really vital social processes of production and distribution heavily injured by the financial combat and carnage which rages ever over and among them.

The real development of the people, the forming of finer physiques, finer minds, a higher level of efficiency, a broader range of enjoyment and accomplishment—is hindered and not helped by this artificially maintained "struggle for existence," this constant endeavor to eliminate what, from a masculine standard, is "unfit."

That we have progressed thus far, that we are now moving forward so rapidly, is in spite of and not because of our androcentric culture.

XIV. A HUMAN WORLD.

In the change from the dominance of one sex to the equal power of two, to what may we look forward? What effect upon civilization is to be expected from the equality of womanhood in the human race?

To put the most natural question first—what will men lose by it? Many men are genuinely concerned about this; fearing some new position of subservience and disrespect. Others laugh at the very idea of change in their position, relying as always on the heavier fist. So long as fighting was the determining process, the best fighter must needs win; but in the rearrangement of processes which marks our age, superior physical strength does not make the poorer wealthy, nor even the soldier a general.

The major processes of life to-day are quite within the powers of women; women are fulfilling their new relations more and more successfully; gathering new strength, new knowledge, new ideals. The change is upon us; what will it do to men?

No harm.

As we are a monogamous race, there will be no such drastic and cruel selection among competing males as would eliminate the vast majority as unfit. Even though some be considered unfit for fatherhood, all human life remains open to them. Perhaps the most important feature of this change comes in right here; along this old line of sex-selection, replacing that power in the right hands, and using it for the good of the race.

The woman, free at last, intelligent, recognizing her real place and responsibility in life as a human being, will be not less, but more, efficient as a mother. She will understand that, in the line of physical evolution, motherhood is the highest process; and that her work, as a contribution to an improved race, must always involve this great function. She will see that right parentage is the purpose of the whole scheme of sex-relationship, and act accordingly.

In our time, his human faculties being sufficiently developed, civilized man can look over and around his sex limitations, and begin to see what are the true purposes and methods of human life.

He is now beginning to learn that his own governing necessity of Desire is not the governing necessity of parentage, but only a contributory tendency; and that, in the interests of better parentage, motherhood is the dominant factor, and must be so considered.

In slow reluctant admission of this fact, man heretofore has recognized one class of women as mothers; and has granted them a varying amount of consideration as such; but he has none the less insisted on maintaining another class of women, forbidden motherhood, and merely subservient to his desires; a barren, mischievous unnatural relation, wholly aside from parental purposes, and absolutely injurious to society. This whole field of morbid action will be eliminated from human life by the normal development of women.

It is not a question of interfering with or punishing men; still less of interfering with or punishing women; but purely a matter of changed education and opportunity for every child.

Each and all shall be taught the real nature and purpose of motherhood; the real nature and purpose of manhood; what each is for, and which is the more important. A new sense of the power and pride of womanhood will waken; a womanhood no longer sunk in helpless dependence upon men; no longer limited to mere unpaid house-service; no longer blinded by the false morality which subjects even motherhood to man's dominance; but a womanhood which will recognize its pre-eminent responsibility to the human race, and live up to it. Then, with all normal and right competition among men for the favor of women, those best fitted for fatherhood will be chosen. Those who are not chosen will live single—perforce.

Many, under the old mistaken notion of what used to be called the "social necessity" of prostitution, will protest at the idea of its extinction.

"It is necessary to have it," they will say.

"Necessary to whom?"

Not to the women hideously sacrificed to it, surely.

Not to society, honey-combed with diseases due to this cause.

Not to the family, weakened and impoverished by it.

To whom then? To the men who want it?

But it is not good for them, it promotes all manner of disease, of vice, of crime. It is absolutely and unquestionably a "social evil."

An intelligent and powerful womanhood will put an end to this indulgence of one sex at the expense of the other; and to the injury of both.

In this inevitable change will lie what some men will consider a loss. But only those of the present generation. For the sons of the women now entering upon this new era of world life will be differently reared. They will recognize the true relation of men to the primal process; and be amazed that for so long the greater values have been lost sight of in favor of the less.

This one change will do more to promote the physical health and beauty of the race; to improve the quality of children born, and the general vigor and purity of social life, than any one measure which could be proposed. It rests upon a recognition of motherhood as the real base and cause of the family; and dismisses to the limbo of all outworn superstition that false Hebraic and grossly androcentric doctrine that the woman is to be subject to the man, and that he shall rule over her. He has tried this arrangement long enough—to the grievous injury of the world. A higher standard of happiness will result; equality and mutual respect between parents; pure love, undefiled by self-interests on either side; and a new respect for Childhood.

With the Child, seen at last to be the governing purpose of this relation, with all the best energies of men and women bent on raising the standard of life for all children, we shall have a new status of family life which will be clean and noble, and satisfying to all its members.

The change in all the varied lines of human work is beyond the powers of any present day prophet to forecast with precision. A new grade of womanhood we can clearly foresee; proud, strong, serene, independent; great mothers of great women and great men. These will hold high standards and draw men up to them; by no compulsion save nature's law of attraction. A clean and healthful world, enjoying the taste of life as it never has since racial babyhood, with homes of quiet and content—this we can foresee.

Art—in the extreme sense will perhaps always belong most to men. It would seem as if that ceaseless urge to expression, was, at least originally, most congenial to the male. But applied art, in every form, and art used directly for transmission of ideas, such as literature, or oratory, appeals to women as much, if not more, than to men.

We can make no safe assumption as to what, if any, distinction there will be in the free human work of men and women, until we have seen generation after generation grow up under absolutely equal conditions. In all our games and sports and minor social customs, such changes will occur as must needs follow upon the rising dignity alloted to the woman's temperament, the woman's point of view; not in the least denying to men the fullest exercise of their special powers and preferences; but classifying these newly, as not human—merely male. At present we have pages or columns in our papers, marked as "The Woman's Page" "Of Interest to Women," and similar delimiting titles. Similarly we might have distinctly masculine matters so marked and specified; not assumed as now to be of general human interest.

The effect of the change upon Ethics and Religion is deep and wide. With the entrance of women upon full human life, a new principle comes into prominence; the principle of loving service. That this is the governing principle of Christianity is believed by many; but an androcentric interpretation has quite overlooked it; and made, as we have shown, the essential dogma of their faith the desire of an eternal reward and the combat with an eternal enemy.

The feminine attitude in life is wholly different. As a female she has merely to be herself and passively attract; neither to compete nor to pursue; as a mother her whole process is one of growth; first the development of the live child within her, and the wonderful nourishment from her own body; and then all the later cultivation to make the child grow; all the watching, teaching, guarding, feeding. In none of this is there either desire, combat, or self-expression. The feminine attitude, as expressed in religion, makes of it a patient practical fulfillment of law; a process of large sure improvements; a limitless comforting love and care.

This full assurance of love and of power; this endless cheerful service; the broad provision for all people; rather than the competitive selection of a few "victors;" is the natural presentation of religious truth from the woman's viewpoint. Her governing principle being growth and not combat; her main tendency being to give and not to get; she more easily and naturally lives and teaches these religious principles. It is for this reason that the broader gentler teaching of the Unitarian and Universalist sects have appealed so especially to women, and that so many women preach in their churches.

This principle of growth, as applied and used in general human life will work to far other ends than those now so painfully visible.

In education, for instance, with neither reward nor punishment as spur or bait; with no competition to rouse effort and animosity, but rather with the feeling of a gardener towards his plants; the teacher will teach and the children learn, in mutual ease and happiness. The law of passive attraction applies here, leading to such ingenuity in presentation as shall arouse the child's interest; and, in the true spirit of promoting growth, each child will have his best and fullest training, without regard to who is "ahead" of him, or her, or who "behind."

We do not sadly measure the cabbage-stalk by the corn-stalk, and praise the corn for getting ahead of the cabbage—nor incite the cabbage to emulate the corn. We nourish both, to its best growth—and are the richer.

That every child on earth shall have right conditions to make the best growth possible to it; that every citizen, from birth to death, shall have a chance to learn all he or she can assimilate, to develop every power that is in them—for the common good—this will be the aim of education, under human management.

In the world of "society" we may look for very radical changes.

With all women full human beings, trained and useful in some form of work; the class of busy idlers, who run about forever "entertaining" and being "entertained" will disappear as utterly as will the prostitute. No woman with real work to do could have the time for such petty amusements; or enjoy them if she did have time. No woman with real work to do, work she loved and was well fitted for, work honored and well-paid, would take up the Unnatural Trade. Genuine relaxation and recreation, all manner of healthful sports and pastimes, beloved of both sexes to-day, will remain, of course; but the set structure of "social functions"—so laughably misnamed—will disappear with the "society women" who make it possible. Once active members of real Society; no woman could go back to "society," any more than a roughrider could return to a hobbyhorse.

New development in dress, wise, comfortable, beautiful, may be confidently expected, as woman becomes more human. No fully human creature could hold up its head under the absurdities our women wear to-day—and have worn for dreary centuries.

So on through all the aspects of life we may look for changes, rapid and far-reaching; but natural and all for good. The improvement is not due to any inherent moral superiority of women; nor to any moral inferiority of men; men at present, as more human, are ahead of women in all distinctly human ways; yet their maleness, as we have shown repeatedly, warps and disfigures their humanness. The woman, being by nature the race-type; and her feminine functions being far more akin to human functions than are those essential to the male; will bring into human life a more normal influence.

Under this more normal influence our present perversities of functions will, of course, tend to disappear. The directly serviceable tendency of women, as shown in every step of their public work, will have small patience with hoary traditions of absurdity. We need but look at long recorded facts to see what women do—or try to do, when they have opportunity. Even in their crippled, smothered past, they have made valiant efforts—not always wise—in charity and philanthropy.

In our own time this is shown through all the length and breadth of our country, by the Woman's Clubs. Little groups of women, drawing together in human relation, at first, perhaps, with no better purpose than to "improve their minds," have grown and spread; combined and federated; and in their great reports, representing hundreds of thousands of women—we find a splendid record of human work. They strive always to improve something, to take care of something, to help and serve and benefit. In "village improvement," in traveling libraries, in lecture courses and exhibitions, in promoting good legislation; in many a line of noble effort our Women's Clubs show what women want to do.

Men do not have to do these things through their clubs, which are mainly for pleasure; they can accomplish what they wish to through regular channels. But the character and direction of the influence of women in human affairs is conclusively established by the things they already do and try to do. In those countries, and in our own states, where they are already full citizens, the legislation introduced and promoted by them is of the same beneficent character. The normal woman is a strong creature, loving and serviceable. The kind of woman men are afraid to entrust with political power, selfish, idle, over-sexed, or ignorant and narrow-minded, is not normal, but is the creature of conditions men have made. We need have no fear of her, for she will disappear with the conditions which created her.

In older days, without knowledge of the natural sciences, we accepted life as static. If, being born in China, we grew up with foot-bound women, we assumed that women were such, and must so remain. Born in India, we accepted the child-wife, the pitiful child-widow, the ecstatic suttee, as natural expressions of womanhood. In each age, each country, we have assumed life to be necessarily what it was—a moveless fact.

All this is giving way fast in our new knowledge of the laws of life. We find that Growth is the eternal law, and that even rocks are slowly changing. Human life is seen to be as dynamic as any other form; and the most certain thing about it is that it will change. In the light of this knowledge we need no longer accept the load of what we call "sin;" the grouped misery of poverty, disease and crime; the cumbrous, inefficacious, wasteful processes of life today, as needful or permanent.

We have but to learn the real elements in humanity; its true powers and natural characteristics; to see wherein we are hampered by the wrong ideas and inherited habits of earlier generations, and break loose from them—then we can safely and swiftly introduce a far nobler grade of living.

Of all crippling hindrances in false ideas, we have none more universally mischievous than this root error about men and women. Given the old androcentric theory, and we have an androcentric culture—the kind we so far know; this short stretch we call "history;" with its proud and pitiful record. We have done wonders of upward growth—for growth is the main law, and may not be wholly resisted. But we have hindered, perverted, temporarily checked that growth, age after age; and again and again has a given nation, far advanced and promising, sunk to ruin, and left another to take up its task of social evolution; repeat its errors—and its failure.

One major cause of the decay of nations is "the social evil"—a thing wholly due to the androcentric culture. Another steady endless check is warfare—due to the same cause. Largest of all is poverty; that spreading disease which grows with our social growth and shows most horribly when and where we are most proud, keeping step, as it were, with private wealth. This too, in large measure, is due to the false ideas on industry and economics, based, like the others mentioned, on a wholly masculine view of life.

By changing our underlying theory in this matter we change all the resultant assumptions; and it is this alteration in our basic theory of life which is being urged.

The scope and purpose of human life is entirely above and beyond the field of sex relationship. Women are human beings, as much as men, by nature; and as women, are even more sympathetic with human processes. To develop human life in its true powers we need full equal citizenship for women.

The great woman's movement and labor movement of to-day are parts of the same pressure, the same world-progress. An economic democracy must rest on a free womanhood; and a free womanhood inevitably leads to an economic democracy.

End